GREAT WRITERS STUDENT

THE
ROMANTIC PERIOD

EXCLUDING THE NOVEL

GREAT WRITERS STUDENT LIBRARY

1. The Beginnings to 1558
2. The Renaissance Excluding Drama
3. Renaissance Drama
4. Restoration and 18th-Century Prose and Poetry
   Excluding Drama and the Novel
5. Restoration and 18th-Century Drama
6. The Romantic Period Excluding the Novel
7. The Victorian Period Excluding the Novel
8. The Novel to 1900
9. 20th-Century Poetry
10. 20th-Century Fiction
11. 20th-Century Drama
12. American Literature to 1900
13. 20th-Century American Literature
14. Commonwealth Literature

Editor: James Vinson
Associate Editor: D. L. Kirkpatrick

GREAT WRITERS STUDENT LIBRARY

THE
ROMANTIC PERIOD

EXCLUDING THE NOVEL

INTRODUCTION BY
KENNETH MUIR

© by The Macmillan Press Ltd., 1980

All rights reserved. No part of this publication
may be reproduced or transmitted in any form
or by any means, without permission.

First published 1980 by
THE MACMILLAN PRESS LIMITED
London and Basingstoke
Associated companies in New York, Dublin
Melbourne, Johannesburg and Madras

ISBN 0333 28338 4

CONTENTS

EDITOR'S NOTE   page vii

INTRODUCTION   1

THE ROMANTIC PERIOD   19

NOTES ON CONTRIBUTORS   129

EDITOR'S NOTE

The entry for each writer consists of a biography, a complete list of his published books, a selected list of published bibliographies and critical studies on the writer, and a signed critical essay on his work.

In the biographies, details of education, military service, and marriage(s) are generally given before the usual chronological summary of the life of the writer; awards and honours are given last.

The Publications section is meant to include all book publications, though as a rule broadsheets, single sermons and lectures, minor pamphlets, exhibition catalogues, etc. are omitted. Under the heading Collections, we have listed the most recent collections of the complete works and those of individual genres (verse, plays, novels, stories, and letters); only those collections which have some editorial authority and were issued after the writer's death are listed; on-going editions are indicated by a dash after the date of publication; often a general selection from the writer's works or a selection from the works in the individual genres listed above is included.

Titles are given in modern spelling, though the essayists were allowed to use original spelling for titles and quotations; often the titles are "short." The date given is that of the first book publication, which often followed the first periodical or anthology publication by some time; we have listed the actual year of publication, often different from that given on the title-page. No attempt has been made to indicate which works were published anonymously or pseudonymously, or which works of fiction were published in more than one volume. We have listed plays which were produced but not published, but only since 1700; librettos and musical plays are listed along with the other plays; no attempt has been made to list lost or unverified plays. Reprints of books (including facsimile editions) and revivals of plays are not listed unless a revision or change of title is involved. The most recent edited version of individual works is included if it supersedes the collected edition cited.

In the essays, short references to critical remarks refer to items cited in the Publications section or in the Reading List. Introductions, memoirs, editorial matter, etc. in works cited in the Publications section are not repeated in the Reading List.

vii

INTRODUCTION

The writers included in this volume are classed as romantics because they flourished at a particular time rather than because of what they wrote. Some of the writers, indeed, were apparently untouched by the general characteristics of the romantic movement. John O'Keefe, for example, is a dramatist who belongs in spirit to the 18th century; Samuel Rogers, who lived on into mid-Victorian times, continued to write mainly in a neo-classical idiom; neither Frere nor Praed could be described justly as a romantic poet; and Landor, although he displayed some romantic tendencies, liked to think of his work as "classical" in style and content.

But the best writers of the period, apart from Jane Austen, were romantic. Despite this the poets had a difficult task to achieve recognition because of the entrenched attitudes of the reviewers and the conservatism of most educated readers. Scott was an exception to this generalisation; and so was Byron, who woke up to find himself famous when the first two cantos of *Childe Harold's Pilgrimage* were published. Wordsworth acquired a large public only after he had ceased to write his best poetry; Blake's public could be counted on the fingers of both hands; and Keats and Shelley died before their work attracted a large public.

Critics are hopelessly divided when they attempt to define romanticism, and it is doubtful whether definitions are helpful. It will be convenient to assume that the characteristics of romanticism are those which are shared, in whole or in part, by the major writers of the period. It is important, nevertheless, to notice that every one of these characteristics is to be found in writers of the neo-classical period between 1660 and 1780.

To some critics, influenced by Wordsworth's famous Preface to the second edition of the *Lyrical Ballads,* the essential thing about the romantic revival was the return to nature, both in style and content. Wordsworth himself complained that with slight exceptions (Cotton and Lady Winchilsea), no English poets introduced into their work images drawn directly from nature. He implied that the poetry of that period was too imitative, too bookish, too much concerned with society, too intellectualised. It does not require much knowledge to realise that Wordsworth was unduly prejudiced by the style in which 18th-century poets expressed their appreciation of nature. One has only to read through any good anthology to see how widespread nature poetry was. *The Seasons* by James Thomson is entirely concerned with nature in its various aspects, as in these lines from *Autumn* on the migration of birds:

> Or where the Northern ocean, in vast whirls,
> Boils round the naked melancholy isles
> Of farthest Thule, and th'Atlantic surge
> Pours in among the stormy Hebrides;
> Who can recount what transmigrations there
> Are annual made? what nations come and go?
> And how the living clouds on clouds arise?
> Infinite wings! till all the plume-dark air
> And rude resounding shore are one wild cry.

Or consider these lines by Mark Akenside, which the unwary might ascribe to Wordsworth, as David Nichol Smith pointed out in *The Oxford Book of Eighteenth-Century Verse:*

> O ye Northumbrian shades, which overlook
> The rocky pavement and the mossy falls
> Of solitary Wensbeck's limpid stream;

2 INTRODUCTION

> How gladly I recall your well-known seats
> Belov'd of old, and that delightful time
> When all alone, for many a summer's day,
> I wander'd through your calm recesses, led
> In silence by some powerful hand unseen.
> Nor will I e'er forget you: nor shall e'er
> The graver tasks of manhood, or the advice
> Of vulgar wisdom, move me to disclaim
> These studies which possess'd me in the dawn
> Of life, and fix'd the colour of my mind
> For every future year.

A third and last example (from *The Oxford Book of Eighteenth-Century Verse*) is by a certain John Brown who died in 1766. It describes a night scene:

> Now every eye
> Oppress'd with toil, was drown'd in deep repose;
> Save that the unseen shepherd in his watch,
> Propt on his crook, stood list'ning to the fold
> And gaz'd the starry vault and pendant moon;
> Nor voice nor sound broke on the deep serene,
> But the soft murmur of swift-gushing rills,
> Forth-issuing from the mountain's distant steep,
> (Unheard till now, and now scarce heard) proclaim'd
> All things at rest, and imag'd the still voice
> Of quiet whispering in the ear of Night.

It is not a return to Nature that constitutes romanticism, declare some critics, but a return to the past, displayed not merely in the revival of interest in the Middle Ages and the Renaissance, but also in imitation of the genres and forms of those periods. Byron, Shelley, and Keats, for example, used the Spenserian stanza. But Dryden and Pope had imitated Chaucer; Thomson in *The Castle of Indolence,* Beattie in *The Minstrel,* and several other 18th-century poets had used the Spenserian stanza, sometimes using archaic language; and Chatterton had written imitations of medieval poetry. Joseph Warton, writing in 1756, had ranked Pope's poetry below that of Spenser, and Richard Hurd in 1762 had defended Gothic romances: "You will find that the manners they paint, and the superstitions they adopt, are the more poetical for being Gothic" (*Letters on Chivalry and Romance*). Gray wrote two Norse odes, Collins one on the superstitions of the Highlands, and Macpherson's Ossian was immensely popular. Equally important was Thomas Warton's pioneer work on the *History of English Poetry* (1774–81) and Bishop Percy's *Reliques of Ancient English Poetry* (1765), an anthology of pre-Augustan verse. This last had a considerable impact on the poets of the late 18th century. This is apparent not merely in the adolescent poems in Blake's first volume, but equally in the verse of such a minor poet as Thomas Russell:

> When thirst and hunger griev'd her most,
> If any food she took,
> It was the berry from the thorn,
> The water from the brook.
>
> Now hurrying o'er the heath she hied,
> Now wander'd thro' the wood,
> Now o'er the precipice she peep'd,
> Now stood and eyed the flood.

From every hedge a flower she pluck'd,
And moss from every stone,
To make a garland for her Love,
Yet left it still undone.

Other critics have argued that the chief distinguishing mark of romantic literature is "sensibility"; but, of course, the 18th century, with the sentimental comedies of Kelly and Cumberland, and the still greater popularity of the sentimental novel, culminating in Sterne's *Sentimental Journey,* is the real age of sensibility.

Then it is argued that the essential difference between classical and romantic is related to the difference between objectivity and subjectivity. The classical poet describes things as they are; the romantic poet as modified by his feelings, or as he would like them to be. But this, like all the other supposed characteristics of Romanticism, is to be found in the Age of Reason. It is simply a matter of degree. The two major poets, Dryden and Pope, dominated the poetic scene. Matthew Arnold, who was out of sympathy with the kind of poetry they wrote, absurdly referred to them as "classics of our prose." Some later critics have discovered elements of romanticism even in them − in Dryden's heroic plays, in *Annus Mirabilis,* in Pope's lines beginning:

What beckoning ghost along the moon-light shade
Invites my steps and points to yonder glade? ...
Is there no bright reversion in the sky
For those who greatly think, or bravely die?

But it is obviously true that the dominant trend throughout the century was not romantic. It has even been suggested that poets who tried to write in a different manner suffered from a sense of alienation. They complained of the spleen (as Matthew Green and Lady Winchilsea did), or of its psychological counterpart, melancholia (Thomson and Gray), or they went mad (Collins, Cowper, Smart), or even committed suicide.

The simultaneous publication of the Odes of Joseph Warton and Collins in 1746 has been called (by H. W. Garrod) an abortive romantic revival, for the preface to Warton's book could be regarded as a joint manifesto:

The public has been so much accustomed of late to didactic poetry alone, and essays on moral subjects, that any work where the imagination is much indulged will perhaps not be relished or regarded. The author, therefore, of these pieces is in some pain, lest certain austere critics should think them too fanciful or descriptive. But he is convinced that the fashion of moralising in verse has been carried too far, and he looks upon invention and imagination to be the chief faculties of a poet, so he will be happy if the following odes may be looked upon as an attempt to bring back poetry into its right channel.

Unfortunately Joseph Warton himself was lacking in invention and imagination − he is a bookish and derivative poet; and Collins, who had both, went mad. More than a generation passed before William Blake, with only a handful of readers, had the necessary toughness and independence to carry out a revolution single-handed; and soon afterwards Robert Burns, whose English-language work is feeble and conventional, escaped from the neo-classical strait-jacket by writing in Scots.

Although definitions prove unhelpful, it is possible to point to some characteristics which are shared by nearly all writers of the period. One such characteristic was the revolt against neo-classical dogmas − the supremacy of the writers of Greece and Rome; the barbarism of Gothic art and literature, including presumably the cathedrals of Durham and Chartres; the belief that Shakespeare, although a great genius, was spoilt by the barbarous age in which he lived; that the poet should generalise rather than particularise − write of flowers, rather than

4 INTRODUCTION

of daffodils or the lesser celandine; that good poetry depended on the exercise of intelligence and craftsmanship, the cultivation of "taste," and the imitation of the Ancients. Johnson began his *Lives of the Poets,* not with Chaucer or Spenser, but with Cowley: there is no evidence that he objected to this decision by his publishers. But the *Lives* were a final expression of neo-classical views which were already under attack. The song in Blake's satire "The Island in the Moon" (1784) takes off what he regarded as Johnson's blinkered criticism:

> Lo the Bat with Leathern wing,
> Winking & blinking,
> Winking & blinking,
> Winking & blinking,
> Like Doctor Johnson.

Ten years later the Fairy who ostensibly dictated *Europe* is described as seated on a striped tulip – a deliberate rejoinder to Johnson's statement in *Rasselas* that it was not the business of a poet to number the streaks of a tulip. Blake continued throughout his life to deplore the effect of neo-classicism on poetry and art from the early address "To the Muses" in *Poetical Sketches* to Milton's claim (in the poem of that title) that he comes in "the grandeur of inspiration":

> To cast off the rotten rags of Memory by Inspiration ...
> To cast aside from Poetry all that is not Inspiration,
> That it no longer shall dare to mock with the aspersion of Madness
> Cast on the Inspired by the tame high finisher of paltry Blots
> Indefinite, or paltry Rhymes, or paltry Harmonies....

Blake's most comprehensive attack on neo-classical theory is to be found in the furious annotations on the *Discourses* of Sir Joshua Reynolds, written probably in 1808. He described the work as "A Pretence of Art, To destroy Art." He objected to Reynolds's alleged opinion that genius may be taught, and that pretence to inspiration is a lie and deceit. Above all he objected to Reynolds as "a great generalizer" since he thought that "To Particularize is the Alone Distinction of Merit.... Ideas cannot be given but in their minutely appropriate words, nor can a design be made without its minutely appropriate execution. It is impossible to separate design from execution." When he wrote *Jerusalem* Blake was still stressing the necessity of seeing things in their minute particulars. As late as 1820 in his statement about Homer Blake declared "The Classics! it is the Classics, & not Goths nor Monks, that Desolate Europe with Wars."

Wordsworth in the Preface to the second edition of *Lyrical Ballads* – a preface which Coleridge said was half the child of his own brain – was also concerned to establish the fact that poetry was the spontaneous overflow of powerful feelings; it came, in Blake's terminology, from energy rather than from reason. Wordsworth also argued that the poetic diction of the 18th century was deplorable, and that there was no essential difference between the language of prose and the language of poetry. He chose to write of "low and rustic life" because he believed that

> in that situation the essential passions of the heart find a better soil in which they can attain their maturity, are less under restraint, and speak a plainer and more emphatic language, because in that situation our elementary feelings exist in a state of greater simplicity ... and lastly, because in that situation the passions of men are incorporated with the beautiful and permanent forms of nature.

Wordsworth was reacting against the artificial diction of most 18th-century poetry, but also against its concentration on aristocratic and city life. Although his first two volumes, *An Evening Walk* and *Descriptive Sketches,* belonged to popular 18th-century genres, and were written in conventional couplets, the *Lyrical Ballads* were revolutionary in content as well as in style. They were poems of protest. "The Female Vagrant," extracted from "Salisbury Plain," was a fierce indictment of social injustice and war, and reminds one of Wordsworth's early sympathies with the French Revolution. (That the new purified diction was necessary for what Wordsworth wanted to say may be seen by comparing the continental tour as described in *Descriptive Sketches,* and the same tour as described in *The Prelude.* One is faced with three explanations: that Wordsworth did not realise until years later the full meaning of his experiences; that *The Prelude* is partly fiction; that the meaning could not be expressed until Wordsworth had broken away from the poetic diction of his youth. There may be some truth in all three explanations.)

The age of the romantic revival significantly coincided with the age of revolution. Blake, Wordsworth, Coleridge, and Southey lived through the American War of Independence, the French Revolution, the Napoleonic war and its aftermath. The second generation of romantic poets – Byron, Hunt, Shelley, and Keats – were all, to a greater or lesser degree, politically involved. Wordsworth, Coleridge, and Southey began by enthusiastically supporting the French Revolution. Wordsworth was in France at its inception, in love with Annette Vallon, and he was bitterly opposed to England's declaration of war. Even as late as the 1805 version of *The Prelude* he could declare that members of the British government in 1795

> Thirsted to make the guardian Crook of Law
> A tool of Murder; they who ruled the State,
> Though with such awful proof before their eyes
> That he would sow death, reaps death, or worse,
> And can reap nothing better, child-like long'd
> To imitate, not wise enough to avoid,
> Giants in their impiety alone,
> But, in their weapons and their warfare base
> As vermin working out of reach, they leagu'd
> Their strength perfidiously, to undermine
> Justice, and make an end of liberty.

Coleridge similarly declared that "In order to oppose Jacobinism they imitated it in its worst features: in personal slander, in illegal violence, and even in the thirst for blood" (*The Friend*). By this time all three poets, horrified by the Reign of Terror, and by what they regarded as the way the revolutionary armies had changed from defence to aggression, had abandoned their revolutionary sympathies. Coleridge wrote his retraction in "France: An Ode" (1798):

> The Sensual and the Dark rebel in vain
> Slaves by their own compulsion! In mad game
> They burst their manacles and wear the name
> Of Freedom, graven on a heavier chain.

Wordsworth's retraction is scattered through a series of sonnets attacking France for her treatment of Toussaint L'Ouverture, for the conquest of Switzerland and Venice. When Napoleon became emperor, there seemed to be little left of the principles of liberty, equality, and fraternity. Wordsworth became fervently patriotic and before the end of the war had become a convinced Tory. The man who admired Charles James Fox and had written "Salisbury Plain" against capital punishment, now wrote sonnets in its favour; and he was a staunch opponent of the Reform Bill of 1832. Coleridge and Southey followed much the same course.

Blake, however, who had hailed the liberation of the American colonies and written a poem on the French Revolution – which was withdrawn before publication, either because he or the publisher feared prosecution or because Blake was opposed to the reign of terror –

6 INTRODUCTION

remained a radical to the end of his life. He was opposed to war, he deplored the miseries caused by the Industrial Revolution, and he attacked the injustices of society in *Songs of Experience* and elsewhere, denouncing the hypocritical and reactionary views of the established church. His intransigent position is as apparent in the last prophetic books, *Milton* and *Jerusalem*, as in the early Lambeth books. It has been argued (by J. Bronowski) that the increasing obscurity of Blake's later work was due to his fear of prosecution for sedition; but it is more likely to be due to the complexity of the mythology he had invented.

The second generation of poets came to maturity in the years following the final defeat of Napoleon. Byron's first major poem, *Childe Harold's Pilgrimage*, was published in 1812. After the breakdown of his marriage, Byron lived in exile; he supported the liberals until the end of his life, and he died fighting for Greek independence. His literary tastes, however, remained at odds with his politics. He mocked at Wordsworth and was obscenely scathing about Keats until Shelley remonstrated with him. Only in *Don Juan* did he invent a genre in which his satirical powers, his romantic tendencies, and his political convictions could all be accommodated. His attacks on Southey were partly political.

Shelley was another aristocratic rebel. He, like Byron, wrote on the arch-rebel Prometheus, and its heterodoxy was the main reason, no doubt, why he overpraised *Cain*. Shelley's life was a continuous crusade against the real (or imaginary) oppressors of mankind. He rebelled against his father and Oxford; he rescued Harriet from her father's supposed tyranny; he poured out pamphlets on political topics; and most of his verse is explicitly or implicitly political. *Queen Mab*, among other things, is an attack on kings and priests. *The Revolt of Islam* is an inquest on the French Revolution which failed, he thought, because of its use of violence. In *Prometheus Unbound* he again advocated non-violent resistance as a means of achieving a better society:

> To suffer wrongs which Hope thinks infinite,
> To forgive wrongs darker than death or night;
> To defy Power, which seems omnipotent;
> To love, and bear; to hope, till Hope creates
> From its own wreck the thing it contemplates.

To offer the same advice is the purpose of *The Masque of Anarchy*, written after the Peterloo Massacre; and its setting is not a mythological Caucasus but the England of 1819. In *A Philosophical View of Reform* Shelley drafted a liberal manifesto, although it was not published for a century. Even some of his lyrics are directly political; and the "Ode to the West Wind," in asking the question "If winter comes can spring be far behind?," was clearly alluding to the spring of freedom.

Just before he died, Shelley arranged for Leigh Hunt to come to Italy, there to edit a radical periodical with Byron as chief contributor. Hunt was a very minor poet, but a friend of both Keats and Shelley, and a notable journalist who had been imprisoned for his views. His political views left a permanent impression on his two friends. Keats, in one of his letters, mentions his intention to make a living by journalism, and to write on the liberal side of the question for anyone who would pay him; and in another he expressed the hope that before he died he would be able to "put a mite of help to the liberal side of the question." In October 1818 and in September 1819 he has two long disquisitions on politics. This is one of the reasons for believing that *Hyperion*, the poem he was writing between these dates, had political undertones. Unlike Hazlitt, who remained an admirer of Napoleon, Keats felt that Napoleon had done "more harm to the life of Liberty" than any one else could have done. It may be added that Ebenezer Elliott, the Corn Law rhymer, was a political propagandist in all his best verse; and the Chartist poets were all directly influenced by Shelley. Hood's best poems are an attack on exploitation.

This discussion of the politics of the romantic poets will serve to show that there was a connection, if only psychological, between the revolt against the neo-classical tradition and

INTRODUCTION 7

the revolt against the political ideology which fostered it. This did not prevent some writers from being neo-classical in their style and radical in politics.

We are now in a position to consider the peculiar contributions of each of the main writers of the period to the nature of romanticism. Blake's 1783 volume exhibits the influence of several of the pre-romantic works of the mid-18th century. The poems on the seasons, for example, seem to derive from the unrhymed "Ode to Evening" of William Collins. The rhymed poems that follow show that Blake had been reading Gray and Percy's *Reliques*. There is an avowed imitation of Spenser, and scenes from *King Edward III*, deriving from Shakespeare's histories. The volume concludes with several prose poems in the manner of Macpherson's Ossian. Although the book as a whole is clearly romantic, the best poem, "To the Muses," deploring the barrenness of contemporary poetry, is purely classical in style. Already, 15 years before the publication of *Lyrical Ballads*, Blake had abandoned poetic diction, and he was never tempted, as Wordsworth sometimes was, to return to it. Indeed his own poem on the lamb in the *Songs of Innocence*, when compared with Wordsworth's sentimental "The Pet Lamb," has been used to illustrate his own aphorism, "How wide the gulf and unpassable! between Simplicity and Insipidity" (*Milton*). We have seen how Blake rebelled against the orthodoxy of his age on political and social questions. He was equally heretical on matters of art and religion, if only because he believed that all these areas of human life were one. He was the arch-romantic in that he was the complete individualist, creating his own system to avoid being enslaved by another's, creating his own mythology (of Orc, Enitharmon, Luvah, etc.) so that the characters could express his own philosophy without distortion. It is characteristic that he should object to Wordsworth's nature mysticism. His own was quite different. He regarded the outward creation as a hindrance:

"What," it will be Question'd, "When the Sun rises, do you not see a round disk of fire somewhat like a Guinea?". O no, no, I see an Innumerable company of the Heavenly host crying "Holy, Holy, Holy is the Lord God Almighty."

Blake, for better or worse, also created his own verse forms. The free verse in "A Song of Liberty" was quite original, and the verse of *Milton* and *Jerusalem*, derived no doubt from the prose of the Authorised Version, is sometimes a vehicle of noble eloquence.

Lascelles Abercrombie, while admitting that there are some manifestations of romanticism in Wordsworth, denied that he was a romantic poet. One sees what he means. In the Preface to *Peter Bell*, written as a friendly retort to "The Ancient Mariner," Wordsworth claimed that the Imagination "does not require for its exercise the intervention of supernatural agency," but can be called forth "in the humblest departments of daily life." Then in the Prologue he declares:

A potent wand doth Sorrow wield;
What spell so strong as guilty Fear!
Repentance is a tender Sprite;
If aught on earth have heavenly might,
'Tis lodged within her silent tear.

Nevertheless the choice of Peter as a hero was more of a challenge to neo-classical orthodoxy than the noble Michael, who, despite the naturalistic manner of his portrait, could be accommodated in the frame of the pastoral. There are, moreover, many passages in Wordsworth's poetry, particularly in his great decade (1797–1807), which would be accepted by everyone as romantic:

the cuckoo bird,
Breaking the silence of the seas
Among the farthest Hebrides.

8 INTRODUCTION

> Hence in a season of calm weather
> Though inland far we be,
> Our souls have sight of that immortal sea
> Which brought us hither,
> Can in a moment travel thither,
> And see the children sport upon the shore,
> And hear the mighty waters rolling evermore.
> The light that never was, on sea or land,
> The consecration, and the Poet's dream....

These lines are particularly interesting since the "Elegiac Stanzas" from which they come are, in a sense, a farewell to romance. He would no longer, in 1805, invest Peele Castle with a romantic gleam, because his soul has been humanised by a deep distress – the drowning of his brother at sea. The happiness, based on a dream, "Is to be pitied; for 'tis surely blind." Nevertheless, although *The Excursion* is a natural development of the didactic poem of the previous century – *Night Thoughts, The Pleasures of the Imagination* – the best parts of that poem, such as the tale of Margaret, and the whole of his masterpiece, *The Prelude,* belong in spirit to the new age. Wordsworth's ideas of education and his mystical attitude to nature, are expressions of his personal convictions; and if it is true that an essential difference between neo-classical and romantic is that the former tends to express the traditional views of society and the latter the possibly heterodox views of the individual, then Wordsworth, at least during the period when he was writing his masterpieces, must be regarded as a romantic. Yet such distinctions have only a limited meaning. When one is confronted with the "sublime epitaph," as Coleridge called it, one is forced to admit that it is supremely classical, as well as supremely romantic:

> A slumber did my spirit seal;
> I had no human fears:
> She seemed a thing that could not feel
> The touch of earthly years.

> No motion has she now, no force;
> She neither hears nor sees;
> Rolled round in earth's diurnal course,
> With rocks, and stones, and trees.

Coleridge wrote no verse of importance until his meeting with Wordsworth. His early effusions or his admiration for Bowles would not lead anyone to suppose that he could develop into a great poet, a great romantic poet. As late as 1796, the year previous to his *annus mirabilis,* , his lines to a primrose contain the tired personifications of 18th-century poetasters:

> When timorous Hope the head uprears,
> Still drooping and still moist with tears,
> If, through dispersing grief, be seen
> Of Bliss the heavenly spark serene.

> And sweeter far the early blow,
> Fast following after storms of woe,
> Than (Comfort's riper season come)
> Are full-blown joys and Pleasure's gaudy bloom.

A year later he was writing "The Ancient Mariner."

It has been argued that it was Coleridge's example that transformed the versifier of

Descriptive Sketches into the great poet of "Tintern Abbey," an idea embodied in Garrod's epigram: "Wordsworth was Coleridge's greatest work; and like all his work he left it unfinished." Nevertheless we know that in "Salisbury Plain" Wordsworth had begun his self-transformation, and it seems certain that the friendship of the two poets was mutually stimulating and mutually educative. Coleridge's new way of looking at nature − or his Wordsworthian way of expressing it − is apparent in "This Lime-tree bower my prison," and still more in the masterly conclusion of "Frost at Midnight":

> Therefore all seasons shall be sweet to thee,
> Whether the summer clothe the general earth
> With greenness, or the redbreast sit and sing
> Betwixt the tufts of snow on the bare branch
> Of mossy apple-trees, while the nigh thatch
> Smokes in the sun-thaw; whether the eave-drops fall
> Heard only in the trances of the blast,
> Or if the secret ministry of frost
> Shall hang them up in silent icicles
> Quietly shining to the quiet Moon.

Yet it is "The Ancient Mariner," begun in 1797, that revealed Coleridge in all his glory as the quintessential romantic. The style purports to be that of the old ballads but, as Lowes amply demonstrated in *The Road to Xanadu,* almost every stanza is a tissue of probably unconscious reminiscences of the poet's multifarious reading. The supernatural is made to seem natural, as Coleridge wished; but, most significantly, the poem becomes a profound parable on guilt and repentance, hate and forgiveness, alienation and its overcoming by confession. In "Kubla Khan," written in the same year, Coleridge combined an exotic setting and a mysterious atmosphere with a strange and original music. The poem's very obscurity carries hints of things beyond the reaches of our souls. It was based, allegedly, on a dream; but in it Coleridge had miraculously managed to tap the springs of the unconscious mind. "Christabel," the third of Coleridge's masterpieces, was left unfinished; and this is more damaging to it than it had been to "Kubla Khan." It has some of the characteristics of the Gothic novel; but Coleridge's reference to Crashaw's poem on Saint Theresa, and the name he gave to his heroine, make it clear that the theme of vicarious suffering underlies the Gothic trappings. A year after abandoning "Christabel," Coleridge wrote "Dejection," his virtual farewell to poetry, although he continued to write verse for another 30 years. In this poem he explains that his afflictions (his marriage and his love for Sarah Hutchinson) suspend his "shaping spirit of Imagination," and that his attempt "not to think of what [he] needs must feel" has become "the habit of [his] soul."

Landor was a friend of Southey and Wordsworth, and, in his old age, of Browning and Tennyson. He was even an admirer of Keats and Shelley, and the subject of an elegy by Swinburne. He was a violent and lovable man, the model for Dickens's Boythorn, a rebel, republican and radical, a supporter of revolutions abroad, and he seemed the model of a romantic poet in his life and character. Yet in his writings he was comparatively untouched by romanticism. The exotic setting and melodramatic plot of *Gebir* does not turn it into a romantic epic. Although his *Imaginary Conversations* are varied in content − historical, philosophical, dramatic, critical, humorous − most of them are neo-classical in style. The feebleness and pomposity of many of them have been overlooked because of the beauty of others. In a devastating analysis, Vernon Lee (in *The Handling of Words*) concluded by comparing Landor to a schoolboy faced with the painful task of writing on a set theme. Some of the conversations on classical subjects remind one of stilted translations of the duller classics. The exquisite cadences of his best prose embody commonplaces rather than individual moments of perception, and this has led to charges of sentimentality:

It is better to repose in the earth betimes than to sit up late; better, than to cling

10 INTRODUCTION

pertinaciously to what we feel crumbling under us, and to protract an inevitable fall. We may enjoy the present while we are insensible of decay: but the present, like a note in music, is nothing but as it appertains to what is past and what is to come. There are no fields of amaranth on this side of the grave; there are no voices, O Rhodope, that are not soon mute, however tuneful; there is no name, with whatever emphasis of passionate love repeated, of which the echo is not faint at last.

Too often Landor's classicism led him to say that the poet should not be stirred by a spontaneous overflow of powerful feelings, and he even suggested that when Priam goes to Achilles to beg for the corpse of Hector, "Homer stands unmoved." His verse is also neo-classical for the most part. The *Hellenics,* as the title suggests, take their inspiration from Greece. Even the short lyrics, of which there are hundreds, read like a supplement to the Greek Anthology. One famous example appeared in the rather dull prose work, *Pericles and Aspasia:*

> Stand close around, you Stygian set,
> With Dirce in one boat conveyed,
> Or Charon, seeing, may forget
> That he is old, and she a shade.

To read these short poems in bulk is to become aware that many of them are uninspired exercises; but the best of them combine purity of diction with classical restraint. "Rose Aylmer" is one of the undoubted successes, a perfect example of a poem which is romantic in sentiment and classical in form:

> Ah! what avails the sceptred race?
> Ah! what the form divine?
> What every virtue, every grace?
> Rose Aylmer, all were thine.

> Rose Aylmer, whom these wakeful eyes
> May weep but never see,
> A night of memories and sighs
> I consecrate to thee.

Sir Walter Scott wrote a handful of beautiful lyrics – Lucy Ashton's song in *The Bride of Lammermoor,* Proud Maisie in *The Heart of Midlothian* – but his romantic verse narratives, popular as they were, were hastily written and loosely constructed. As W. M. Rossetti said, "he is not, and never can be, the poet of literary readers." *The Lay of the Last Minstrel* and *Marmion,* the best of the narratives, are filled with a romantic nostalgia for the past. As Scott was able to exploit this much more successfully in the Waverley Novels, we cannot be sorry that the poet was driven by the still greater success of Byron's narratives to the other harmony of prose.

Byron was an unwilling romantic. Throughout his life he proclaimed the superiority of Pope's poetry to anything written by himself and his contemporaries. Pope, he said, was ineffably superior "in point of sense, harmony, effect, and even Imagination, passion, and Invention." Pope was the "parent of English *real* poetry – poetry without faults," and, if the attacks on Pope continued, Byron feared, "it will destroy what little good writing or taste remains amongst us!" So Byron attacked the Lake Poets and Keats for their attacks on Pope, although he was persuaded by Shelley to see some good in Wordsworth and to admit that *Hyperion* was as sublime as Aeschylus. Byron's own attempts to write in the neo-classical manner are, despite some amusing passages in *English Bards and Scotch Reviewers,* nearer to Churchill's satires than Pope's. "Hints from Horace," which he brought back from his travels with the first two cantos of *Childe Harold's Pilgrimage*, is curiously dull; and so is *The Age of Bronze*. It was not until Byron got away from classical models and wrote *Beppo, The Vision of Judgement*, and *Don Juan* that he really found himself as a satirist. Some of his narrative poems are in formal heroic couplets (*The Corsair, Lara*) instead of in the irregularly rhymed stanzas which Scott had used (*The Giaour, The Siege of Corinth*), but only one of the couplet poems, *The Island*, is now regarded as a success.

Meanwhile Byron had become immensely popular with the first instalment of *Childe Harold's Pilgrimage* and with the romantic tales just mentioned, with "Byronic" heroes who were mistakenly thought to be self-portraits. They ranged from Gothic villains to noble outlaws, from misanthropes to men of sensibility. The style of the poems owes a great deal to Scott; and their additional popularity was partly due to their melodramatic plots and their exotic settings, and partly to the thrill of the supposed confessional nature of the poems. The third and fourth Cantos of *Childe Harold* are a great improvement on the first two. Byron has dropped the misanthropic pose of his hero, becomes indeed identified with his hero. By this time he had greater reason to be a misanthrope because of his treatment by society on the breakdown of his marriage. The poem becomes something more than a travelogue in verse. The stanzas about Waterloo, Venice, and Rome are genuinely eloquent and the nature descriptions show how effectively Shelley had "dosed" him with Wordsworth.

Yet it was in *Don Juan* that Byron was able to exploit all his varied talents – his narrative and descriptive power, his wit and satire, his enjoyment of love, his mocking philosophy. The poem breaks all the rules, or rather sets up its own rules, however much they were derived from Italian poetry, or from Frere. Its relaxed mastery makes it one of the masterpieces of the romantic movement, worthy to stand beside *The Prelude* (belatedly published in 1850), a bigger thing, if not a better, than "The Ancient Mariner," *Adonais,* or "The Eve of St. Agnes."

English lovers of poetry would put Byron below Wordsworth and Keats, and perhaps below Coleridge and Shelley. Yet in the rest of the world Byron is the dominant figure of the English Romantic movement. This is party because the peculiar poetic qualities of Wordsworth or Keats are as untranslatable as those of Racine. Byron loses much less among readers whose native language is other than English. So the phenomenon of Byron impressed itself on European, and American, consciousness. This is how he comes to figure in the second part of Goethe's *Faust* as the representative of modern poetry.

Byron was the most popular poet of the age; Shelley, in his lifetime was as little read as Blake, his poems published at his own expense, and he was known mainly for his "atheism" and for scandals about his private life. He was in some important ways more classical than the neo-classical poets, more classical, C. S. Lewis insisted (in *Revaluations*), than Dryden. He translated Plato, Homer, Bion, and Moschus as enthusiastically as he did Goethe and Calderón. He wrote a sequel to *Prometheus Bound*, and *Hellas* is clearly modelled on *The Persians. Swellfoot the Tyrant*, feeble though it is, was inspired by Aristophanes. Much of his work is influenced by Plato far more than by Godwin. Yet, with some justification he is regarded as the most romantic of the romantics. Although, as he said, didactic poetry was his abhorrence, all his longer poems were written to convert his readers to his passionately held beliefs – nakedly in *Queen Mab*, more circumspectly in *Prometheus Unbound* and *The Triumph of Life*. His views on the function of poetry as expressed in his reply to Peacock, *A Defence of Poetry*, are essentially romantic, both when he argues that poetry increases our capacity to love by strengthening our imagination, and in the sweeping claim at the end of the essay:

> It is impossible to read the compositions of the most celebrated writers of the present day without being startled with the electric life which burns within their words. They measure the circumference and sound the depths of human nature with a comprehensive and all-penetrating spirit, and they are themselves perhaps the most sincerely astonished at its manifestations; for it is less their spirit than the spirit of the age. Poets are the hierophants of an unapprehended inspiration; the mirrors of the gigantic shadows which futurity casts upon the present; the words

12 INTRODUCTION

which express what they understand not; the trumpets which sing to battle, and feel not what they inspire; the influence which is moved not, but moves. Poets are the unacknowledged legislators of the world.

Nevertheless the Victorians liked to think of Shelley as (in Arnold's words) an "ineffectual angel beating in the void his luminous wings in vain"; or, like his own skylark, pouring forth his heart "In profuse strains of unpremeditated art." But this supposition could not survive a glance at his tangled manuscripts. It is true that many of his lyrics appear to be spontaneous and direct expressions of his feelings, without the interposition of *persona* or mask. He appears to reveal himself without disguise. He was, we are told, as the Madman in *Julian and Maddalo* described himself, "as a nerve o'er which do creep/The else unfelt oppressions of this earth." But, of course, the Madman was a *persona,* as was Ariel in the poems addressed to Jane Williams.

Among poets and critics of our day, Shelley is the least admired of all the romantic poets. His reputation has not fully recovered from the attacks by Graves, Eliot, Leavis, and Auden – although Eliot later recanted. All these four found his verse as shrill as his voice, his character selfish and caddish. Above all, they said, he was immature. Immature he certainly was. But he was drowned at the age of 29, after a very rapid development during the previous eight years, between *Queen Mab* and *The Triumph of Life*. If Shakespeare, Milton, and Wordsworth had died at the age of 29 they would not be numbered among the great poets: nor would T. S. Eliot.

One of the characteristics of romantic poets – perhaps, as Bacon thought, of all poets – is that they submit the shows of things to the desires of the mind. The Utopian dreams at the end of several of Shelley's longer works – *Queen Mab, The Revolt of Islam, Prometheus Unbound,* even *The Masque of Anarchy* – can be taken as a sign of his romanticism, as the pessimism of the last chorus of *Hellas* and of *The Triumph of Life* have been thought to show his increasing realism about human nature. But it should be remembered that his shorter poems are steeped in melancholy, and that his longer poems were written – and published, as the lyrics were not – to fulfil his high conception of the poet's function.

Shelley was more influenced by the real classics than by neo-classical writers. He used the Spenserian stanza in *The Revolt of Islam* and *Adonais. The Cenci* and several dramatic fragments are too Shakespearean in form and style. His lyrics, and the lyrical passages in *Prometheus Unbound,* are astonishingly varied and original in form. That at least 70 of his lyrics were left unfinished may support his statement that the mind in creation was like a fading coal. The lyrics depended on sudden and intermittent bursts of inspiration. In this respect, as well as in his passionate enthusiasms which he acted out in life and in his use of poetry as a continuous confession, Shelley was a romantic poet; but this is an adjective, as with other poets celebrated in this volume, which requires qualification.

If Shelley's development as a poet was crowded into ten years, that of Keats covered only two, from the publication of the 1817 volume, with its single great poem – the sonnet on Chapman's Homer – to the ode "To Autumn" in 1819. Among his contemporaries Keats was first influenced by Hunt who had introduced his work to the public; and "Sleep and Poetry," written in Hunt's cottage, contains an attack on the use of the heroic couplet in the 18th century:

> with a puling infant's force,
> They swayed about upon a rocking horse
> And thought it Pegasus –

the image being taken from an essay by Hazlitt which had appeared in Hunt's *Examiner* in the previous year. *Endymion,* though Huntian in some of its defects, owes more to Michael Drayton and William Browne. "Hyperion," which followed in 1818, is Miltonic in style, as Keats afterwards regretted. "The Eve of St. Agnes" owes something to the example of Coleridge's *Christabel,* and something to the Gothic fantasies of Mrs. Radcliffe. For the couplets of "Lamia," as a corrective to the loose couplets of *Endymion*, Keats went to Dryden.

If one reads his letters, one realises how Keats, as he developed, became dissatisfied with his contemporaries, both as models and absolutely. *The Excursion*, once hailed as the chief poem of the age, was soon dismissed as an example of the egotistical sublime. In the same way, Keats outgrew his own poems one by one. The Preface to *Endymion* shows that he had outgrown that poem while it was still in the press:

> The imagination of a boy is healthy, and the mature imagination of a man is healthy; but there is a space of life between, in which the soul is in a ferment, the character undecided, the way of life uncertain, the ambition thick-sighted: thence proceeds mawkishness, and all the thousand bitters which those men I speak of must necessarily taste in going over the following pages.

"Isabella," and even that very lovely poem "The Eve of St. Agnes," were regarded by him as too romantic, too remote from real life; and the style of "Hyperion" came to seem too artificial – this was the reason for his attempt to turn the poem into "The Fall of Hyperion."

If one examines the shorter poems written by Keats in the Spring and Summer of 1819, one can observe a gradual move towards a more "classical" style. "La Belle Dame sans Merci," inspired equally by medieval poems and by the Paolo and Francesca canto of Dante's *Inferno*, is a poem about romantic enchantment, contrasting with its celebration in "The Eve of St. Agnes." The first of the great odes, "To Psyche," inspired by the tale of Cupid and Psyche in *The Golden Ass*, , is a dual celebration: of sexual love and of pagan deities. In the "Ode to a Nightingale" Keats contrasts the immortality of the song with the mortality of the poet, his sense of mortality being coloured by the death of his brother; but the poem also contains a poignant account of human misery, from which he wishes to escape:

> Where youth grows pale, and spectre-thin, and dies;
> Where but to think is to be full of sorrow
> And leaden-eyed despairs.

In the "Ode on a Grecian Urn" the imperfections of human life are contrasted with the cold perfections of art, with the message on the Urn, "Beauty is Truth, Truth Beauty," implying wistfully that the sorrows of life could be transcended, that the disagreeables could evaporate in life, as they do in a great work of art. "To Autumn," although more objective than the other odes, is not merely a description of the season; it is also, as Arnold Davenport pointed out (in *Keats: A Reassessment*, 1958), a poem on the idea behind Edgar's words in *King Lear*: "Men must endure/Their going hence even as their coming hither:/Ripeness is all." With such a poem the label of romantic or classical is meaningless.

John Clare was a voluminous poet, so that, despite the efforts of Blunden, the Tibbles, and Geoffrey Grigson, a large proportion of his work remains in manuscript. Nearly all his poems are loving descriptions of the Northamptonshire countryside and it is easy to see why they appealed to readers in 1820, who found Keats odd and difficult. Clare is still the best of nature poets, if only because he did not use Nature either as decoration or as the foundation of a philosophical system. Keats touched on his limitations when he remarked of one of Clare's poems that the description too much prevailed over the sentiment. This is true of his early work; but some of his best poems, such as "Song's Eternity," on much the same theme as the "Ode to a Nightingale," and the lines beginning "I lost the love of heaven," written in his madness, go beyond description.

With the deaths of Keats, Shelley, and Byron, all within the space of three years, and with the deterioration, poetically speaking, of Wordsworth and Coleridge, romantic poetry seemed to have reached a dead end. Tennyson did not emerge as a substantial poet until 1832. In the interval there were two minor poets who could be used to illustrate the weaknesses of romantic literature. George Darley's *Sylvia* is chaotic and undisciplined, and *Nepenthe*,

14   INTRODUCTION

obscurely allegorical, comes alive only in a few lyrical passages. Darley is like the early Keats, but without any powers of self-criticism. The other poet who emerged in the interregnum, Beddoes, wrote two preposterous neo-Jacobean plays and fragments of others. They contain a few exquisite songs, worthy of the Elizabethan lyrics they imitate, and images, lines, and even whole scenes, which, detached from their contexts, might delude the reader into thinking that Beddoes was an important dramatist. In fact, he had some ability to write effective dramatic rhetoric, but his imagination was morbid, his plots read like parodies of the more melodramatic Jacobean and Caroline dramatists, he could not create convincing characters, and he had no sense of dramatic construction.

Three essayists of the period, Lamb, Hazlitt, and De Quincey, have close links with the great romantic poets. Charles Lamb was at Christ's Hospital with Coleridge and remained a friend and admirer all his life; and he was a discriminating admirer of Wordsworth. Hazlitt, as his brilliant essay on his first acquaintance with poets describes, met Coleridge and Wordsworth in his youth. In *The Spirit of the Age* he wrote on Wordsworth, Coleridge, and Southey, disappointed that two of them had not fulfilled their promise. Of the younger poets, Hazlitt was severe on Byron and failed to appreciate *Don Juan;* he disliked Shelley; but he was one of the first to appreciate Keats, who was much influenced by Hazlitt's critical opinions.

All three essayists had a wide knowledge of literature. Lamb had a particular fondness for writers of earlier periods who were little known to his contemporaries. He was an unsuccessful dramatist who became known as an essayist only in his middle forties. In spite of obvious objections to giving extracts from plays, his anthology of passages from Elizabethan drama introduced them to many readers. Hazlitt's knowledge of past literature is apparent in his lectures on the English comic writers and on the poets, but still more in the echoes from his reading which occur on every page of his prose. He began life as a philosopher, and then failed as a painter: art and philosophy are two subjects about which he frequently wrote in his essays. He was also one of the best drama critics. De Quincey was an omnivorous reader, and he too wrote on philosophical topics.

All three essayists appreciated the best writers of the 18th century, but Hazlitt regretted the decline of poetry during that period: "It degenerated into the poetry of mere commonplaces, both in style and thought." This deterioration was reversed, at least partially, by Burns and Wordsworth. It is sometimes said that Hazlitt was too prejudiced politically to be a good judge of his contemporaries: but it is noteworthy that he praised Wordsworth without complaining of his politics, that he admitted that Coleridge was the only man from whom he learnt something, and, on the other hand, that despite his agreement with Byron and Shelley on political matters he underestimated the quality of their work. He was quite justified in flaying Gifford, whose own attacks were politically motivated; and although the last paragraph of his essay on Scott deplores his reactionary attitudes, Hazlitt had paid an enthusiastic tribute to the Waverley novels.

It is in their very different prose styles that these essayists show a complete break with neo-classicism. Lamb does not merely adopt the *persona* of Elia as a means of giving a series of personal confessions, as frank as Montaigne's, but he deliberately uses archaic words and constructions. De Quincey's best work, too, is mostly autobiographical; but there are a number of passages of ornate prose, magnificently rhythmed, and to find anything comparable we should have to go back to the 17th century. Hazlitt prided himself on his plain style and sometimes he is as plain as Swift or Defoe; but, as we have indicated, his prose is more usually a tissue of quotations, misquotations, and echoes from a wide variety of poets; and there is one paragraph, of which he was justifiably proud, in *The Principles of Human Action,* where he speaks of the discovery by a solitary thinker, which is perhaps one of the grandest passages of prose in the language.

We have briefly surveyed the work of the chief authors of the period in order to show in what respects they can be regarded as romantic writers. Our conception of romanticism would not be altered by a consideration of Joanna Baillie, Richard Barham, Felicia Hemans, or Anna Seward, or even by Southey and Moore.

INTRODUCTION 15

It is sometimes claimed that the difference between classical and romantic is between maturity and immaturity; that the romantic poets either died young or, if they lived, ceased to write good poetry. Moreover it is pointed out that all their greatest works were left unfinished: *The Recluse,* of which only a third was completed; *Christabel,* left unfinished; *Kubla Khan* a mere fragment; *Don Juan* and *The Triumph of Life* cut short by death. It is claimed, on the other hand, that the great poets arranged their lives more successfully. Shakespeare completed no less than forty works; Milton, despite twenty years of poetical abstinence, and despite his blindness, completed his three major poems, with a year or two to spare; Dryden finished a number of major poems and a translation of Virgil, Pope *The Dunciad* and a translation of Homer. These cases are conveniently selective: both Chaucer and Spenser left their masterpieces unfinished; and, on the other hand, one can point to *The Ancient Mariner, The Prelude, The Eve of St. Agnes,* and *Adonais* as examples of completed masterpieces; and where in the whole of neo-classical poetry can one find any lyrics to compare with the ones produced by the romantic poets from Blake to Keats?

All the romantic writers were engaged in a rediscovery of the past, either as a subject of their poems, their prose, or their criticism, or as an influence on their style of writing; and, in addition to their concern with the past, they were fascinated with places remote in time and space. Even those poets who disagreed with Wordsworth's views on poetic diction avoided the periphrastic clichés and stereotyped personifications, and used a simpler language than they would have done a generation before.

Along with a more natural language went an increasing knowledge of nature in its minute particulars. Wordsworth's retirement to the Lake District would have been unthinkable a hundred years earlier, when it was regarded as beyond the pale of civilisation.

All the writers broke with neo-classical dogmas, sometimes shamefacedly, sometimes defiantly, and sometimes not fully aware of what they were doing. All of them used their work to express their own ideas and feelings, which were often those of the spirit of the age, but which met with considerable opposition from the entrenched conservatism of the reviewers and of the reading public for which they catered. This conflict was exacerbated by political considerations. All the poets, except Scott, began with radical and even revolutionary sympathies; and if they were influenced by the past, they had a passion for reforming the world. If none would have agreed with Blake that "mere enthusiasm was all in all," it has been argued that enthusiasm, which had once been a derogatory word, had become the distinguishing feature of romantic literature.

When Wordsworth quoted lines from *The Recluse* in the preface to *The Excursion,* he was claiming that the subject of his poem, the mind of man, "My haunt and the main region of my song," was of greater importance than the theme of *Paradise Lost,* as Milton himself had claimed that his epic had a more important theme – the Fall – than either the *Iliad* or the *Aeneid.* Of course Wordsworth was not simply shifting the emphasis from the external to the internal world, since *The Prelude,* the successful part of *The Recluse,* though concerned with the growth of a poet's mind, is equally concerned with the impact of nature and society on that mind. Yet it is probably true that the most important revolution in romantic literature was its turning inwards to the mind of the poet, even to his unconscious mind. A few examples must suffice. It is apparent in "The Mental Traveller" of Blake, as well as in the best of his prophetic books; it is apparent in Shelley's remarks in the preface to *Prometheus Unbound* where he declares that his imagery is frequently drawn "from the operations of the human mind"; it is apparent in "Dejection" and even in "The Ancient Mariner"; it is apparent in Keats, but more in his letters than in his poems. Even *Don Juan* is not primarily concerned with its hero, or even with the satirising of society as such: it is about Byron and his thoughts and feelings, the main region of his song.

16 READING LIST

READING LIST

1. Bibliographies, handbooks, etc.
Bernbaum, Ernest, *Guide Through the Romantic Movement*, 1930; revised edition, 1954.
Sper, F., *The Periodical Press of London: Theatrical and Literary 1800–30*, 1938.
Dyson, H. V. D., and John Butt, *Augustans and Romantics 1689–1830*, 1940; revised edition, 1961.
Raysor, Thomas M., editor, *The English Romantic Poets: A Review of Research*, 1950; revised edition, 1956; revised edition, edited by Frank Jordan, 1972.
Houtchens, C. W., and L. H., editors, *The English Romantic Poets and Essayists: A Review of Research and Criticism*, 1957; revised edition, 1966.
Fogle, R. H., "The Romantic Movement," in *Contemporary Literary Scholarship*, edited by Lewis Leary, 1958.
Green, D. G., and E. G. Wilson, *Keats, Shelley, Byron, Hunt, and Their Circles: A Bibliography 1950–1962*, 1964.
Ward, William S., *Literary Reviews in British Periodicals 1798–1820*, 2 vols., 1972.

2. General histories
Elton, Oliver, *A Survey of English Literature 1780–1830*, 2 vols., 1912.
Ward, A. W., and A. R. Waller, editors, *Cambridge History of English Literature*, vol. 11: *The Period of the French Revolution*, 1914.
Law, Marie H., *The English Familiar Essay in the Early Nineteenth Century*, 1934.
Dyson, H. V. D., and John Butt, *Augustans and Romantics 1689–1830*, 1940; revised edition, 1961.
Hough, Graham, *The Romantic Poets*, 1953.
Nicoll, Allardyce, *A History of English Drama*, vol. 4: *Early Nineteenth Century Drama 1800–1850*, 1955.
Wellek, René, *A History of Modern Criticism 1750–1950*, vol. 2: *The Romantic Age*, 1955.
Battenhouse, H. M., *English Romantic Writers*, 1958.
Jack, Ian, *English Literature 1815–1832*, 1963.
Renwick, W. L., *English Literature 1789–1815*, 1963.
Booth, Michael R., and others, *The Revels History of Drama in English*, vol. 6: *1750–1880*, 1975.

3. Topics, themes, short periods, etc.
Brailsford, H. N., *Shelley, Godwin, and Their Circle*, 1913.
Havens, R. D., *The Influence of Milton on English Poetry*, 1922.
Partridge, E. H., *Eighteenth-Century English Romantic Poetry*, 1924.
Praz, Mario, *The Romantic Agony*, 1933.
Lovejoy, A. O., *The Great Chain of Being*, 1936.
Beach, Joseph Warren, *The Concept of Nature in Nineteenth-Century English Poetry*, 1936.
Bush, Douglas, *Mythology and the Romantic Tradition in English Poetry*, 1937.
Knight, G. Wilson, *The Starlit Dome*, 1941.
Elwin, M., *The First Romantics*, 1947.
Fairchild, H. N., *Religious Trends in English Poetry*, vol. 3: *1780–1830: Romantic Faith*, 1949.
Hayden, John O., editor, *Romantic Bards and British Reviewers*, 1952.
Abrams, M. H., *The Mirror and the Lamp: Romantic Theory and the Critical Tradition*, 1953.

READING LIST 17

Wain, John, editor, *Contemporary Reviews of Romantic Poetry*, 1953.

Read, Herbert, *The True Voice of Feeling: Studies in English Romantic Poetry*, 1953.

Watson, W. R., *Magazine Serials and the Essay Tradition 1746–1820*, 1956.

Thorpe, C. D., Carlos Baker, and B. Weaver, editors, *The Major Romantic Poets: A Symposium in Reappraisal*, 1957.

Foakes, R. A., *The Romantic Assertion: A Study of the Language of Nineteenth-Century Poets*, 1958.

Brand, C. P., *Italy and the English Romantics*, 1958.

Wasserman, E. R., *The Subtler Language: Critical Readings of Neoclassic and Romantic Poems*, 1959.

Weinstein, L., *The Metamorphosis of Don Juan*, 1959.

Perkins, D., *The Quest for Permanence: The Symbolism of Wordsworth, Shelley, and Keats*, 1959.

Abrams, M. H., editor, *English Romantic Poets: Modern Essays in Criticism*, 1960; revised edition, 1975.

Kroeber, K., *Romantic Narrative Art*, 1960.

Bloom, Harold, *The Visionary Company: A Reading of English Romantic Poetry*, 1961.

Thorslev, P. L., *The Byronic Hero: Types and Prototypes*, 1962.

Piper, H. W., *The Active Universe: Pantheism and the Concept of Imagination in the English Romantic Poets*, 1962.

Frye, Northrop, editor, *Romanticism Reconsidered*, 1963.

Bostetter, E. E., *The Romantic Ventriloquists: Wordsworth, Coleridge, Keats, Shelley, and Byron*, 1963.

Rodway, A. E., *The Romantic Conflict*, 1963.

Hodgart, P., and Theodore Redpath, editors, *Romantic Perspectives*, 1964.

Stone, P. W. K., *The Art of Poetry 1750–1820: Theories of Poetic Composition and Style*, 1967.

Hayter, Alethea, *Opium and the Romantic Imagination*, 1968.

Furst, Lillian R., *Romanticism*, 1969; revised edition, 1976.

Abrams, M. H., *Natural Supernaturalism: Tradition and Revolution and Romantic Literature*, 1971.

Bloom, Harold, *The Ringers in the Tower: Studies in Romantic Tradition*, 1971.

Reiman, Donald H., editor, *The Romantics Reviewed*, 9 vols., 1972.

Eichner, Hans, editor, *"Romantic" and Its Cognates*, 1972.

Thorburn, David, and Geoffrey Hartman, editors, *Romanticism: Vistas, Instances, Continuities*, 1973.

Redpath, Theodore, *The Young Romantics and Critical Opinion*, 1973.

Fogle, R. H., *The Permanent Pleasure: Essays on Classics of Romanticism*, 1974.

Ryals, Clyde de L., editor, *Nineteenth-Century Literary Perspectives*, 1974.

Donohue, Joseph, *Theatre in the Age of Kean*, 1975.

Albrecht, W. P., *The Sublime Pleasures of Tragedy: A Study of Critical Theory from Dennis to Keats*, 1975.

Davies, R. T., and B. G. Beatty, editors, *Literature of the Romantic Period 1750–1850*, 1977.

4. Anthologies of Primary Works

Bryan, William F., and R. S. Crane, editors, *The English Familiar Essay: Representative Texts*, 1916.

Smith, David Nicol, editor, *The Oxford Book of Eighteenth-Century Verse*, 1926.

Milford, H. S., editor, *The Oxford Book of Regency Verse 1798–1837*, 1928; revised edition, as *The Oxford Book of Romantic Verse*, 1935.

Campbell, O. J., J. F. A. Pyre, and B. Weaver, editors, *Poetry and Criticism of the Romantic Movement*, 1932.

Noyes, Russell, editor, *English Romantic Poetry and Prose*, 1956.

Hugo, H. E., editor, *The Romantic Reader*, 1957.

18   READING LIST

Woodring, C., editor, *Prose of the Romantic Period,* 1961.
Grigson, Geoffrey, editor, *The Romantics: An Anthology of English Prose and Poetry,* 1962.
Bloom, Harold, editor, *English Romantic Poetry,* 1963.
Creeger, G. R., and J. W. Reed, editors, *Selected Prose and Poetry of the Romantic Period,* 1964.
Perkins, D., editor, *English Romantic Writers,* 1967.
Booth, Michael R., editor, *English Plays of the Nineteenth Century,* 5 vols., 1969–76.
Bloom, Harold, and Lionel Trilling, editors, *Romantic Poetry and Prose,* 1973.
Bennett, Betty T., editor, *British War Poetry in the Age of Romanticism 1793–1815,* 1977.

BAILLIE   19

BAILLIE, Joanna.   Scottish.   Born at the Manse of Bothwell, Lanarkshire, 11 September 1762. Educated at schools in Glasgow. Settled with her family in London, 1783: lived with her sister, in Hampstead, 1806 until her death. *Died 23 February 1851.*

PUBLICATIONS

Plays

A Series of Plays in Which It Is Attempted to Delineate the Stronger Passions of the Mind (includes *Count Basil, The Trial, De Monfort, The Election, Ethwald, The Second Marriage, Orra, The Dream, The Siege, The Beacon*).   3 vols., 1798–1812.
De Monfort (produced 1800).   In *A Series of Plays 1,* 1798.
The Election, music by Charles Edward Horn (produced 1817).   In *A Series of Plays 2,* 1802.
Miscellaneous Plays (includes *Rayner, The Country Inn, Constantine, Paleologus*).   1804.
The Family Legend (produced 1810).   1810.
The Beacon (produced 1815).   In *A Series of Plays 3,* 1812.
The Martyr.   1826.
The Bride.   1828.
Dramas (includes *The Martyr, Romiero, The Alienated Manor, Henriquez, The Separation, The Stripling, The Phantom, Enthusiasm, Witchcraft, The Homicide, The Bride, The Match*).   3 vols., 1836.
Henriquez (produced 1836).   In *Dramas,* 1836.
The Separation (produced 1836).   In *Dramas,* 1836.

Verse

Fugitive Verses.   1790(?); revised edition, 1840.
Metrical Legends of Exalted Characters.   1821.
Complete Poetical Works.   1832.
Ahalya Baee.   1849.

Other

A View of the General Tenor of the New Testament Regarding the Nature and Dignity of Jesus Christ.   1831.
Dramatic and Poetical Works.   1851.

Editor, *A Collection of Poems from Living Authors.*   1823.

Reading List: *The Life and Works of Baillie* by Margaret S. Carhart, 1923 (includes bibliography); "The Plays of Baillie" by M. Norton, in *Review of English Studies,* 1947.

*   *   *

The long-lived Joanna Baillie as a young girl won Burns's admiration for her substantially original revision of the folk-song "Saw ye Johnie Comin'?," which Burns called

20   BAILLIE

"unparalleled ... for genuine humour in the verses, and lively originality in the air." She scored a similar success with her versions of other folk-songs, notably "The Weary Pund o' Tow," "Tam o' the Linn," and "Woo'd and Married an' a'." As it was thought unseemly for ladies who, like herself, came from an old Scottish family to acknowledge authorship, both her *Fugitive Verses* and the first two volumes of her "Plays on the Passions" appeared anonymously.

So wide was the spread of Burns's genius, and so great the shade it cast, that few seedlings grew up in its vicinity. Joanna Baillie, however, did achieve one original lyric in Scots, "A Scottish Song," unaided by echoes from the common stock:

> The gowan glitters on the sward,
>   The lav'rock's in the sky,
> And Collie on my plaid keeps ward,
>   And time is passing by.
>   Oh no! sad an' slow
> And lengthen'd on the ground
>   The shadow of our trysting bush,
> It wears so slowly round.

The themes of her plays were historical. She scored a success with *De Monfort* in London in 1809, mainly because of the acting of John Kemble and Mrs. Siddons. By then, however, she enjoyed the support of Scott, who did much to promote the enthusiastic success of her Highland drama *Family Legend* in Edinburgh the following year, again starring Kemble and Mrs. Siddons, with a prologue by Scott and an epilogue by Henry Mackenzie. In spite of Scott's praise, reinforced by that of David Hume and Robert Blair, the success was not repeated. The fustian, pseudo-Shakespearean blank verse seems dead to us today, and all that retains life is an occasional lively song, like "The Chough and the Crow" from *Orra*.

Joanna Baillie won the lifelong friendship of Scott, whose "Halidon Hill" was written at her request, and who salutes and eulogises her in the introduction to Canto iii of *Marmion* in the passage beginning "When she, the bold enchantress, came/ With fearless hand and heart on flame...." She lived into her ninetieth year, at the centre of an admiring literary circle in her Hampstead cottage.

—Maurice Lindsay

BARHAM, Richard Harris.   English.   Born in Canterbury, Kent, 6 December 1788. Educated at St. Paul's School, London; Brasenose College, Oxford, 1807–10. Ordained priest, 1813; obtained the living of Snargate in Romney Marsh, 1817, and St. Mary Magdalene and St. Gregory, 1824–42; appointed priest-in-ordinary of the chapels royal, 1824; received minor canonry, St. Paul's Cathedral, London, 1821; Lecturer in Divinity at St. Paul's, 1842; Rector, St. Augustine, Watling Street, 1843–45. *Died 17 June 1845.*

PUBLICATIONS

Verse

Verses Spoken at St. Paul's School.   1807.

The Ingoldsby Legends; or, Mirth and Marvels. 3 vols., 1840–47 (vol. 3 edited by R. H. D. Barham); edited by D. C. Browning, 1960.
The Ingoldsby Lyrics, edited by R. H. D. Barham. 1881.

Fiction

Baldwin; or, A Miser's Heir: A Serio-Comic Tale. 1820.
Some Account of My Cousin Nicholas. 1841.

Other

Personal Reminiscences by Barham, Harness, and Hodder, edited by R. H. Stoddard. 1875.
The Garrick Club. 1896.

Reading List: *The Life and Letters of Barham* by R. H. D. Barham, 2 vols., 1870; *A Concordance to The Ingoldsby Legends* by George W. Sealy, 1882; *Barham* by William G. Lane, 1968.

* * *

Richard Harris Barham is better known as Thomas Ingoldsby, pseudonymous author of *The Ingoldsby Legends,* published in three series, the last of them posthumously. A few of the legends (mainly in the first series) are in prose, but most of them are in verse. The legends embody a type of humour popular in the Victorian era. The starting point for their humour is the invention of the persona of Thomas Ingoldsby, Esquire, the scion of an ancient and prolific family, the heir to a traditionally haunted manor-house, Tappington Everard. The legends presented by Ingoldsby purport to stem from the "family memoranda" stored in an old oak chest, and their varying style is accounted for by their having been written by various of Ingoldsby's ancestors.

In truth the tales are humorous, but generally grotesque, stories, peppered with parodies and burlesques of other writers, chiefly, though not entirely, of Barham's near contemporaries. On the surface the world of Ingoldsby is one of nightmare horror, of violence and of mystery – ghosts and witches, hauntings and cursings, hangings, murders and suicides. All is told, however, with such verve and gaiety that the predominant emotion is not fear, but amusement. Sometimes the humorous side prevails entirely, a ghost turns out to be a somnambulist ("The Spectre of Tappington"); witches, the drunken imaginings of a lover disappointed of his tryst ("The Witches' Frolic"); a jewel thief, nothing but a frightened jackdaw ("The Jackdaw of Rheims"). When murder does, in fact, occur, it is recounted with a nonchalant humour that precludes any sense of horror, as, for instance, in "The Tragedy," when the heroine's husband murders her lover and her page:

> Catherine of Cleves Roar'd "Murder!" and "Thieves!"
> From the window above While they murder'd her love;
> Till, finding the rogues had accomplished his slaughter,
> She drank Prussic acid without any water,
> And died like a Duke-and-a-Duchess's daughter!

In lines such as these the romantic and heroic are mocked by the use of the inelegant word "Roar'd" and the lady's suicide is reduced to anti-climax by the cliché "without any water." Barham was an accomplished story teller and had a gift for rollicking rhythms and absurd rhymes. Much of his humour has now become somewhat dated, but a number of his tales give pleasure to the modern reader, and his parodies, though not of the quality of those of the Smith brothers before him nor of Calverley after him, are skilful and amusing. He has a small but secure niche in the history of nineteenth-century light verse.

—Hilda D. Spear

BEDDOES, Thomas Lovell. English. Born in Clifton, Bristol, Somerset, 20 July 1803. Educated at Bath Grammar School; Charterhouse School, London, 1817–20; Pembroke College, Oxford, 1820–25, B.A. 1825, M.A. 1828; studied medicine at the University of Göttingen, 1825–29, and University of Wurzburg, 1829–32, M.D. 1832. Physician and anatomist; visited England, 1842, 1846, but otherwise lived on the Continent; involved in various radical movements in Germany and Switzerland: settled in Zurich, 1835–40, Frankfurt, 1847. *Died* (by suicide) *26 January 1849*.

PUBLICATIONS

Collections

 Letters, edited by Edmund Gosse. 1894.
 Works, edited by Henry W. Donner. 1935.
 Plays and Poems, edited by Henry W. Donner. 1950.
 Selected Poems, edited by J. Higgins. 1976.

Verse

 The Improvisatore, in Three Fyttes, with Other Poems. 1821.
 Poems Posthumous and Collected. 2 vols., 1851.

Plays

 The Bride's Tragedy. 1822.
 Death's Jest-Book; or, The Fool's Tragedy. 1850.

Reading List: *Beddoes: The Making of a Poet* by Henry W. Donner, 1935; *Beddoes* by Edward H. W. Meyerstein, 1940; *Beddoes: A Psychiatric Study* by Hiram K. Johnson, 1943.

* * *

It would be easy to see in Thomas Lovell Beddoes's work no more than a series of particularly skilful variations on the stock Gothic themes of late Romantic poetry. As he himself writes (in "Song: A Cypress-Bough, and a Rose-Wreath Sweet"), "Death and Hymen both are here," and this combination of the morbid and the sexual characterized most of his best poems, furnishing them with an imagery as lovingly detailed as it is repellent. Webster and Tourneur are obvious models here; the Keats of "Lamia" and "Isabella" is a nearer antecedent. And Beddoes himself may well be counted an influence on Browning, for the complex of ambivalent attitudes which animates Beddoes's work is sometimes fused (as in "The Ghost's Moonshine") into a coherent psychological whole which puts one in mind of such dramatic monologues as "Porphyria's Lover."

Although Beddoes can thus be defined as a minor contributor to a tradition which was itself all too literary by the nineteenth century, it should be emphasised that his best work possesses an idiosyncratic force which sometimes deserves the name of originality. His own unhappy life gave personal meaning to the conventional pseudo-Jacobean death-obsession: his father died when he was an infant, his beloved mother just as he entered adulthood. He spent his later years wandering in Germany, where his wild drinking and his radicalism made him unpopular with the authorities, and his eventual suicide was the end of a lonely and eccentric existence. It seems likely that he was a homosexual, and his feelings of guilt on this score, together with the anatomical knowledge he acquired studying medicine, may have helped to endow the Gothic imagery of his poetry with its conviction and emotional force.

Despite the *succès d'estime* enjoyed by his play *The Bride's Tragedy*, published when he was not yet twenty, Beddoes never completed any major work, and in his belief that his was a dramatic talent he shared a common delusion of his time. But although *Death's Jest-Book*, the semi-dramatic work whose obsessive revision occupied the poet's later life, fails as a whole, its incidental lyrics (of which "Old Adam, The Carrion Crow" is the best-known), together with a number of other poems and verse-letters, constitute a body of verse which confirms Beddoes's own deathbed self-estimate, according to which he "ought to have been a good poet." Modern readers who take the trouble to look at Beddoes's work are likely to regret that this distinctive and compelling voice never found more ample utterance.

—James Reeves

BLAKE, William. English. Born in London, 28 November 1757. Studied at Pars' Drawing School, Strand, London, 1767; apprentice to the engraver James Basire, 1772–79; subsequently studied at the Royal Academy of Arts, London. Married Catharine Boucher in 1782. Worked as an illustrator and graphic designer, and gave drawing lessons, London, after 1778; moved to Felpham, Sussex, under the patronage of William Hayley, 1800; returned to London, 1803; after unsuccessful one-man show of his works in 1809 retreated into obscurity; in the 1820's attracted a group of young painters. *Died 12 August 1827.*

PUBLICATIONS

Collections

> *Writings,* edited by Geoffrey Keynes. 3 vols., 1925; revised edition, as *Poetry and Prose,* 1927, 1939; as *Complete Writings,* 1957, 1966.
> *Letters,* edited by Geoffrey Keynes. 1956; revised edition, 1968.

24 BLAKE

Poetry and Prose, edited by David Erdman.   1965.
Complete Poems, edited by W. H. Stevenson.   1973.
The Illuminated Blake, edited by David Erdman.   1974.
Complete Poems, edited by A. Ostriker.   1977.
Writings, edited by G. E. Bentley, Jr.   2 vols., 1978.

Verse

Poetical Sketches.   1783.
The Book of Thel.   1789.
Songs of Innocence.   1789; expanded edition, as *Songs of Innocence and of Experience, Shewing the Two Contrary States of the Human Soul,* 1794.
The French Revolution.   1791.
The Marriage of Heaven and Hell.   1793.
For Children: The Gates of Paradise.   1793; revised edition, as *For the Sexes,* 1818(?).
Visions of the Daughters of Albion.   1793.
America: A Prophecy.   1793.
Europe: A Prophecy.   1794.
The First Book of Urizen.   1794.
The Book of Ahania.   1795.
The Book of Los.   1795.
The Song of Los.   1795.
Milton.   1804–09(?).
Jerusalem: The Emanation of the Giant Albion.   1804–20(?).
The Ghost of Abel: A Revelation in the Visions of Jehovah Seen by William Blake.   1822.
Tiriel.   1874; edited by G. E. Bentley, Jr., 1967.
Vala, edited by H. M. Margoliouth.   1956; as *The Four Zoas,* edited by G. E. Bentley, Jr., 1963.

Other

Notebook, edited by Geoffrey Keynes.   1935; edited by David Erdman, 1973.
Engravings, edited by Geoffrey Keynes.   1950.
The Blake-Varley Sketchbook of 1819, edited by Martin Butlin.   1969.
The Complete Graphic Works, edited by David Bindman.   1977.

Bibliography: *A Blake Bibliography: Annotated Lists of Works, Studies, and Blakeana* by G. E. Bentley, Jr., and M. K. Nurmi, 1964, revised by Bentley, as *Blake Books,* 1977.

Reading List: *The Life of Blake* by Mona Wilson, 1927, revised editon, 1948, edited by Geoffrey Keynes, 1971; *Fearful Symmetry* by Northrop Frye, 1947; *Infinity on the Anvil: A Critical Study of Blake's Poetry,* 1954, and *Blake,* 1968, both by Stanley Gardner; *Blake, Prophet Against Empire* by David Erdman, 1954, revised edition, 1969; *The Everlasting Gospel: A Study in the Sources of Blake* by Arthur L. Morton, 1958; *The Valley of Vision: Blake as Prophet and Revolutionary* by Peter F. Fisher, edited by Northrop Frye, 1961; *Blake's Apocalypse: A Study in Poetic Argument* by Harold Bloom, 1963; *Innocence and Experience: An Introduction to Blake* by E. D. Hirsch, Jr., 1964; *Blake's Humanism,*1968, and *Blake's Visionary Universe,* 1969, both by John B. Beer; *Blake: The Lyric Poetry* by John Holloway, 1968; *Blake and Tradition* by Kathleen Raine, 2 vols., 1969; *A Blake Dictionary: The Ideas and Symbols of Blake* by S. Foster Damon, 1973; *Blake: The Critical Heritage* edited by G. E. Bentley, Jr., 1976.

It is hardly too much to say that William Blake achieved greatness in several different fields. He was not merely one of the best lyrical poets of the last five hundred years. His engravings for *Job*, and the unfinished series for Dante's *Divine Comedy*, are generally recognised as one of the peaks of English art. As a painter his quality is still a matter of controversy: he was in violent reaction against the fashionable portraits by Sir Joshua Reynolds, his own visionary pictures being regarded as crazy. In his old age, however, he acquired several disciples, including Richmond and Palmer. He was, finally, a prophet, convinced that he had rediscovered the truth of Christianity, which had become perverted by the Churches.

Blake was a radical who supported the French Revolution before the Reign of Terror. He was horrified by the results of the Industrial Revolution and he was almost alone in his outright condemnation of the age, in which he saw "A pretence of Art to destroy art; a pretence of liberty/To destroy liberty; a pretence of religion to destroy religion." He believed that "the arts of life had been changed into the arts of death"; that a world had been created "In which Man is by his nature the enemy of man," a world in which the poor were mercilessly exploited. But although Blake was a passionate critic of social evils, he was also a mystic. This can be illustrated by the experience related in a letter to Thomas Butts (22 November 1802) or by the opening quatrain of "Auguries of Innocence":

> To see a World in a Grain of Sand,
> And heaven in a Wild Flower,
> To hold Infinity in the palm of your hand,
> And Eternity in an hour.

Blake had many brilliant insights which he expressed in marginalia, in note-books, in letters, and most incisively in *The Marriage of Heaven and Hell*, but he also picked up a number of eccentric ideas. He believed, for example, that the English were the lost Ten Tribes, and he had curious notions about Druids. But the silliness is often transformed by the poetry. Not many who sing his most famous verses really believe that Jesus visited Britain, but they rightly accept that the building of Jerusalem in "England's green and pleasant land" is a powerful symbol of their social aspirations.

For two reasons it is impossible to consider Blake's poetry in isolation from his work as an artist and from his social and political ideas. First, because nearly all his verse was printed by himself from engraved copper plates, with hand-coloured illustrations, and these often give a necessary clue to the meaning; and, secondly, because even some of his simple songs embody his religious and political views.

Blake's first book, *Poetical Sketches*, written in his nonage, shows him imitating the precursors of romanticism – Gray, Collins, Ossian – and, inspired by Percy's *Reliques*, producing songs in the Elizabethan style. But the finest poem in the book, and arguably the best poem of the second half of the eighteenth century, is an address "To the Muses," lamenting their departure from England, and unconsciously proving their return. It might serve as a model of pure classical style.

Songs of Innocence, Blake's first illustrated poems, are simple without being naive, childlike without being childish, innocent without being insipid. Their subject is childhood as a symbolic representation of the Kingdom of Heaven; but, as we can see from the illustrations to "Infant Joy" and "The Blossom," several of the poems are concerned with sex and procreation. *Songs of Experience*, published five years later, are written in deliberate contrast. There love is treated as a crime; religion is mere hypocrisy; society is in the grip of a tyrannical class system; instead of the Divine Image of Mercy, Pity, Peace, and Love, we have Cruelty, Jealousy, Terror, and Secrecy; instead of sexual freedom there is enforced virginity; instead of the Lamb there is the Tyger.

Blake published no more lyrical verse, although he continued to write it for another ten years. A few of these later poems are as lucid as the *Songs*, but "The Mental Traveller" is as

26 BLAKE

difficult as any of the prophetic books, and "The Everlasting Gospel," in which Blake gives his plainest statement of his disagreements with the Churches, was left unfinished. He probably came to feel that the propagation of his gospel could best be accomplished by means of the prophetic books.

It is characteristic of Blake's dialectical method that after the contrast in the *Songs* between the two contrary states of the human soul – good and bad – he should declare in *The Marriage of Heaven and Hell* that without contraries there is no progression. The marriage is that of energy and reason. Satan symbolises energy, and Blake's famous epigram that Milton "was a true Poet and of the Devil's party without knowing it" means in its context almost what Wordsworth meant when he said that poetry was "the spontaneous overflow of powerful feelings." The book, apart from prefatory and concluding poems in free verse, is written in witty and humorous prose: it is the most entertaining of Blake's writings. It was followed soon afterwards by *Visions of the Daughters of Albion*, a plea for the sexual emancipation of women, written in vigorous and eloquent verse. Blake rejected the use of blank verse, "derived from the modern bondage of rhyming," and he claimed later that in *Jerusalem* "Every word and every letter is studied and put into its fit place; the terrific numbers are reserved for the terrific parts, the mild & gentle for the mild & gentle parts, and the prosaic for inferior parts." This seems to conflict with his other statement that the poem was dictated to him, he being merely the secretary. Some critics have suspected that the verse of the prophetic books is really prose cut up into length. This may be true of the prosaic parts: Blake's chief model was the King James Bible. But it is important to recognize that there are many passages where rhythm, alliteration, and assonance bear out Blake's claims.

A more serious obstacle to enjoyment is the mythology, invented by Blake to avoid the misleading associations of classical mythology. (Keats, it will be remembered, found some discrepancy between the story of Hyperion and the meaning he wished to convey in his poem.) Blake's names, such as Urizen, Oothoon, Theotormon, Bromion, need a key; and the need is increased by the fact that the significance of the characters varies from poem to poem. Yet the difficulties can easily be exaggerated. Years ago, a recital of the last part of *Jerusalem* in Masefield's private theatre was enthusiastically received by an audience who did not know the difference between Enitharmon and Palamabron.

Although their strictly poetical qualities have usually been undervalued, the greatness of *Milton* and *Jerusalem* depends largely on their prophetic message. *Milton* originated in Blake's difficulties with Hayley and in his wish to correct the "errors" of *Paradise Lost*. On these foundations Blake constructed a metaphysical drama of great profundity, in which the religion, the art, the morality, and the literature of his time were tried and found wanting. The climax of his attack comes in the splendid speech beginning "Obey thou the words of the Inspired Man" (Plate 40), in which he goes on to protest at "the aspersion of Madness/Cast on the Inspired" by the poetasters of the day.

In *Jerusalem* Blake introduces Scofield, the soldier who had accused him of sedition, but he is mainly concerned with the necessity of mutual forgiveness and of self-annihilation, which to him were the essentials of Christ's teaching, and the conditions for the establishment of the Kingdom of Heaven on earth, and specifically in England. In *Milton* Bacon, Locke, and Newton were treated as symbols of barren rationalism, but towards the end of *Jerusalem*, no longer enemies of the imagination, they are welcomed alongside Chaucer, Shakespeare, and Milton as part of the English tradition.

Bronowski argued in *The Man Without a Mask* that Blake turned from political to religious subjects because he was afraid of prosecution, and that he adopted the obscure style of the prophetic books for the same reason. But, despite the repressive age in which he lived, Blake did not become obscure for this reason. He continued to advertise two of his most radical works (*America* and *Europe*); some of his earlier prophecies are much more obscure than *Milton*; and his move away from politics was more likely due to his disappointment with the course of the French Revolution. We should remember, too, that Blake's politics and religion are inseparable: art, poetry, and politics are all part of his religion. It is significant that in *America* he uses the resurrection as a symbol of political emancipation, and in *Jerusalem* he asks: "Are not Religion & Politics the same Thing? Brotherhood is Religion." Jesus in the same poem declares that Man cannot "exist but by Brotherhood."

Blake's message fell on deaf ears. The one coloured copy of *Jerusalem* – artistically his most beautiful book – was unsold at his death; and it was not until the present century that critics and readers began to understand him.

—Kenneth Muir

BLOOMFIELD, Robert. English. Born in Honington, near Bury St. Edmunds, Suffolk, 3 December 1766. No formal education other than from his mother; apprenticed to a shoemaker in London. Married; four children. Worked as a shoemaker, London; given the post of undersealer in the Seal Office, then an allowance, by the Duke of Grafton, 1802; thereafter worked at making Aeolian harps, and as a bookseller, but went bankrupt; visited Wales, 1811; settled in Shefford, Bedfordshire, 1812, and died there in poverty. *Died 19 August 1823.*

PUBLICATIONS

Collections

Works. 1883.
A Selection from the Poems, edited by J. L. Carr. 1966.

Verse

The Farmer's Boy: A Rural Poem, edited by Capel Lofft. 1800.
Rural Tales, Ballads, and Songs. 1802.
Good Tidings; or, News from the Farm. 1804.
Wild Flowers; or, Pastoral and Local Poetry. 1806.
The Poems. 2 vols., 1809.
The Banks of Wye. 1811.
The History of Little Davy's New Hat (juvenile). 1815; edited by Walter Bloomfield, 1878.
Collected Poems. 2 vols., 1817.
May Day with the Muses. 1822.

Play

Hazelwood Hall: A Village Drama. 1823.

Other

Selections from the Correspondence, edited by W. H. Hart. 1870.

28   BLOOMFIELD

Editor, *Nature's Music, Consisting of Extracts from Several Authors in Honour of the Harp of Aeolus.* 1808.

Reading List: *The Farmer's Boy, Robert Bloomfield: His Life and Poems* by William Wickett and Nicholas Duval, 1971.

*   *   *

Robert Bloomfield achieved overnight fame with the publication of *The Farmer's Boy* in 1800; while this volume thoroughly deserves to be remembered, the neglect of his other work is a loss to the lover of simple but accomplished poetry.

The Farmer's Boy follows the tradition of Thomson's *The Seasons*, of "L'Allegro" and "Il Penseroso," and the English georgics such as Somerville's *The Chase*. It is also redolent of the atmosphere which informs *The Compleat Angler* or *The Natural History of Selbourne*, offering an uncomplicated description of a farm labourer's daily round through each season of the year. The poem gains a freshness from Bloomfield's personal experience as jack-of-all-trades on a Suffolk farm.

Bloomfield's lines are frequently utilitarian though seldom banal. The heroic couplet is a medium rather than an ornament to him, and the charm of his poem lies in the freshness of his descriptions rather than in the exercise of a lush or individualised lyrical power, though moments like "Stopped in her song, perchance the starting thrush/Shook a white shower from the blackthorn bush ..." show that he was not deficient in delicacy of apprehension. He describes the dairy "with pails bright scoured and delicately sweet" and the shepherd who "idling lies,/And sees tomorrow in the marbling skies," and even his humblest tasks are dignified by the powers of observation with which they are described.

He has moments of "romantic" awareness, as in his Turner-esque appreciation of colour and movement in the gathering stormclouds:

> Now eve o'erhangs the western cloud's thick brow:
> The far-stretch'd curtain of retiring light,
> With fiery treasures fraught; that on the sight
> Flash from its bulging sides, where darkness lowers,
> In Fancy's eye, a chain of mouldering towers;
> Or craggy coasts just rising into view,
> Midst javelins dire, and darts of streaming blue.

Occasionally he shows a nice critical apprehension of the dangers inherent in employing georgic language to realistic descriptions, as when the ploughman trudges along his furrows "till dirt usurp the empire of his shoes."

Throughout *The Farmer's Boy* Bloomfield maintains a steady balance of common sense and delicacy of feeling. If his sociological comments are unoriginal they are still interesting. He feels that Nature has a double rapport with man: there is a mystic, poetic communion, but this is not prejudiced by a shrewd delight in commerce and in the time-honoured daily round of labour. At times his feelings for the land remind one of Cobbett's *Rural Rides*.

Bloomfield's later volumes − especially *Rural Tales* and *Wild Flowers* − have an honourable place among those poems which sought to link country stories and ballad measures to a higher purpose, an aspiration realised in Wordsworth's *Lyrical Ballads*. Purely as ballads, pieces like "The Broken Crutch" or "The Horkey" hold their own very well, managing rustic dialogue with a skill which avoids archness or stereotype. Bloomfield has more power to please than is consistent with the neglect into which he has fallen, and he offers a healthy corrective to those sociologists who regard the agricultural labourer's lot as one of unmitigated misery at the turn of the century. Bloomfield's stories of village revels and agricultural pursuits sometimes depend too much on squirarchal benevolence for their happy endings, but at his best he can achieve a comic dignity which looks forward to the Hardy of *Under the Greenwood Tree.*

—T. Bareham

BYRON, Lord; George Noel Gordon, 6th Baron Byron, of Rochdale. English. Born in London, 22 January 1788; lame at birth. Educated at Aberdeen Grammar School, 1794–98; Harrow School, 1801–05; Trinity College, Cambridge, 1805–08, M.A. Married Annabella Milbanke, 1815; had one daughter, Augusta Ada; had affair with Mary Godwin Shelley's step-sister Claire Clairmont, 1816–17, who bore him daughter Allegra; settled with Teresa Guiccioli, 1819. With his friend, John Cam Hobhouse, toured Portugal, Spain, Malta and Greece, 1809–11; returned to London and took his seat in the House of Lords and was briefly active on the extreme liberal wing of the Whig Party. Ostracized by English society for his supposed incestuous affair with his half-sister, Augusta Leigh, he left England permanently, 1816; lived with Shelley, his wife Mary Godwin, and Claire Clairmont, Geneva, 1816; moved to Venice, 1817; joined Shelley at Pisa, 1818, and remained there as part of the "Pisan Circle" until 1822; organized an expedition to assist in Greek war of independence from the Turks, 1823, and died in Missolonghi. *Died 19 April 1824.*

PUBLICATIONS

Collections

The Works, edited by E. H. Coleridge and Rowland E. Prothero. 13 vols., 1898–1904.
Poems, edited by G. Pocock. 3 vols., 1948; revised by V. de Sola Pinto, 1963.
Letters and Journals, edited by Leslie Marchand. 1973–

Verse

Fugitive Pieces. 1806.
Poems on Various Occasions. 1807.
Hours of Idleness: A Series of Poems, Original and Translated. 1807; revised edition, 1808.
English Bards and Scotch Reviewers: A Satire. 1809; revised edition, 1809, 1816.
Childe Harold's Pilgrimage, cantos 1–2, 1812; *Canto the Third,* 1816; *Canto the Fourth,* 1818; complete edition, 2 vols., 1819.
The Curse of Minerva. 1812.
Waltz: An Apostrophic Hymn. 1813.
The Giaour: A Fragment of a Turkish Tale. 1813; 4 revised editions, 1813.
The Bride of Abydos: A Turkish Tale. 1813.

30   BYRON

The Corsair: A Tale.   1814.
Ode to Napoleon Buonaparte.   1814.
Lara: A Tale.   1814.
Hebrew Melodies Ancient and Modern.   2 vols., 1815.
The Siege of Corinth; Parisina.   1816.
Poems.   1816.
The Prisoner of Chillon and Other Poems.   1816.
Monody on the Death of Sheridan.   1816.
The Lament of Tasso.   1817.
Beppo: A Venetian Story.   1818; revised edition, 1818.
Mazeppa.   1819.
Don Juan, cantos 1–2.   1819; cantos 3–5, 1821; cantos 6–14, 3 vols., 1823; cantos
    15–16, 1824; complete edition, 2 vols., 1826; *Dedication,* 1833; edited by Truman
    Guy Steffan and Willis W. Pratt, 4 vols., 1957.
The Irish Avatar.   1821.
The Vision of Judgment.   1822.
The Age of Bronze; or, Carmen Seculare et Annus Haud Mirabilis.   1823.
The Island; or, Christian and His Comrades.   1823.
A Political Ode.   1880.
A Version of Ossian's Address to the Sun.   1898.

Plays

Manfred (produced 1834).   1817.
Marino Faliero, Doge of Venice (produced 1821).   With *The Prophecy of Dante: A Poem,*
    1821.
Sardanapalus; The Two Foscari; Cain: A Mystery.   1821.
The Two Foscari (produced 1837).   In *Sardanapalus ...,* 1821.
Heaven and Earth: A Mystery.   1823.
Werner (produced 1830).   1823.
The Deformed Transformed.   1824.

Other

A Letter to John Murray on Bowles' Strictures on the Life and Writings of Pope.   1821.
The Parliamentary Speeches.   1824.
Correspondence of Byron with a Friend, edited by R. C. Dallas.   1824.
Letters and Journals of Byron, with Notices of His Life by Thomas Moore.   2 vols., 1830.
Astarte, edited by Mary, Countess of Lovelace.   1921.
Correspondence, edited by John Murray.   2 vols., 1922.
Byron in His Letters, edited by V. H. Collins.   1927.
The Ravenna Journal, 1821, edited by Rowland E. Prothero.   1928.
The Self Portrait: Letters and Diaries 1798 to 1824, edited by Peter Quennell.   2 vols.,
    1950.
His Very Self and Voice: Collected Conversations, Medwin's Conversations with Byron,
    and *Lady Blessington's Conversations of Byron,* edited by Ernest J. Lovell.   3 vols.,
    1954–69.

Bibliography: in *The Works,* 1898–1904; *A Bibliography of the Writings of Byron* by T. J.
Wise, 2 vols., 1932–33; *Byron: A Comprehensive Bibliography of Secondary Materials in
English* by O. J. Santucho, 1977.

Reading List: *Byron: The Years of Fame*, 1935, and *Byron in Italy*, 1940, both volumes revised in 1967, both by Peter Quennell; *Byron: Christian Virtues* by G. Wilson Knight, 1953; *Byron: A Biography*, 3 vols., 1957, *Byron's Poetry: A Critical Introduction*, 1965, and *Byron: A Portrait*, 1971, all by Leslie Marchand; *Byron and the Spoiler's Art* by Paul West, 1960; *The Style of Don Juan* by G. M. Ridenour, 1960; *The Late Lord Byron* by Doris L. Moore, 1961; *The Structure of Byron's Major Poems* by W. H. Marshall, 1962; *The Byronic Hero: Types and Prototypes* by P. L. Thorslev, 1962; *Byron: A Critical Study* by A. Rutherford, 1962; *Byron the Poet* by M. K. Joseph, 1964; *Byron and the Ruins of Paradise* by R. Gleckner, 1967; *Fiery Dust* by J. J. McGann, 1968; *Byron and Shelley* by J. Buxton, 1968; *Byron* by B. Blackstone, 3 vols., 1970–71; *Byron* by J. D. Jump, 1972.

*   *   *

The vast reputation Byron enjoyed as a poet during his life suffered some diminution during the high Victorian era as a consequence of Matthew Arnold's rating of Wordsworth as the supreme poet of the Romantic Movement, and the gradual promotion of other poets of that Movement to high critical esteem. During the twenties and thirties of this century, a new poetic practice – in which irony, reticence, ambiguity were aims, in sharpest contrast to those of Byron – accelerated the decline of a reputation which was once pre-eminent. Rightly, I think, the initial great reputation of Byron is now being restored, though with some redistribution of emphases. Meanwhile, the discovery by a wide readership of Byron's letters and journals has forced a recognition of virtues – for example, an engaging, rakish frankness and generous humour – scarcely found in such radiant abundance in other writers.

In contrast to the irony, reticence and cautious verse of the middle of this century, Byron's is wonderfully robust, charged with vigour and colour, and it has a bold rhythmic movement. This description may be incomplete where *Beppo* or his comic masterpiece *Don Juan* are concerned, but it applies to the bulk of his early work. The early poetry is declamatory and deserves to be declaimed. If this is to concede that it is rhetorical, this is no denigration: Byron was the last English poet who, with an assured audience in mind – a large audience of cultured men and women, informed in matters of public interest – spoke out boldly to that audience, and held that audience spellbound. If this poetry lacks subtlety in syntax, nuance of rhythm, complexity of thought, these are the necessary defects of the virtues of a poetic voice and style demanding a strong and immediate effect at a first hearing. Byron does not mince matters; he knows what he wants to say; he says it bravely and magnificently; and the simple but grand surge of the rhythm matches the strength of his convictions and is its appropriate organ. Whereas the subtle rhythms and tones of a Keats resist translation, Byron can be largely rendered into other languages successfully, and this helps to account for a fame and influence on the continent scarcely less than in England during his life and, after his death, in Greece.

Much recent criticism has been concerned with dividing the poet Byron from the man Byron who lived a poetic – if at times wickedly glamourous – life. Such a dissociation is not easy, and perhaps should not be attempted. For, eminently, Byron is the poet who lived his poetry. Prime evidence for this oneness of the man and his writing is the image of the chief figure, the hero, who appears again and again in the poems. This Byronic hero, it has been alleged, is less of a projection of Byron as he actually was than a projection of the figure he liked to consider himself to be, and wished others to accept as his true self. It is a saturnine figure, "pathetic, statuesque, posturing," conscious of his suffering, remorseful for some obscure sin with which he is tainted, yet proud, whether as "an outlaw of his own dark mind" or as wrongfully ostracized by others. He is mysterious, attractive to women, yet self-sufficient, lonely. He is capable of brave acts. No doubt such a figure, especially if he is handsome, and old enough to have had, as the saying is, a "past," can engage the romantic speculations of women and an envious, if undeclared, rivalry of those women's men. Childe Harold, the Giaour, Manfred, and the others, are recognizably akin: fascinating, yet repelling of pity, disdainful even of a larger sympathy. So it must not be thought therefore that this real

32 BYRON

or phantasied self-projection made, or makes, his poems less attractive on account of their author's self-absorption. At the time of their publication they had an immense appeal. Many like Captain Benwick, in Jane Austen's novel *Persuasion*, would indulge and magnify their own sorrow by identifying with the Byronic hero, appropriating to themselves "all the impassioned descriptions of hopeless agony." Moreover, a hero, like Childe Harold, was conveyed through a variety of scenes in a Europe, contemplating actual events or historic occasions, that were the concern of all educated men and women. If these heroes have a fascination today, it may well be that they have a strange resemblance to some modern terrorist leaders or others who, however viciously destructive their acts, may sincerely picture themselves, though wrongly and romantically, as heroes, hated and outlawed became of their noble ideals.

All of Byron is worth reading, but the first production which brought him overnight fame continues as a massive testament of his poetic vitality. Yet *Childe Harold* was published by instalments from 1812 to 1818. The management of the Spenserian stanza is, at first, occasionally awkward and the archaisms annoy, but gradually, as the thought becomes more sombre, the authentic Byronic assurance, weight, and impetus are established. But excellencies glow even in Cantos I and II, narrating the Childe's travels in Portugal, Spain, Greece, and Albania. The stanzas on the bull-fight in Cadiz are superb in the concrete vividness of the realization of the *corrida*, its sights, sounds, movements of those in the arena and of the spectators. Superb too is the honesty of the report of the reactions of the Childe – he is stirred by the ritual but he deplores the cruel sufferings of the animals. However, it is in the closing stanzas of Canto IV, by which time the mask of Harold has been dropped and the poet is speaking in his own person, that one of the most assured and sonorous voices in English poetry is heard.

With the oriental tales, some of them in octosyllabic metres, we are reminded of the poet's narrative skills, and especially of one he was to use to such effect later: he was a master in the skill of creating diversions with the intent of increasing suspense in the issue of the main story.

Yet the Byron who has received the most acclaim in the last two decades is not the Romantic poet of *Childe Harold* or the oriental tales, but the satirical and comic poet of *The Vision of Judgment, Beppo*, and *Don Juan*. His early *English Bards and Scotch Reviewers*, a biting attack on those who had upbraided his juvenilia, had revealed his gift for invective, the existence of another aspect of Byron's personality – more in tune with Pope and the Augustans than with what is commonly regarded as Romantic, even though Byron can also, and rightly, be regarded as *the* type of the Romantic poet. But it is this anti-romantic side which emerged to dominance in *The Vision of Judgment, Beppo*, and, above all, in *Don Juan*.

Auden has said that *Don Juan* is the only long poem which is nowhere boring. It is the only great comic poem in English. Don Juan is, of course, Byron, who can now see himself with detachment as a frequently ludicrous and exploited figure. On the back of the MS of Canto I are some poignant lines in which Byron cries "for God's sake – hock and soda water." This mixture alleviated the effects of the excesses of the night before, a hangover. It is with a "morning after" sanity that the poem was conceived. With its writing came the discovery that the Italian *ottava rima* form, used by early Italian poets for solemn purposes, was, especially when employing di- or tri-syllabic rhymes, ideally suited for comic effects in English. But the lines "If that I laugh at any mortal thing/'Tis that I may not weep" warn us of the seriousness of the comedy of *Don Juan*. If the long, though unfinished, mock-epic is conceived in a mainly comic spirit, that comedy embraces good-natured burlesque, banter, angry invective, the fiercest indignation, light-hearted gaiety. Byron chooses mainly to laugh at mortal things that he may not weep. There are many different kinds of laughter.

It has been right to have concentrated on *Childe Harold*, representative of one mode, and on *Don Juan*, representative of the other mode, but mention should be made of Byron's lyrics. Unlike those of most other Romantic poets, but like those of his friend, Thomas Moore, these (for instance, "She walks in beauty like the night" or "So we'll go no more a-roving") appear not to be the utterances of a singular individual – though they are that – but the utterances of sociable Regency mankind. They are turned for rendering in song in an Assembly room. The private anguish and the class interest in their themes are combined.

The poet's immense production includes the plays which, though ostensibly not for production, make profound searchings into political and family themes. And his prose, as already observed, affords almost matchless interest and entertainment.

—Francis Berry

CAMPBELL, Thomas. Scottish. Born in Glasgow, 27 July 1777. Educated at Glasgow Grammar School, 1785–91; University of Glasgow, 1791–96; studied law in Edinburgh, 1797. Married Matilda Sinclair in 1803 (died, 1828); two sons. Tutor at Downie, near Lochgilphead, 1796–97; worked for the publishers Mundell and Company, and as a private tutor, Edinburgh, 1797–1800; toured Germany and Denmark, 1800–01; lived in London and Edinburgh, 1801–03, and settled in London, 1803, having refused a chair at Wilna, to pursue a literary career: lectured at the Royal Institution, 1810, and the Surrey Institution, 1820; Editor, *The New Monthly Magazine*, London, 1820–30, and *The Metropolitan*, London, 1831–32. Advocate and planner of a university for London, 1825; Founder, Polish Association, 1832. Lord Rector, University of Glasgow (elected three times), 1826–29. Granted Crown pension, 1805. *Died 15 June 1844.*

PUBLICATIONS

Collections

    Poetical Works, edited by J. Logie Robertson.   1907.

Verse

    The Wounded Hussar. 1799.
    The Pleasures of Hope with Other Poems.   1799; revised edition, 1800, 1803.
    Poems. 1803.
    Gertrude of Wyoming: A Pennsylvanian Tale, and Other Poems.   1809.
    Miscellaneous Poems. 1824.
    Theodoric: A Domestic Tale, and Other Poems.   1824.
    Poland; Lines on the View from St. Leonard's.   1831.
    The Pilgrim of Glencoe and Other Poems.   1842.

Other

    Life of Mrs. Siddons. 2 vols., 1834.
    Letters from the South. 2 vols., 1837; as *The Journal of a Residence in Algiers,* 1842.
    Memoir of Dugald Stewart. 1838.
    Life of Petrarch. 2 vols., 1841.

34 CAMPBELL

Editor, *Specimens of the British Poets.*   7 vols., 1819.
Editor, *The Dramatic Works of Shakespeare.*   1838.
Editor, *The Scenic Annual for 1838.*   1838.

Reading List: *Life and Letters of Campbell* by William Beattie, 3 vols., 1849; *Campbell* by James C. Hadden, 1899; *Campbell: An Oration* by W. Macneille Dixon, 1928.

*   *   *

Like his contemporary, the Irish poet Thomas Moore, Thomas Campbell gives the impression of having worked from the outside. He did not, therefore, achieve the highest flights of his art. Like Moore, Campbell specialised in cantering metres. Like Moore too, he scored outstanding success in one, though not the same, department of poetry. Campbell's gusto found perfect expression in "Ye Mariners of England," generally regarded with the "Marseillaise" and "Scots wha hae" as one of the three greatest war songs ever written. "Hohenlinden" and "The Battle of the Baltic" are other striking examples of his ability to achieve memorability in action poetry. He scored another success, too, in the field of the lighter lyric. Everyone knows the poem beginning "How delicious is the winning/Of a kiss at Love's beginning," though the less familiar "Florine," set to music by the Scottish composer Francis George Scott, is finer still.

For the rest, Campbell is a poet of remembered words and phrases, mostly from his youthful poem in heroic couplets, modelled on Milton and on Thomson's *Seasons*, "The Pleasures of Hope." To that poem, which quickly ran through four editions, we are indebted for: "Tis distance lends enchantment to the view," "like angels' visits, few and far between," and "what millions died – that Caesar might be great." Scott thought that Campbell's achievement so scantily lived up to its promise because Campbell "feared the shadow his own fame cast before him." W. Macneille Dixon, on the other hand, believed the poet "had a fear of the world's best," adding "and there can be no more wholesome type of alarm."

"Lord Ullin's Daughter" is as good as anything Scott himself achieved in the Scots ballad vein, while in its different way "Lochiel" is very little inferior. "Gertrude of Wyoming," a tale of the destruction of Pennsylvanian settlers, lacks narrative force, difficult in any case to keep moving in the Spenserian stanza. It also perpetrates numerous scientific errors and anachronisms, such as locating tigers on the shores of Lake Erie, and panthers in Ohio.

As an editor and critic, Campbell was cool towards the Lake Poets, especially Coleridge, but warm in his defence and attempted restitution of Pope. This led Byron to record in his journal: "[Campbell's] defence of Pope is glorious; to be sure it is his *own cause* too – but no matter, it is very good, and does him much credit."

While Campbell was editor of *The Metropolitan*, the novelist Captain Marryat submitted a contribution on the merits of flogging to maintain naval discipline. Campbell printed it, followed by his own lines:

> Ingenious author of this article,
> I believe in your doctrine not one particle,
>   But if e'er the power be mine
> To flog contributors, my boy,
> Your back shall be the first to enjoy
>   The benefit of the Nine.

It is impossible not to warm to that.

—Maurice Lindsay

CLARE, John. English. Born in Helpston, Northamptonshire, 13 July 1793. Educated at a local dame school, and at schools in Glinton, Northamptonshire, to age 16. Married Martha Turner in 1820; seven children. Farm labourer; worked for Francis Gregory, 1809–10, and as gardener at Burghley House, 1810–11; attracted brief celebrity as "peasant-poet" on publication of his first volume, 1820; ill after 1830: committed to High Beech asylum for the insane, Epping, Essex, 1837–41, and to St. Andrew's Asylum, near Northampton, 1841–64. *Died 20 May 1864.*

PUBLICATIONS

Collections

Poems, edited by J. W. Tibble.   2 vols., 1935.
Poems of Clare's Madness, edited by Geoffrey Grigson.   1949.
Prose, Letters, edited by J. W. and Anne Tibble.   2 vols., 1951.
Later Poems, edited by Eric Robinson and Geoffrey Summerfield.   1964.
Selected Poems and Prose, edited by Eric Robinson and Geoffrey Summerfield.   1966

Verse

Poems Descriptive of Rural Life and Scenery.   1820.
The Village Minstrel and Other Poems.   2 vols., 1821.
The Shepherd's Calendar, with Village Stories and Other Poems.   1827; edited by Eric Robinson and Geoffrey Summerfield, 1964.
The Rural Muse.   1835.
Poems Chiefly from Manuscript, edited by Edmund Blunden and Alan Porter.   1920.
Madrigals and Chronicles, Being Newly Found Poems, edited by Edmund Blunden.   1924.
The Midsummer Cushion, edited by Anne Tibble.   1978.

Other

Sketches in the Life of Clare by Himself, edited by Edmund Blunden.   1931.

Reading List: *Clare: A Life,* 1932, revised edition, 1972, and *Clare: His Life and Poetry,* 1956, both by J. W. and Anne Tibble; *The Idea of Landscape and the Sense of Place 1730–1840: An Approach to the Poetry of Clare* by John Barrell, 1972; *Clare: The Critical Heritage* edited by Mark Storey, 1973, and *The Poetry of Clare* by Storey, 1974.

*   *   *

John Clare was born in the village of Helpston (then Helpstone) in Northamptonshire. In that rural setting, except for a move three miles to the fen village of Northborough in 1832, he remained until he was incarcerated in first one asylum and then a second where he spent 27 years of his life. Clare's father was a flail-thresher who, Clare said, could recite over a hundred ballads and songs. His mother, a shepherd's daughter, also sang ballads and told traditional stories.

Contemporary with Blake, Keats, Shelley, and Byron, Clare is still not recognized as a poet

36   CLARE

of the first standing; yet he is the foremost English poet of the countryside. His poetry divides into two kinds. Most was descriptive, often repetitive, verse concerning an England changing, after 500 years of stability under a system of "common fields," to a system of "enclosure." Bigger "enclosed" farms were already beginning to use the mechanical methods that have resulted in today's "factory" farming with less of the hard labour in which leisure was an important part of work. Beside the major part of his poetry on country life and on nature, Clare wrote a small but important amount of reflective, visionary poetry.

His first poems were attempts at "imitations of my father's songs," but he burnt them during the many years of the long apprenticeship he set himself. In 1820 Clare's first book of poems was published by the London publisher of Keats, Lamb, and Hood – John Taylor. This, with the clumsy title of *Poems Descriptive of Rural Life and Scenery*, caught the end of a temporary vogue in country verse, went into four editions within a year, and was an undoubted success. Clare visited London, was "lionized," and returned to inevitable isolation at Helpston. His other books, *The Village Minstrel, The Shepherd's Calendar*, and *The Rural Muse*, did not, however, sell. An important manuscript, *The Midsummer Cushion*, having lain unprinted for a century and a half, was published in 1978.

By 1837 the strain of writing, poverty, and the needs of his parents and growing family began to tell on Clare. He developed illusions – that he was Lord Byron (the *successful* poet), a wrestler Tom Spring, a boxer Jack Randall; that his childhood love, Mary Joyce, was his first wife, while Patty, mother of his children, was but his second. With the help of his publisher Clare was sent to High Beech, a private asylum in Essex – he was there for four years. In the summer of 1841 he escaped "those jailors called warders" and walked the 80 miles home to Northborough. For five months he was at home, finishing two long poems with Byronic titles, "Don Juan" and "Child Harold." His physical health improved but his delusions were as strong as ever. In December 1841 Clare was certified insane by two doctors and confined to St. Andrew's asylum near Northampton. He was allowed freedom to walk into the town and encouraged to continue to write. Here he wrote over a thousand verses, some traditional jingle, but a few important to his achievement.

Edmund Blunden introduced Clare to the present century with *Poems Chiefly from Manuscript* of 1920. Clare's half-dozen or so reflective lyrics of his St. Andrew's period contain "Love Lies Beyond the Tomb," "An Invite to Eternity," "I Am," "A Vision," "Hesperus," "Love's Story," "I Hid My Love," and "Love's Pains." A few more mystical, reflective poems lie scattered among the bulk of his country, descriptive work. This handful of lyrics, rhythmically new, Edmund Blunden writes, places Clare where "William Blake and only he can be said to resemble him." Geoffrey Grigson believes that they push Clare into "greatness, however circumscribed that greatness." They are concerned with the confusion into which, during man's civilized development, sexual love has fallen, from its original innocence.

From "An Invite to Eternity":

> Wilt thou go with me, sweet maid,
> Say, maiden, wilt thou go with me
> Through the valley-depths of shade,
> Of night and dark obscurity;
> Where the path has lost its way,
> Where the sun forgets the day,
> Where there's no life nor light to see,
> Sweet maiden, wilt thou go with me?...
>
> The land of shadows wilt thou trace,
> And look – nor know each other's face;
> The present mixed with reason gone,
> And past and present all as one?
> Say, maiden, can thy life be led

To join the living with the dead?
Then trace thy footsteps on with me;
We're wed to one eternity.

Clare's major work, his country verse, with, as De Quincey wrote, scarcely one "commonplace image," remains: sonnets on the blackcap, the reed-bird, the redcap, in fact hundreds on animals, flowers, birds, in what he saw as an "Eternity of Nature." He was a non-scientific but excellent naturalist:

Within a thick and spreading hawthorn bush
  That overhung a mole-hill large and round,
I heard from morn to morn a merry thrush
  Sing hymns to sunrise, while I drank the sound
With joy; and often an intruding guest,
  I watched her secret toils from day to day —
How true she warped the moss to form a nest,
  And modelled it within with wood and clay;
And by and by, like heath-bells gilt with dew,
  There lay her shining eggs, as bright as flowers,
Ink-spotted over shells of greeny blue;
  And there I witnessed, in the sunny hours,
A brood of nature's minstrels chirp and fly,
Glad as that sunshine and the laughing sky.

Clare's mental disorder was cyclothymic. He endured this form of insanity in common with Hölderlin, Smart, Cowper, Newton, Goethe, and Samuel Johnson. It is a sickness to which men of broad general powers coupled with a sensitive imagination are naturally exposed.

—Anne Tibble

COBBETT, William. English. Born in Farnham, Surrey, 9 March 1763. Largely self-taught. Worked as a solicitor's clerk in London, 1783, then joined the 54th Foot, and served at Chatham, Kent, 1784, then as a corporal and sergeant-major in Nova Scotia and New Brunswick, 1784–91. Married Ann Reid in 1792; seven children. Teacher in Philadelphia, 1792–96; bookseller and publisher on the loyalist side, Philadelphia, 1796–1800; began the monthly *The Censor*, 1796, and its successor, the daily newspaper *Porcupine's Gazette*, 1797–99; prosecuted for libel, moved to New York, started a new magazine, *The Rush-Light*, then abandoned the project and returned to England, 1800; Editor, *The Porcupine*, London, 1801–02; proprietor of a bookshop in Pall Mall, 1801–03; Founder/Editor, *Cobbett's Weekly Political Register*, 1802 until his death; farmer in Botley, Hampshire, 1804–17; imprisoned for his criticism of the flogging of militiamen, 1810–12; fled to the United States to avoid arrest; farmed on Long Island, 1817–19; returned to England, 1820; published *Corbett's Evening Post*, 1820; established a seed farm at Kensington, 1821; stood as candidate for Parliament for Coventry, 1821, and Preston, 1826; tried for sedition, 1831; Member of Parliament for Oldham, 1832–34. *Died 18 June 1835.*

38   COBBETT

PUBLICATIONS

Collections

The Opinions of Cobbett, edited by G. D. H. and Margaret Cole.   1944.
Letters, edited by Gerald Duff.   1974.

Prose (selection)

Le Tuteur Anglais; ou, Grammaire Regulière de la Langue Anglaise.   1795.
The Works of Peter Porcupine.   1795.
The Life and Adventures of Peter Porcupine.   1796; as *The Life of Cobbett,* 1809.
The Life of Thomas Paine.   1796.
Porcupine's Works (reprints pamphlets and periodical writings).   2 vols., 1797; revised
    edition, 12 vols., 1801.
A Collection of the Facts and Observations Relative to the Peace with Bonaparte.   1801.
Cobbett's Political Register (periodical with varying title).   89 vols., 1802–35.
*The Political Proteus: A View of the Public Character and Conduct of R. B.
    Sheridan.*   1804.
Letters on the Late War Between the United States and Great Britain.   1815.
The Pride of Britannia Humbled.   1815.
*Paper Against Gold and Glory Against Prosperity; or, An Account of the Rise, Progress,
    Extent, and Present State of the Funds and of the Paper-Money of Great Britain.*   2
    vols., 1815; revised edition, 1821.
A Year's Residence in the United States of America.   3 vols., 1818–19.
A Grammar of the English Language.   1818; revised edition, 1823.
A Letter from the Queen to the King.   1820.
The American Gardener.   1821.
Sermons.   1822.
Cottage Economy.   1822.
Collective Commentaries.   1822.
A French Grammar.   1824.
A History of the Protestant "Reformation" in England and Ireland.   2 vols., 1826–27.
Poor Man's Friend.   5 vols., 1826–27.
The Woodlands.   1828.
The English Gardener.   1828.
A Treatise on Cobbett's Corn.   1828; revised edition, 1831.
The Emigrant's Guide.   1829.
*On the Present Prospects of Merchants, Traders, and Farmers, and on the State of the
    Country in General* (lectures).   1829.
Three Lectures on the State of the Country.   1830.
Good Friday; or, The Murder of Jesus Christ by the Jews.   1830.
Rural Rides.   1830; *Tour in Scotland,* 1832; edited by G. D. H. and Margaret Cole, 3
    vols., 1930.
*Advice to Young Men and (Incidentally) to Young Women in the Middle and Higher
    Ranks of Life.*   1830.
*Eleven Lectures on the French and Belgian Revolutions, and English
    Boroughmongering.*   1830.
History of the Regency and Reign of King George the Fourth.   2 vols., 1834.
Two-Penny Trash; or, Politics for the Poor.   2 vols., 1831–32.
A Spelling Book.   1831.
Manchester Lectures in Support of His Fourteen Reform Propositions.   1832.

A Geographical Dictionary of England and Wales. 1832.
The Speeches of Cobbett, M.P. for Oldham. 2 vols., 1833.
A New French and English Dictionary. 2 vols., 1833.
Three Lectures on the Political State of Ireland. 1834.
Legacy to Labourers. 1835.
Legacy to Parsons. 1835.
Selections from Cobbett's Political Works, edited by John Morgan and James Paul Cobbett. 6 vols., 1835–37.
Legacy to Peel. 1836.
Legacy to Lords, edited by William Cobbett, Jr. 1863.
Thomas Paine: A Sketch of His Life and Character, in *The Life of Thomas Paine* by Moncure Daniel Conway. 1892.
A History of the Last Hundred Days of Freedom, edited by J. L. Hammond. 1921.
Life and Adventures of Peter Porcupine with Other Records of His Early Career in England and America, edited by G. D. H. Cole. 1927.
The Progress of a Plough-Boy to a Seat in Parliament, edited by William Reitzel. 1933.
Letters to Edward Thornton 1797 to 1800, edited by G. D. H. Cole. 1937.

Plays

Big O. and Sir Glory; or, Leisure to Laugh. 1825.
Mexico; or, The Patriot Bondholders, in *Political Register*, 1830.
Surplus Population and Poor-Law Bill. 1835(?).

Verse

French Arrogance; or, The Cat Let Out of the Bag. 1798.

Other Works

Editor, *An Answer to Paine's Rights of Man*, by Henry Mackenzie. 1796.
Editor, *The History of Jacobinism*, by William Playfair. 1796.
Editor, *A View of the Causes and Consequences of the Present War with France*, by Thomas Erskine. 1797.
Editor, *Observations on the Dispute Between the United States and France*, by Robert Goodloe Harper and others. 1798.
Editor, *A Treatise on the Culture and Management of Fruit Trees*, by William Forsyth. 1802.
Editor, *Spirit of the Public Journals for the Year 1804*. 1805.
Editor, with John Wright and Thomas Bayley Howell, *Complete Collection of State Trials*. 33 vols., 1809–26 (Cobbett was co-editor until 1812 only).
Editor, *An Essay on Sheep*, by R. R. Livingston. 1811.
Editor, *The Horse-Hoeing Husbandry*, by Jethro Tull. 1822.
Editor, *The Curse of Paper-Money and Banking; or, A Short History of Banking in the United States*, by William M. Gouge. 1833.
Editor, *Life of Andrew Jackson*, by John Henry Eaton. 1834.

Translator, *Impeachment of Mr. Lafayette*. 1793.
Translator, *A Compendium of the Law of Nations*, by G. F. Von Martens. 1795.
Translator, *A Topographical and Political Description of the Spanish Port of Saint Domingo*, by M. L. E. Moreau de Saint-Mery. 1796.

40 COBBETT

Translator, *The Empire of Germany*, by Jean Gabriel Peltier. 1803.
Translator, *Elements of the Roman History* (bilingual edition), by J. H. Sievrac. 1828.
Translator, *An Abridged History of the Emperors* (bilingual edition), by J. H. Sievrac. 1829.

Bibliography: *Cobbett: A Bibliographical Account of His Life and Times* by M. L. Pearl, 1953.

Reading List: *Life and Letters of Cobbett* by Lewis Melville, 2 vols., 1913; *The Life of Cobbett* by G. D. H. Cole, 1924, revised edition, 1947; *Cobbett* by W. Baring Pemberton, 1949; *Cobbett* by A. J. Sambrook, 1973; *Cobbett: An Introduction to His Life and Writings* by Simon Booth, 1975.

*   *   *

William Cobbett found his vocation as a political commentator in America in the 1790's when he patriotically opposed Democratic attempts to ally the United States with France in her war against England. In addition to his newspaper *Porcupine's Gazette* he wrote some forty pamphlets, collected later into twelve fat volumes of *Porcupine's Works*; but the most enduring work of those years is *The Life and Adventures of Peter Porcupine*, where Cobbett blends his sense of the unique value of his own life into an attractive, idealized vision of Old England, and, like his Romantic contemporaries in that age of autobiographies, discovers that his own life has a representative significance.

Back in England, Cobbett gradually moved into opposition to the Government, joined the Radicals, and pressed for Parliamentary reform. In this cause he wrote scores of pamphlets, many of which were first published serially in the *Political Register*, the newspaper which he conducted practically single-handed and with a few interruptions (for prison and exile) from 1802 to his death in 1835. He wrote books on many other subjects from grammar to agriculture, all with a marked political bias; his *History of the Protestant "Reformation"* was one of the most widely influential of all the nineteenth-century works which idealized the Middle Ages; but his best writing is to be found in the largely autobiographical *Rural Rides* and *Advice to Young Men*. Cobbett has a political purpose in comparing the condition of England in the 1820's with his idealized view of the 1770's, but his writing about his own childhood conveys an urgent sense of personal wholeness within a landscape of memory. The power, vigour, and beauty of Cobbett's best work, like Wordsworth's, arise from recollected emotion.

—A. J. Sambrook

COLERIDGE, Samuel Taylor. English. Born in Ottery St. Mary, Devon, 21 October 1772. Educated at the Blue Coat School, Christ's Hospital, London, 1782–90; Jesus College, Cambridge (Christ's Hospital Exhibitioner; Greek Verse Medal), 1791–94; attended classes at the University of Göttingen, 1798. Married Sara Fricker, sister-in-law of the poet Robert Southey, in 1794. Involved with Southey in an abortive scheme for a "pantisocracy" in America, 1794; lived in Bristol, 1794–97; settled at Nether Stowey, Somerset, near the Wordsworths at Alfoxden, 1797; spent winter in Germany with the Wordsworths, 1798;

COLERIDGE   41

given an annuity by the Wedgwood family, 1798; moved to Greta Hall, Keswick, near Southey, and the Wordsworths at Grasmere, 1800; became addicted to opium and lived in Malta in an effort to restore his health, 1804–06: Secretary to the Governor, Sir Alexander Bell, 1804–05; quarrelled with Wordsworth, 1810; final residence at Highgate, near London, under the care of Dr. James Gillman, 1816 until his death; reconciled with Wordsworth and toured the Rhineland with him, 1828. Lecturer and journalist: Editor, *The Watchman*, 1796; wrote for the *Morning Post*, 1799; lectured extensively in London, 1808–19; Editor, *The Friend*, 1809–10; Assistant Editor, *The Courier*, 1810–11. Associate of the Royal Society of Literature (with pension), 1824. *Died 25 July 1834.*

PUBLICATIONS

Collections

Complete Works, edited by W. G. T. Shield.   7 vols., 1853.
Complete Poetical Works, edited by W. H. Coleridge.   2 vols., 1912.
Collected Letters, edited by E. L. Griggs.   6 vols., 1956–68.
Collected Works, edited by Kathleen Coburn.   1969 –

Verse

Ode on the Departing Year.   1796.
Poems on Various Subjects.   1796; revised edition, as *Poems*, with Charles Lamb and Charles Lloyd, 1797; revised edition, by Coleridge alone, 1803.
Fears in Solitude, France: An Ode, and Frost at Midnight.   1798.
Lyrical Ballads, with a Few Other Poems, with William Wordsworth.   1798; revised edition, 2 vols., 1800; edited by W. J. B. Owen, 1967.
Christabel, Kubla Khan: A Vision, The Pains of Sleep.   1816.
Sybilline Leaves: A Collection of Poems.   1817.
Poetical Works.   3 vols., 1828.
The Devil's Walk, with Robert Southey, edited by H. W. Montagu.   1830.

Plays

The Fall of Robespierre, with Robert Southey.   1794.
Wallenstein, from the play by Schiller.   1800.
Remorse, music by Michael Kelly (produced 1813).   1813; earlier version, *Osorio*, edited by R. H. Shepherd, 1873.
Zapolyta: A Christmas Tale (revised version by T. J. Dibdin produced 1818).   1817.
Dramatic Works, edited by Derwent Coleridge.   1852.
The Triumph of Loyalty, in *Complete Poetical Works.*   1912.

Other

Omniana; or, Horae Otiosiores, with Robert Southey.   2 vols., 1812; edited by Robert Gittings, 1969.
The Friend.   1812; revised edition, 3 vols., 1818; edited by Barbara E. Rooke, in *Collected Works*, 2 vols., 1969.

42 COLERIDGE

Biographia Literaria; or, Biographical Sketches of My Literary Life and Opinions. 2 vols., 1817; edited by George Watson, 1956.
On Method. 1818; as *Mental Science,* 1855; edited by A. D. Snyder, 1934.
Aids to Reflection in the Formation of a Manly Character. 1825; edited by H. N. Coleridge, 1839.
On the Constitution of the Church and State According to the Idea of Each. 1830; edited by John Colmer, in *Collected Works,* 1975.
Specimens of the Table-Talk, edited by H. N. Coleridge. 2 vols., 1835.
Literary Remains, edited by H. N. Coleridge. 4 vols., 1836–39; reprinted in part as *Notes on English Divines,* 2 vols., 1853.
Letters, Conversations, and Recollections of Coleridge, by T. Allsop. 2 vols., 1836.
Confessions of an Inquiring Spirit, edited by H. N. Coleridge. 1840.
Hints Toward the Formation of a More Comprehensive Theory of Life, edited by S. B. Watson. 1848.
Notes and Lectures upon Shakespeare and Some of the Old Poets and Dramatists, with Other Literary Remains, edited by Mrs. H. N. Coleridge. 2 vols., 1849; as *Essays and Lectures ...,* 1907.
Essays on His Own Time, edited by Sara Coleridge. 3 vols., 1850; edited by David V. Erdman, with additional material, in *Collected Works,* 3 vols., 1975.
Notes Theological, Political, and Miscellaneous, edited by Derwent Coleridge. 2 vols., 1853.
Anima Poetae, from the Unpublished Notebooks, edited by E. H. Coleridge. 1895.
Biographia Epistolaris, Being the Biographical Supplement of Biographia Literaria, edited by A. Turnbull. 2 vols., 1911.
Coleridge on Logic and Learning, with Selections from the Unpublished Manuscripts, edited by A. D. Snyder. 1929.
Shakespearean Criticism, edited by T. M. Raysor. 2 vols., 1930.
Miscellaneous Criticism, edited by T. M. Raysor. 1936.
The Philosophical Lectures, edited by Kathleen Coburn. 1949.
Coleridge on the Seventeenth Century, edited by Roberta Florence Brinkley. 1955.
Notebooks, edited by Kathleen Coburn. 1957–

Bibliography: *A Bibliography of the Writings in Prose and Verse of Coleridge,* by T. J. Wise, 1913, supplement, 1919; *An Annotated Bibliography of Criticism and Scholarship,* vol. 1, 1793–1899 by Josephine and Richard Haven and Maurianne Adams, 1976.

Reading List: *The Road to Xanadu* by John Livingston Lowes, 1927, revised edition, 1930; *Coleridge* by Humphrey House, 1953; *Coleridge* by Kathleen Raine, 1953; *Coleridge the Visionary* by J. B. Beer, 1959; *Coleridge, Critic of Society* by John Colmer, 1959; *The Idea of Coleridge's Criticism* by R. H. Fogle, 1962; *Coleridge: A Collection of Critical Essays* edited by Kathleen Coburn, 1967; *The Waking Dream* by Patricia M. Adair, 1967; *Coleridge: The Work and the Relevance* by William Walsh, 1967; *Coleridge and the Pantheist Tradition* by Thomas McFarland, 1969; *Coleridge: The Critical Heritage* edited by J. R. de J. Jackson, 1970; *Coleridge* by John Cornwell, 1973; *Coleridge's Meditative Art* by Reeve Parker, 1975; *Coleridge and the Idea of Love* by Anthony John Harding, 1977.

*   *   *

Samuel Taylor Coleridge, in *Biographia Literaria,* describes in an oft-quoted passage what was to be his part in the *Lyrical Ballads,* the book of verses which he and Wordsworth planned together: "my endeavours should be directed to persons and characters supernatural, or at least romantic." Wordsworth on the other hand was to "propose to himself as his object, to give the charm of novelty to things of everyday, and to excite a feeling analogous to the supernatural, by awakening the mind's attention from the lethargy of custom, and directing it to the loveliness and the wonders of the world before us." When the volume appeared in 1798 this intention of Coleridge's was realised in one poem, "The Rime of the Ancient Mariner" (in its original form).

If Coleridge had written nothing else, this poem would be enough to establish his greatness as a Romantic poet. Essentially it is an imitation of the traditional ballads, a tale of adventures and of the supernatural, and can be read simply as such. But it is full of wider overtones, and we can see it as both a presentation of the Romantic archetype of Man as wanderer, and as a record of Coleridge's own spiritual pilgrimage. The Mariner's shooting of the albatross is an affront to the spirit of Nature, who pursues the Mariner and his companions with its vengeance. The thirst which torments them may be taken as a symbol of spiritual as well as physical drought, and the Life-in-Death to which the Mariner is given over is a state which Coleridge himself experienced continually and tragically. The redemption of the Mariner begins when he spontaneously blesses the water-snakes – a gratuitous act which complements the previous gratuitous slaying of the bird. But the redemption is not finally complete. The Mariner is still compelled to wander, and compulsively to relive his experience in recounting it. These and a great many other complexities of meaning are to be discovered in the poem, whether Coleridge intended them consciously or no. But the whole is given a sense of reality, especially by the use Coleridge makes of his wide reading in books of voyages and travelling.

Two other poems of the *annus mirabilis* 1797 have the same kind of imaginative power, but both of them, as with so much of Coleridge's work, are unfinished. Coleridge's account of the composition of "Kubla Khan," which he tells us was presented to him in a vision induced by laudanum and which he was unable to complete owing to the interruption of the person from Porlock, may be open to question. But the poem, represented by Coleridge as a "psychological experiment," is the forerunner of that imaginative exploitation of the subconscious which was to issue in later Symbolist and Surrealist poetry. Like "The Ancient Mariner," "Kubla Khan" can be made to reveal many levels of meaning. Its genesis is from the contemporary genre of Oriental romance. Its controlling images of a Dome associated with the permanence of Art, and moving waters suggestive of the world of shifting phenomena, point backwards to Chaucer's *Hous of Fame* and forward to Yeats' "Byzantium."

In "Christabel" we are superficially in the world of Gothic romance, though Coleridge's metrical originality in reviving the stressed or sprung rhythms of earlier English poetry is noteworthy. But the real subject of the poem is the mystery of iniquity – the pure and innocent Christabel obsessed by the vampire Geraldine, another figure of Life-in-Death. Coleridge's inability to find an answer to this may account for the poem's unfinished state. It is true that many years later he gave an account of how it was to be finished: Geraldine, after all, was to turn out to be a good spirit, sent by Christabel's dead mother – but this, though in line with Coleridge's later thinking that all things work together for good, is difficult to square with the text of the poem as it stands.

Nothing in the rest of Coleridge's poetical works quite lives up to the promise of these three relatively early poems. A number of reasons have been adduced to account for this, and all perhaps contributed. There is the debilitating effect of his use of opium, the temptation to abstraction which his study of philosophy brought, the breakdown of his marriage to Sara Fricker, and the quarrel with Wordsworth. Coleridge himself suffered deeply from the sense that he had not fulfilled his potentiality, in particular in not creating that synthesis of philosophy, theology, and poetry at which he aimed. If anyone in the nineteenth century could have brought about such a synthesis it might well have been Coleridge – but the sense that a unified vision of all knowledge is within one's grasp may itself be part of the false riches which narcotic addiction offers. Nevertheless, one should not underestimate what he actually did achieve. Shelley called Coleridge "a mighty poet/And a subtle-souled psychologist." Indeed he was in many ways the originator of psychology as a science, and

44   COLERIDGE

this enters into his poetry continually. The poem entitled "Love," which begins

> All thoughts, all passions, all delights,
> Whatever stirs this mortal frame,
> All are but ministers of Love,
>   And feed his sacred flame.

in fact enunciates a principle later to be formulated by Freud. What on a cursory reading appears to be a rather facile sentimental narrative is in fact a study in psychology, where the poet in the poem through his poetry elicits from the lady feelings she has not been previously aware of.

Very characteristic of Coleridge are his blank verse conversational poems, in which the form of thought, moving on from association to association, itself creates the form of the poem. Fine examples are "Frost at Midnight," "The Nightingale," and "This Lime-Tree Bower My Prison." These poems are full of natural observation, which relates them to yet also differentiates them from the poems of Wordsworth. Coleridge's sensibility to Nature is in some ways more subtle and delicate than that of his friend. He is particularly aware of atmospheric effects of light and of clouds, in which indeed he evinced a scientific interest. "Fears in Solitude" also belongs among the conversational poems, though it takes on a more oratorical and public tone. It was written at a time when a French invasion was widely expected, and Coleridge's analysis of the state of England may well present the modern reader with present day analogies.

In its opening lines "Dejection" begins as if it also were to be a conversational poem. But it is worked out in terms of the free pseudo- or Pindaric ode. Coleridge had already attempted the ode form in such early political poems as the *Ode to the Departing Year* and "France." But these are on the whole unsuccessful, being over-rhetorical and full of vague abstractions. It is the deep personal crisis which makes of "Dejection" a far greater poem. Originally addressed to Wordsworth, it was intended as a reply to the latter's "Ode on Intimations of Immortality." In both poems the poet is aware of the drying up of the sources of his earlier inspiration. Wordsworth feels that he has somehow moved away from the reality of living Nature, whereas for Coleridge the cause is subjective and psychological:

> we receive but what we give,
> And in our life alone does Nature live:
> Ours is her wedding garment, ours her shroud!
>   And would we aught behold, of higher worth,
> Than that inanimate cold world allowed
> To the poor loveless ever-anxious crowd,
>   Ah! from the soul itself must issue forth
> A light, a glory, a fair luminous cloud
>   Enveloping the Earth—

As Jacob Bronowski has pointed out in his book *The Poet's Defence,* what Coleridge is saying here is really the exact opposite of what Wordsworth believed, and the poem marks the parting of the ways between the two poets. As with Wordsworth's "Ode" the decline of Coleridge as a poet can largely be dated from "Dejection."

Yet, as with Wordsworth, the later years were not wholly barren. Nor were Coleridge's philosophic studies quite unproductive of poetry. We might cite the difficult but very beautiful little allegory of "Time, Real and Imaginary." The extremely obscure fragments "Ne Plus Ultra" and "Limbo" deserve more attention than they receive. They show the influence of Coleridge's reading in Dante and Donne and reach forward to a neo-metaphysical poetry such as was to be characteristic of the twentieth century. There is a surprise of another kind in the late "The Garden of Boccaccio" which exhibits a genial acceptance of sensuality which is otherwise rare in the often rather prudish Coleridge:

O all-enjoying and all-blending sage,
Long be it mine to con thy mazy page,
Where, half-conceal'd, the eye of fancy views
Fauns, nymphs, and winged saints, all gracious to thy muse!

Still in thy garden let me watch their pranks,
And see in Dian's vest between the ranks
Of the trim vines, some maid that half believes
The vestal fires, of which her lover grieves,
With that sly satyr peeping through the leaves!

As with his verse, Coleridge's prose writings are frequently fragmentary and unsystematic. They are full of profound insights, but these are often obscurely or imperfectly expressed. His most important critical work, *Biographia Literaria*, is notable for his definition of the imagination. Coleridge sees the poetic or secondary Imagination as an echo of the primary Imagination, "the prime Agent of all human Perception, and as a repetition in the finite mind of the eternal act of creation in the infinite I AM." His *Lectures on Shakespeare* shift from a preoccupation of earlier critics with the so-called Rules to those matters of psychology and characterisation which were to dominate the nineteenth-century approach. As a metaphysician Coleridge has often been thought of as merely the first interpreter of German Idealistic thought in England, and has even been accused of plagiarism in this respect. But he was deeply grounded in an indigenous British tradition, represented by the Cambridge Platonists and by Berkeley, as well as Hartley's theory of the association of ideas. There is much in Coleridge that anticipates later thinking, as in the evolutionary point of view of *A Theory of Life*.

In religion Coleridge returned by way of Unitarianism and naturalistic pantheism to the Anglican orthodoxy in which he had been brought up. In his *Constitution of Church and State* he puts forward a view of church and state as representing respectively the religious and secular aspects of the nation, organically conceived. This is in the line of conservative and Anglican thinking which stems from Hooker and Burke.

—John Heath-Stubbs

COLMAN, George, the Younger. English. Born in London, 21 October 1762; son of the writer George Colman the Elder. Educated at a school in Marylebone, London, until 1771; Westminster School, London, 1772–79; Christ Church, Oxford, 1779–81; King's College, Aberdeen, 1781–82; Lincoln's Inn, London. Married 1) Clara Morris in 1784 (died); 2) the actress Mrs. Gibbs. Took over management of his father's Haymarket Theatre, 1789–1813 (purchased the Haymarket patent, 1794; disposed of all of his shares to his partner by 1820); appointed Lieutenant of the Yeoman of the Guard by George IV, 1820; Examiner of Plays, 1824 until his death. *Died 17 October 1836.*

46 COLMAN

PUBLICATIONS

Collections

Poetical Works. 1840.
Broad Grins, My Night-Gown and Slippers, and Other Humorous Works, edited by G. B. Buckstone. 1872.

Plays

The Female Dramatist, from the novel *Roderick Random* by Smollett (produced 1782).
Two to One, music by Samuel Arnold (produced 1785). 1784.
Turk and No Turk, music by Samuel Arnold (produced 1785). Songs published 1785.
Inkle and Yarico, music by Samuel Arnold (produced 1787). 1787.
Ways and Means; or, A Trip to Dover (produced 1788). 1788.
The Battle of Hexham, music by Samuel Arnold (produced 1789). 1790.
The Surrender of Calais, music by Samuel Arnold (produced 1791). 1792.
Poor Old Haymarket; or, Two Sides of the Gutter (produced 1792). 1792.
The Mountaineers, music by Samuel Arnold (produced 1793). 1794.
New Hay at the Old Market (produced 1795). 1795; revised version, as *Sylvester Daggerwood* (produced 1796), 1808.
The Iron Chest, music by Stephen Storace, from the novel *Caleb Williams* by William Godwin (produced 1796). 1796; edited by Michael R. Booth, in *Eighteenth Century Tragedy,* 1965.
The Heir at Law (produced 1797). 1800.
Blue Beard; or, Female Curiosity! A Dramatic Romance, music by Michael Kelly, from a play by Michel Jean Sedaine (produced 1798). 1798.
Blue Devils, from a play by Patrat (produced 1798). 1808.
The Castle of Sorrento, with Henry Heartwell, music by Thomas Attwood, from a French play (produced 1799). 1799.
Feudal Times; or, The Banquet-Gallery, music by Michael Kelly (produced 1799). 1799.
The Review; or, The Wags of Windsor, music by Samuel Arnold (produced 1800). 1801.
The Poor Gentleman (produced 1801). 1802.
John Bull; or, An Englishman's Fireside (produced 1803). 1803.
Love Laughs at Locksmiths, music by Michael Kelly, from a play by J. N. Bouilly (produced 1803). 1803.
The Gay Deceivers; or, More Laugh Than Love, music by Michael Kelly, from a play by Theodore Hell (produced 1804). 1808.
The Children in the Wood (produced 1805?). 1805.
Who Wants a Guinea? (produced 1805). 1805.
We Fly by Night; or, Long Stories (produced 1806). 1808.
The Forty Thieves, with Sheridan, music by Michael Kelly (produced 1806). 1808; as *Ali Baba,* 1814.
The Africans; or, War, Love, and Duty, music by Michael Kelly (produced 1808). 1808.
X.Y.Z. (produced 1810). 1820.
The Quadrupeds of Quedlinburgh; or, The Rovers of Weimar (produced 1811).
Doctor Hocus Pocus; or, Harlequin Washed White (produced 1814).
The Actor of All Work; or, First and Second Floor (produced 1817).
The Law of Java, music by Henry Bishop (produced 1822). 1822.

Stella and Leatherlungs; or, A Star and a Stroller (produced 1823).
Dramatic Works. 4 vols., 1827.

Verse

My Nightgown and Slippers; or, Tales in Verse. 1797; revised edition, as *Broad Grins*, 1802.
Poetical Vagaries. 1812.
Vagaries Vindicated; or, Hypocrite Hypercritics. 1813.
Eccentricities for Edinburgh. 1816.

Other

Random Records (autobiography). 2 vols., 1830.

Editor, *Posthumous Letters Addressed to Francis Colman and George Colman the Elder.* 1820.

Reading List: *Colman the Younger* by Jeremy F. Bagster-Collins, 1946; "The Early Career of Colman" by Peter Thomson, in *Essays on Nineteenth-Century British Theatre* edited by Kenneth Richards and Thomson, 1971.

*   *   *

The younger George Colman was a shrewd judge of the theatrical public's taste. As such, he earned for himself a reputation as a superior writer without ever achieving anything more than popularity. His dramatic work was of four main kinds. Firstly, he was the originator of a new kind of play (his contemporary, James Boaden, writes of "a sort of Colman drama of three acts"), in which Elizabethan blank verse and a serious theme are lightened by frequent songs and imported comic characters. *The Battle of Hexham, The Surrender of Calais, The Mountaineers*, and *The Iron Chest* are all in this style, and Colman was still ready to exploit it in 1822, when he wrote *The Law of Java*. They are plays that eased the important passage of traditional tragedy into nineteenth-century melodrama. Secondly, he wrote comedies that were generally saved by his sense of humour from conceding too much to the contemporary vogue for sentimentality. *Inkle and Yarico*, his first striking success and still an interesting piece to stage, is a comedy with songs, *Ways and Means* an imitative comedy of manners, and *The Heir at Law* shows some ingenuity in the creation of Pangloss and an ability to handle the full five-act form. *The Poor Gentleman* is too much in the mawkish shadow of Cumberland's *The West Indian*, but Colman's finest comedy, *John Bull*, merits more attention than it has received. It is robust and not at all mealy-mouthed. Thirdly, there are the ephemeral theatre-pieces, *Doctor Hocus Pocus*, a pantomime, *Blue Beard*, a spectacular, *Love Laughs at Locksmiths*, a farce, and many others. Finally, there are pieces that grew out of his work as a theatre-manager. *Poor Old Haymarket* was a prelude to the new season at the small summer theatre which he had inherited from his ailing father. It reveals a fondness for the Haymarket, and a felt sense of the difference between it and the vast patent houses. *New Hay at the Old Market* exhibits Colman's familiarity with the contemporary theatre, and furnishes us with a lot of information about it.

His autobiographical *Random Records* is honest to its title. It tells regrettably little about his final years as Examiner of Plays. He was much abused for his strictness, not least because his own light verse has prurient edges; but abuse is an inevitable concomitant of the office. Colman's Examinership was unimpressive but not malicious. The submerged tradition that

48 COLMAN

he was the author of *Don Leon*, a witty and obscene poem in heroic couplets proposing an explanation of the collapse of Lord Byron's marriage, may owe its currency to a contemporary delight in taxing with immorality the official guardian of theatrical morals.

—Peter Thomson

DARLEY, George. Irish. Born in Dublin in 1795. Educated at Trinity College, Dublin, 1815–20, B.A. 1820. Moved to London in 1822: wrote, mainly on the drama, for *London Magazine* and the *Athenaeum*. Also a mathematician. *Died 23 November 1846.*

PUBLICATIONS

Collections

Complete Poetical Works, edited by Ramsay Colles. 1908.

Verse

The Errors of Esctasy: A Dramatic Poem, with Other Pieces. 1822.
Nepenthe. 1835.
Poems. 1889.

Plays

Sylvia; or, The May Queen. 1827.
Thomas à Becket. 1840.
Ethelstan; or, The Battle of Brunanburg. 1841.

Other

The Labours of Idleness; or, Seven Nights' Entertainments. 1826.
A System of Popular Geometry, Algebra, Trigonometry. 3 vols., 1826–27.
The Geometrical Companion. 1828.
The New Sketch Book. 2 vols., 1829.
Familiar Astronomy. 1830.

Editor, *The Works of Beaumont and Fletcher.* 2 vols., 1840.

Bibliography: "Some Uncollected Authors 28: Darley" by Cecil Woolf, in *Book Collector 10,* 1961.

Reading List: *Life and Letters of Darley, Poet and Critic* by Claude Colleer Abbott, 1928; *Darley* by Abraham J. Leventhal, 1950; Introduction by James Reeves to *Five Late Romantic Poets*, 1974.

*　　*　　*

George Darley published a good deal of creative work, including prose tales and sketches (*Labours of Idleness*) and plays (among which was *Thomas à Becket*, which Henry Crabb Robinson thought "a work of genius"); and he was also an incisive dramatic critic, writing for the *London Magazine* under the pseudonym of John Lacy, as well as an amateur of painting, a mathematician, and a literary scholar. If he is known today, however, it is for his lyrics, the best of which are to be found in the collection entitled *Nepenthe*.

Although he had firm opinions about the poetry of his time, deprecating in particular the dominant influence of Byron, Darley was never able to realize in his own work the ideals to which he aspired. He spoke in an article called "The Enchanted Lyre" of his "unsystematised" and "heterogeneous" nature, and his verse acquires much of its consistency only insofar as it is derivative, for he sought escape from the impasse of contemporary poetry by turning back to the work of earlier writers – to the middle ages, to the Elizabethans, and to the cavalier lyrists. "It Is Not Beauty I Demand" is a pastiche of seventeenth-century lyric sufficiently accomplished to have been included in early editions of Palgrave's *Golden Treasury* as an anonymous Cavalier piece; "O May, Thou Art a Merry Time" is an effective exercise in the Elizabethan manner; and in such pieces as "The Demon's Cave" we find a quasi-Jacobean fascination with the macabre. There is also an obvious debt to Shelley and Keats, and Darley's best lyric, "O Blest Unfabled Incense-Tree," a vivid fantasy on the self-regeneration of the phoenix, puts one in mind of Coleridge, although Darley here achieves a distinctive idiom and movement of his own.

It must, however, be conceded that his inspiration is almost entirely literary, and, as Ian Jack points out in his *English Literature, 1815–1832*, his diction is enfeebled by its lack of contact with the spoken English of the time. These qualities of his verse reflect the hesitancy and diffidence of his character, and bespeak Darley's withdrawal from life into the less harsh world of books. Darley's work can accordingly be praised only within narrow limits, for it must always evoke an atmosphere of the study; but within these limits we can recognize and take pleasure in the technical artistry and delicacy of perception which are features of his best work.

—James Reeves

DARWIN, Erasmus. English. Born in Elston, Nottinghamshire, 12 December 1731. Educated at Chesterfield School, 1741–50; St. John's College, Cambridge (Exeter Scholar), B.A. 1754, M.B. 1755; studied medicine in Edinburgh, 1754–55. Married 1) Mary Howard in 1757 (died, 1770), three sons; 2) Mrs. Chandos Pole in 1781, four sons, three daughters. Physician: settled in Lichfield, 1756, Derby, 1781, and afterwards at Breadsall Priory. Founder, Philosophical Society, Derby, 1784; Founder, Lichfield Dispensary, 1784; formed a botanical garden near Lichfield, 1778. *Died 18 April 1802.*

50   DARWIN

PUBLICATIONS

Collections

Essential Writings, edited by Desmond King-Hele.   1968.

Verse

The Loves of the Plants.   1789.
The Botanic Garden.   2 vols., 1791.
The Golden Age: A Poetical Epistle to T. Beddoes.   1794.
The Temple of Nature; or, The Origin of Society.   1803.
Poetical Works.   3 vols., 1806.

Other

Zoonomia; or, The Laws of Organic Life.   2 vols., 1794–96.
A Plan for the Conduct of Female Education in Boarding School.   1797.
Phytologia; or, The Philosophy of Agriculture and Gardening.   1800.

Editor, *Experiments Establishing a Criterion,* by Charles Darwin.   1780.

Translator, *The Families of Plants,* by Carolus Linnaeus.   1787.

Reading List: *Doctor Darwin* by Hesketh Pearson, 1930; *The Poetry and Aesthetics of Darwin* by James V. Logan, 1936; *Darwin,* 1963, and *Doctor of Revolution: The Life and Genius of Darwin,* 1977, both by Desmond King-Hele; *The Comedian as the Letter D: Darwin's Comic Materialism* by Donald M. Hassler, 1973.

*   *   *

Erasmus Darwin was a renowned medical doctor and the grandfather of Charles Darwin. His own early theories of biological evolution and other daring scientific speculations have been overshadowed by the work of his grandson, but his imaginative expressions of these speculations in ornate and comic Popean couplets and vigorous prose notes remain an interesting example of the late 18th-century Age of Sensibility. The literary effects in his verse, in particular, are deliberately contrived both to raise and to evade the notion of limitless fecundity in nature. Darwin was closely associated with other materialists, natural philosophers, and inventors such as Joseph Priestley, Josiah Wedgwood, and James Watt, with whom he founded the famous Lunar Society of Birmingham. His influence on the British romantic poets was considerable, and Coleridge coined the word "Darwinizing" to refer to his imaginative and wide-ranging speculations.

His long poems and prose treatises, world famous in his time but now available only in facsimile, were originally published by the radical London bookseller Joseph Johnson. Most notable among them are the poems *The Botanic Garden* and *The Temple of Nature* and the medical treatise containing evolutionary theory *Zoonomia.* Darwin's influences as a speculator and enthusiast of causes ranging from the French Revolution to the anti-slavery movement also extended to the circle of radicals such as William Godwin; and Godwin's daughter, Mary Shelley, mentions Darwin in her account of the intellectual origins of *Frankenstein.* William Blake illustrated some of Darwin's poems and delighted in his wide-ranging speculations, although he abominated the compressed and rational poetic form. Finally, Darwin should be remembered for his energy, his inventiveness, and his subtle expression of many ideas of the Enlightenment.

—Donald M. Hassler

DE QUINCEY, Thomas. English. Born in Manchester, 15 August 1785. Educated at Bath Grammar School, 1796–99; a private school in Winkfield, Wiltshire, 1799–1800; Manchester Grammar School, 1801–02; Worcester College, Oxford, 1803–08, left without taking a degree; entered Middle Temple, London, 1812. Married Margaret Simpson in 1817 (died, 1837), five sons and three daughters. Opium user from 1804; settled in Grasmere, 1809: associated with the Lake Poets, Wordsworth, Coleridge, and Southey; Editor, *Westmorland Gazette*, 1818–19; contributed to the *London Magazine*, 1821–25, and the *Saturday Post* and *Evening Post*, Edinburgh, 1827–28; moved to Edinburgh, 1828: wrote for *Blackwood's Magazine*, 1826–49, and *Tait's Magazine*, 1832–51. *Died 8 December 1859.*

PUBLICATIONS

Collections

  Collected Writings, edited by David Masson. 14 vols., 1889–90.

Prose Writings

  Confessions of an English Opium Eater. 1822; revised edition, 1865; edited by Alethea Hayter, 1971.
  Walladmor: A Novel Freely Translated from the English of Scott and Now Freely Translated into English, by G. W. H. Haering. 2 vols., 1825 (a German forgery).
  Klosterheim; or, The Masque. 1832; edited by Dr. Shelton-Mackenzie, 1855.
  The Logic of Political Economy. 1844.
  Writings, edited by J. T. Fields. 24 vols., 1851–59.
  Selections Grave and Gay, revised and arranged by De Quincey. 14 vols., 1853–60.
  China. 1857.
  Shakespeare: A Biography. 1864.
  The Wider Hope: Essays on Future Punishment. 1890.
  Uncollected Writings, edited by James Hogg. 2 vols., 1890.
  Posthumous Works, edited by A. H. Japp. 2 vols., 1891–93.
  De Quincey Memorials, Being Letters and Other Records Here First Published, edited by A. H. Japp. 2 vols., 1891.

52 DE QUINCEY

A Diary 1803, edited by H. A. Eaton. 1927.
De Quincey at Work, Seen in 130 Letters, edited by W. H. Bonner. 1936.
Dr. Johnson and Lord Chesterfield. 1945.
Recollections of the Lake Poets, edited by Edward Sackville-West. 1948; edited by J. E.
 Jordan, as *Reminiscences of the English Lake Poets*, 1961; edited by David Wright, as
 Recollections of the Lakes and the Lake Poets, 1970.
De Quincey to Wordsworth: A Biography of a Relationship, edited by J. E.
 Jordan. 1962.
*New Essays: His Contributions to the Edinburgh Saturday Post and the Edinburgh
 Evening Post 1827–1828*, edited by Stuart M. Tave. 1966.
De Quincey as Critic, edited by J. E. Jordan. 1973.

Bibliography: *De Quincey: A Bibliography* by J. A. Green, 1908.

Reading List: *A Flame in Sunlight: The Life and Work of De Quincey* by Edward Sackville-
West, 1936, edited by J. E. Jordan, 1974; *De Quincey, Literary Critic* by J. E. Jordan, 1952;
De Quincey by Hugh S. Davies, 1964; *De Quincey: La Vie – L'Homme – L'Oeuvre* by
Françoise Moreux, 1964 (includes bibliography); *The Mine and the Mint: Sources for the
Writings of De Quincey* by Albert Goldman, 1965; *De Quincey* by Judson S. Lyon, 1969.

*   *   *

Thomas De Quincey shares with Lamb and Hazlitt the distinction of having elevated
journalism to a kind of literature. Much of what he wrote was for *Blackwood's*, *Tait's
Magazine*, and the *London Magazine*. It could be argued that his style possessed neither the
charming oddity, deliberately fostered, of the one, nor the sheer energy of the other. But he
shares with both a sharp eye for physical detail and a curiosity about the mainsprings of
human conduct.

He worked in the belief that the calling of literature is a noble one, claiming indeed, in his
essay on Oliver Goldsmith, that it is not only a fine art, but the highest and most powerful of
all the arts. He differentiated between what he called "the literature of *knowledge* and the
literature of *power*," the function of the first being to teach and the second to move. The first,
however valuable, must inevitably in time be superceded. The second remains "triumphant
for ever as long as the language exists in which it speaks." His contrasting examples are a
cookery book, giving "something new ... in every paragraph," and *Paradise Lost*, providing
"the exercise and expansion to your own latent capacity of sympathy with the infinite."

One of the causes of De Quincey's originality is his interest in his own psychology and its
relation to dreams, an interest heightened by his bouts of addiction to opium. By modern
Freudian standards, his inquiries into "states of mind and levels of consciousness" may seem
elementary, but, allied to his honesty of literary purpose, they give remarkable vividness to
Confessions of an English Opium Eater, which has remained his most widely read
masterpiece, "Autobiography" (1834-53), and "Suspira de Profundis" (1845).

His interest in German metaphysics, resulting in his determination to introduce Kant to
English readers, no doubt stimulated a certain transcendental vagueness to which he was
prone, and which reflects itself in moments of inflated pretention in an otherwise highly
polished style.

His ironic humour is well reflected in "Murder Considered as One of the Fine Arts" (1827).
Out of what would seem as transient a subject as "The English Mail Coach" he builds, quite
unforgettably, what he describes as one of his "dream fugues," based on a near-miss between
the coach and a gig with a girl in it, a glimpse of whom provides the fugue with its counter-
subject. Many of his essays reveal his ability to create imaginative reconstructions of incidents
in history. The best known, "Joan of Arc," culminates in a passage which illustrates De
Quincey's "flying contrapuntal style":

Bishop of Beauvais! thy victim died in fire upon a scaffold – thou upon a down bed. But, for the departing minutes of life, both are oftentimes alike. At the farewell crisis, when the gates of death are opening, and flesh is resting from its struggles, oftentimes the tortured and the torturer have the same truce from carnal torment; both sink together into sleep; together both sometimes kindle into dreams. When the mortal mists were gathering fast upon you two, bishop and shepherd girl – when the pavilions of life were closing up their shadowy curtains about you – let us try, through the gigantic glooms to decipher the flying features of your separate visions.

Not the least valuable of his writings is his *Reminiscences of the English Lake Poets* in which Coleridge (with whom he shared his German metaphysical interests), Southey, and Wordsworth and his sister Dorothy are vividly, and frankly, portrayed. A certain dislike of Wordsworth, which grew up through a coolness between them, comes out in the description of the poet skating "like a cow dancing the cotillion," or impatiently tearing open the pages of a new book with a buttery knife while at table.

The weaknesses of De Quincey's writing are his habit of digression – drawn, perhaps, from his early admiration for the work of Jean-Paul Richter – an over-fondness for exclamatory gesture, and the occasional breaking-off of a subject as if "the printer's devil were waiting at the door" (*A Flame in Sunlight* by Edward Sackville-West, 1936).

Nevertheless, for the 20th-century reader De Quincey is an essayist whose opening sentence is frequently as compelling as presumably it must also have seemed a century and a half ago. His preoccupations, too, remain singularly modern. Through the unlikely medium of journalism, he certainly realised his desire to contribute significantly to England's share of "the literature of *power*."

—Maurice Lindsay

ELLIOTT, Ebenezer. English. Born in Masborough, Rotherham, Yorkshire, 17 March 1781. Attended Hollis School briefly; largely self-educated. Married; had 13 children. Worked in his father's iron-foundry, Rotherham, 1797–1804, and maintained a share in the business until it went bankrupt; bar-iron merchant, Sheffield, 1821–42; retired to Great Houghton, near Barnsley. Active in the Chartist Movement: delegate from Sheffield at the public meeting in Palace Yard, Westminster, 1838; withdrew from the movement when the Chartists refused to support repeal of the corn laws. *Died 1 December 1849.*

PUBLICATIONS

Collections

Poetical Works, edited by Edwin Elliott. 2 vols., 1876.

Verse

The Vernal Walk. 1801.
The Soldier and Other Poems. 1810.

Night: A Descriptive Poem. 1818.
Peter Faultless to His Brother Simon, Tales of Night, in Rhyme, and Other Poems. 1820.
Love: A Poem, The Giaour: A Satirical Poem. 1823.
Scotch Nationality: A Vision. 1824.
The Village Patriarch. 1829.
Corn Law Rhymes: The Ranter. 1830; revised edition, 1831.
The Splendid Village: Corn Law Rhymes and Other Poems. 1833.
Poetical Works. 3 vols., 1834–35.
Poems, edited by R. W. Griswold. 1844.
More Verse and Prose of the Cornlaw Rhymer. 2 vols., 1850.

Bibliography: *Elliott, The Corn Law Rhymer: A Bibliography and List of Letters* by Simon Brown, 1971.

Reading List: *The Life, Poetry and Letters of Elliott* by J. Watkins, 1850; *Two Sheffield Poets: James Montgomery and Elliott* by William Odom, 1929; *Fiction for the Working Man* by Louis James, 1963.

*   *   *

Towards the end of his life it was customary for Ebenezer Elliott to append to his name the initials, C.L.R., standing for Corn Law Rhymer. During the 1830's and 1840's his poems (in particular the *Corn Law Rhymes*) had been quoted from hundreds of political platforms and he himself was an active member of the movement to repeal the Corn Laws. The American poet John Greenleaf Whittier wrote in 1850: "Ebenezer Elliott was to the artisans of England what Burns was to the peasantry of Scotland. His *Corn Law Rhymes* contributed not a little to that overwhelming tide of popular opinion and feeling which resulted in the repeal of the tax on bread." The breadth of his popular appeal may be gauged from the fact that while at one time his work was quoted from Chartist platforms, his poem, "The People's Anthem," slightly altered to remove some prickles of class antagonism, found its way into *Songs of Praise*, the Anglican hymnbook.

Elliott came from the radical autodidactic tradition. He claimed at one time to have most of the Bible and *Paradise Lost* by heart. As an iron-dealer in Sheffield, he kept a bust of Shakespeare amidst the stacked iron in his warehouse, and in his day-book quotations mingled with calculations. His earliest poetry was Romantic and pastoral, but the influence of Crabbe and a first-hand knowledge of working-class life in Sheffield changed the focus of his verse. Like other poets of the time he observed the encroachment of the town on the countryside but saw the problem of pollution in its political perspective: "Cursed with evils infinitely worse than a sooty atmosphere we are bread-taxed."

Corn Law Rhymes was first printed in pamphlet form by order of the Sheffield Mechanics Anti-tax Society. Many of the poems, like Thomas Hood's "The Song of the Shirt," are an attempt to voice directly the complaints of the oppressed. In doing so they both feed from and back into the common stock of industrial and urban folk-song. Their language is in general unliterary and has a rigour and energy coming partly from their urgency of purpose and partly from a presentation of facts and conditions as much as of rhetoric and opinion. In general the lachrymose plaint is avoided in favour of abrasive social satire, as in these lines from "Drone v. Worker":

> How God speeds the tax-bribed plough,
>   Fen and moor declare, man;
> Where once fed the poor man's cow,
>   ACRES drives his share, man.

But he did not *steal* the fen,
  Did not *steal* the moor, man;
If he feeds on starving men,
  Still he loves the poor, man.
Hush! he bullies, State and Throne,
  Quids them in his jaw, man;
Thine and mine he calls *his* own,
  Acres' lie is law, man.
Acres eats his tax on bread,
  Acres loves the plough, man;
Acres' dogs are better fed,
  Beggar's slave! than thou, man.

George Saintsbury in a short piece on Elliott in the *Cambridge History of English Literature* spoke of "the rubbish of partisan abuse which feeds his furnace." It was for helping keep alive a vigorous partisan tradition in English poetry that Elliott can be valued long after the repeal of the Corn Laws. He belongs to the tradition of Burns, Hood, Robert Buchanan, and John Davidson whose eloquence lies in their concrete presentation of the real lives of the majority of the population.

—Bridget O'Toole

FITZBALL, Edward. English. Born in Burwell, near Mildenhall, Cambridgeshire, in 1793. Educated at Albertus Parr's school at Newmarket; apprentice in a printing house in Norwich, 1809–12. Married Adelaide Fitzball in 1814; one daughter. Founded a printing house and magazine in Norwich, which subsequently failed; thereafter wrote for the theatre, first in Norwich, and from 1821 in London, where he wrote numerous melodramas for minor theatres; wrote for the more important London theatres from 1828: Resident Dramatist and Reader at Covent Garden, 1835–38; Reader at Drury Lane from 1838. *Died 27 October 1873.*

PUBLICATIONS

Plays

  Edwin, Heir of Cressingham, from the novel *The Scottish Chiefs* by Jane Porter
    (produced 1817).
  Bertha; or, The Assassins of Istria (produced 1819). 1819.
  The Ruffian Boy (produced 1819; also produced as *Giraldi*).
  Edda (produced 1820).
  Antigone; or, The Theban Sister (produced 1821).
  Alonza and Imogene (produced 1821).

56 FITZBALL

The Innkeeper of Abbeville; or, The Hostler and the Robber (produced 1822). 1822.

The Fortunes of Nigel; or, King James I and His Times, from the novel by Scott (produced 1822; as *George Heriot,* produced 1823). 1830(?).

Joan of Arc; or, The Maid of Orleans (produced 1822). 1823.

The Barber; or, The Mill of Bagdad (produced 1822). 1822.

Peveril of the Peak; or, The Days of King Charles II, from the novel by Scott (produced 1823). 1823.

Iwan; or, The Mines of Ischinski (produced 1823).

Laurette; or, The Forest of Unterwald (produced 1823).

Nerestan, Prince of Persia; or, The Demon of the Flood (produced 1823).

The Three Hunchbacks; or, The Sabre Grinders of Damascus (produced 1823). 1823.

Thalaba the Destroyer; or, The Burning Sword (produced 1823). 1826.

Waverley, music by George Rodwell, from the novel by Scott (produced 1824). 1824.

The Fire-Worshippers; or, The Paradise of the Peris (produced 1824).

The Floating Beacon; or, The Norwegian Wreckers (produced 1824). 1824.

William the Conqueror; or, The Days of the Curfew Bell (produced 1824).

The Koeuba; or, The Indian Pirate's Vessel (produced 1824). 1836(?).

The Burning Bridge; or, The Spectre of the Lake (produced 1824).

Der Freischutz; or, The Demon of the Wolf's Glen and the Seven Charmed Bullets (produced 1824).

Wardock Kennilson; or, The Outcast Mother and Her Son (produced 1824). 1835(?).

Omala; or, Settlers in America (produced 1825). 1826.

Hans of Iceland; or, The Iron Casket (produced 1825).

Father and Son; or, The Rock of La Charbonniere (produced 1825). N.d.

Cupid in Disguise (produced 1825).

The Pilot; or, A Tale of the Sea, from the novel by Cooper (produced 1825). 1825.

The Betrothed (produced 1826).

The Flying Dutchman; or, The Phantom Ship, music by George Rodwell (produced 1827). 1829(?).

The Libertine's Lesson (produced 1827). N.d.

Nelson; or, The Life of a Sailor (produced 1827). 1886.

Antoine the Savage; or, The Outcast (produced 1828).

The Inchcape Bell (produced 1828). 1828(?).

The Earthquake; or, The Spectre of the Nile, music by George Rodwell (produced 1828). 1829(?).

The Red Rover; or, The Mutiny of the Dolphin, from the novel by Cooper (produced 1829). 1831(?).

The Devil's Elixir; or, The Shadowless Man, music by George Rodwell (produced 1829). 1829(?).

The Rauberbraut; or, The Robber's Bride, music by Ferdinand Ries (produced 1829).

The Night Before the Wedding, music by Henry Bishop, from a play by Scribe and J. N. Bouilly, music by Adrien Boieldieu (produced 1829).

Mr. Chairman (produced 1829).

Ninetta; or, The Maid of Palaiseau, music by Henry Bishop, from an opera by G. Gherardini, music by Rossini (produced 1830). 1830; revised version, as *The Maid of Palaiseau* (produced 1838), 1838.

The Maid of the Oaks (produced 1830).

The Black Vulture; or, The Wheel of Death (produced 1830).

Adelaide; or, The Royal William (produced 1830; as *William and Adelaide,* produced 1830).

The Libertine of Poland; or, The Colonel of Hussars (produced 1830).

Hofer, The Tell of the Tyrol, music by Henry Bishop, from an opera by de Jouy and others, music by Rossini (produced 1830; as *Andreas Hofer,* produced 1830). 1832(?).

The Haunted Hulk (produced 1831).

The Sorceress, music by Ferdinand Ries (produced 1831).

The Sea Serpent; or, The Wizard and the Winds, with J. B. Buckstone (produced 1831).

Robert le Diable; or, The Devil's Son, with J. B. Buckstone, from an opera by Scribe and Casimir Delavigne, music by Meyerbeer (produced 1832).

The Alchymist (songs only), libretto by T. H. Bayly, music by Henry Bishop, from an opera by K. Pfeiffer, music by Spohr (produced 1832).

Nina, The Bride of the Galley Slave (produced 1832).

The Dillosk Gatherer; or, The Eagle's Nest (produced 1832).

The Bottle of Champagne, music by Henry Bishop (produced 1832).

The Sedan Chair (produced 1832).

The Maid of Cashmere, music by Henry Bishop, from an opera by Scribe, music by Auber (produced 1833). Songs published 1833.

Margaret's Ghost; or, The Libertine's Ship (produced 1833). 1833(?).

The Felon of New York (produced 1833).

The Soldier's Widow; or, The Ruins of the Mill (produced 1833).

Jonathan Bradford; or, The Murder at the Roadside Inn, music by Jolly (produced 1833). 1833(?).

Mary Glastonbury (produced 1833). 1833(?).

Walter Brand; or, The Duel in the Mist (produced 1833). 1834(?).

Esmeralda; or, The Deformed of Notre Dame, from the novel by Hugo (produced 1834). 1855(?).

Tom Cringle; or, The Man with the Iron Hand (produced 1834). 1834(?).

The Lord of the Isles; or, The Gathering of the Clan, music by George Rodwell, from the novel by Scott (produced 1834).

The Young Courier; or, The Miser of Walden (produced 1834).

The Black Hand; or, The Dervise and the Peri (produced 1834).

The Last Days of Pompeii; or, The Blind Girl of Tessaly, from the novel by Bulwer-Lytton (produced 1835).

The Note Forger (produced 1835). 1835(?).

Carmilhan; or, The Drowned Crew (produced 1835). 1835(?).

Paul Clifford, music by George Rodwell, from the novel by Bulwer-Lytton (produced 1835). 1835(?).

The Siege of Rochelle, music by Michael Balfe, from a novel by the Countess de Genlis (produced 1835). 1843(?).

Inheritance; or, The Unwelcome Guest, from the novel by Susan Ferrier (produced 1835).

The Carmelites; or, The Convent Belles, from a French play (produced 1835). 1836.

The Bronze Horse; or, The Spell of the Cloud King, music by George Rodwell, from an opera by Scribe, music by Auber (produced 1835). 1836(?).

Quasimodo; or, The Gipsy Girl of Notre Dame, from the novel by Hugo (produced 1836). 1836.

Za-Ze-Zi-Zo-Zu; or, Dominoes! Chess!! and Cards!!!, from a French play (produced 1836). 1836(?).

The Assurance Company; or, The Boarding School of Montesque (produced 1836).

The Wood Devil (produced 1836).

The Rose of the Alhambra; or, The Enchanted Lute, from an opera with music by de Pinna (produced 1836).

The Sexton of Cologne; or, The Burgomaster's Daughter, music by George Rodwell (produced 1836).

The Hindoo Robber (produced 1836).

Mutual Expense; or, A Female Travelling Companion (produced 1836).

False Colours! or, The Free Trader! (produced 1837). 1837(?).

The Eagle's Haunt (produced 1837).

58 FITZBALL

Walter Tyrrel (produced 1837). 1837.

Zohrab the Hostage; or, The Storming of Mezanderan (produced 1837).

Joan of Arc, music by Michael Balfe (produced 1837).

The Negro of Wapping; or, The Boat-Builder's Hovel (produced 1838). 1838(?).

Diadeste; or, The Veiled Lady, music by Michael Balfe (produced 1838). Songs published 1838.

Oconesto; or, The Mohawk Chief (produced 1838).

The King of the Mist; or, The Miller of the Hartz Mountains, music by G. F. Stansbury (produced 1839). 1839(?).

Scaramuccia; or, The Villagers of San Quintino, music by Luigi Ricci (produced 1839). Songs published 1839.

Këolanthe; or, The Unearthly Bride, music by Michael Balfe (produced 1841).

The April Fool (produced 1841).

The Robber's Sister; or, The Forge in the Forest (produced 1841).

Charlotte Hanwell; or, Sorrow and Crime (produced 1842).

Ombra; or, The Spirit of the Reclining Stone (produced 1842).

The Trooper's Horn; or, The Goblin of the Chest (produced 1842).

Jane Paul; or, The Victim of Unmerited Persecution (produced 1842).

The Miller's Wife (produced 1842).

The Owl Sisters; or, The Haunted Abbey Ruin (produced 1842).

Mary Melvyn; or, The Marriage of Interest (produced 1843). 1843.

The Queen of the Thames; or, The Anglers, music by John Hatton (produced 1843). 1843.

The Ranger's Daughter (produced 1843).

Ondine; or, The Naid, from a play by Pixérécourt (produced 1843). N.d.

The Favorite, from an opera by Gustave Vaez and Alphonse Roger, music by Donizetti (produced 1843).

Madelaine; or, The Daughter of the Regiment, music by J. H. Tully, from an opera by J. H. V. de Saint-Georges and J. F. A. Bayard, music by Donizetti (produced 1843). 1844(?); revised version (produced 1847), 1886.

Ben Bradshaw; or, A Man Without a Head (produced 1844).

The Momentous Question (produced 1844). 1844(?).

Home Again! or, The Lieutenant's Daughters (produced 1844). 1845(?).

Maritana, music by Vincent Wallace, from a play by A. P. d'Ennery and P. F. Dumanoir (produced 1845). 1845.

The Crown Jewels, music by J. H. Tully, from an opera by Scribe and J. H. V. de Saint-Georges, music by Auber (produced 1846). 1846.

The Desert; or, The Imann's Daughter, music by J. H. Tully, from an opera by Auguste Colin, music by Felicien David (produced 1847).

The Wreck and the Reef (produced 1847).

The Traveller's Room (produced 1847). 1847(?).

The Maid of Honour, music by Michael Balfe (produced 1847).

The Lancashire Witches: A Romance of Pendle Forest (produced 1848). 1897(?).

The Crock of Gold! or, The Murder at the Hall (produced 1848). 1848(?).

Marmion; or, The Battle of Flodden Field, from the poem by Scott (produced 1848). 1848(?).

Quentin Durward, music by H. R. Laurent, from the novel by Scott (produced 1848). 1848.

Corasco; or, The Warrior's Steed (produced 1849).

The White Maiden of California (produced 1849).

Alhamar the Moor; or, The Brother of Valencia (produced 1849).

The Prophet, from an opera by Scribe, music by Meyerbeer (produced 1849).

Harlequin and Humpty Dumpty; or, Robin de Bobbin and the First Lord Mayor of London (produced 1850). 1851.

FITZBALL 59

The Four Sons of Aymon; or, The Days of Charlemagne (produced 1850).
Alonzo the Brave and the Fair Imogene; or, Harlequin and the Baron All Covered with Spangles and Gold (produced 1850).
The Cadi's Daughter, music by Sydney Nelson (produced 1851).
Azael the Prodigal, music by H. R. Laurent, from an opera by Scribe, music by Auber (produced 1851). 1851(?).
Hans von Stein; or, The Robber Knight (produced 1851). 1851(?).
Vin Willoughby; or, The Mutiny of the Isis (produced 1851).
The Greek Slave; or, The Spectre Gambler (produced 1851). 1851(?).
The Last of the Fairies (produced 1852). 1852(?).
The Secret Pass; or, The Khan's Daughter (produced 1852).
Alice May; or, The Last Appeal (produced 1852). 1852(?).
Peter the Great (produced 1852). 1898(?).
The Field of Terror; or, The Devil's Diggings (produced 1852).
Uncle Tom's Cabin; or, The Horrors of Slavery (produced 1852). N.d.
The Rising of the Tide (produced 1853).
Amakosa; or, Kaffir Warfare (produced 1853).
The Miller of Derwent Water (produced 1853). 1853.
Raymond and Agnes, music by Edward Loder (produced 1855). N.d.
Nitocris; or, The Ethiop's Revenge (produced 1855).
The Children of the Castle (produced 1857). 1858(?).
The Husband's Vengeance; or, The Knight of Wharley (produced 1857).
Pierette; or, The Village Rivals, music by W. H. Montgomery (produced 1858). 1858(?).
Auld Robin Gray, music by A. Lee (produced 1858).
The Lancashire Witches; or, The Knight, The Giant, and the Castle of Manchester (produced 1858).
The Widow's Wedding (produced 1859). 1859.
Lurline, music by Vincent Wallace (produced 1860). 1860.
Christmas Eve; or, A Duel in the Snow (produced 1860). 1860.
Robin Hood; or, The Merry Outlaws of Sherwood (produced 1860). 1861(?).
She Stoops to Conquer, music by George Macfarren, from the play by Goldsmith (produced 1864). 1864.
The Magic Pearl, music by T. Pede (produced 1873).
A Sailor's Legacy; or, The Child of a Tar. With *A Soldier and a Sailor, A Tinker and a Tailor*, by William Rogers, 1888(?).

Fiction

The Idiot Boy. 1815.
The Black Robber. 1819.
The Sibyl's Warning. 1822.
Michael Schwartz; or, The Two Runaway Apprentices. 1858.

Verse

Serena of Oakwood; or, Trials of the Heart, and Other Poems. 1815.
The Revenge of Taran. 1821.
The House to Let, with Other Poems. 1857.
Bhanavar; The Story of Fadleen. 1858.
The Wee Craft. 1866.
My Pretty Jane. 1891.

60   FITZBALL

Other

Thirty-Five Years of a Dramatic Author's Life (autobiography).   2 vols., 1859.

*   *   *

Edward Fitzball really has more connection with the early swashbucklers and spectaculars of the cinema than with what we have come to think of as the modern drama. He lives in the tradition of "shake and bake" movie epics (*Earthquake* and *The Towering Inferno*) rather than on the stage, but he was in his long and varied career one of the busiest and most influential popular dramatists, a master of nautical and spectacular melodrama.

To the English stage Fitzball brought the devices of such French playwrights as Pixérécourt, and his theatrically effective pieces were in turn the source of many later melodramas. He knew how to package and present material which could fill the cavernous theatres of his time, and he borrowed widely. He could wring the thrills out of Southey's poem *Thalaba the Destroyer* as well as extract every drop of sensationalism from *Uncle Tom's Cabin*. His adaptations of James Fenimore Cooper have less art but more vitality than the originals: *Red Rover* has a typically Fitzball conclusion: " 'I am slain and will perish with my ship.' *Red fire to burn at the side wing*. CURTAIN FALLS." In *The Pilot*, Fitzball contrived to make Cooper's Americans look silly and the British admirable. From *Edwin, Heir of Cressingham*, based on Jane Porter's *The Scottish Chiefs*, to the libretto for Goldsmith's *She Stoops to Conquer*, his career is practically a summary of the topics and techniques that galvanized the gallery; the accursed Vanderdecken (in *The Flying Dutchman*), appearing and disappearing in bursts of red and blue fire, so captured the theatre-goers' attention that he was still being revived decades later as a vehicle for Sir Henry Irving. Just as the fires and other stage effects were *real*, so were his heroes the genuine melodramatic article: "one that hates cruelty, and defies oppression – one that fears no death like the death of dishonour" (*The Earthquake*) or "my hand is free from bloodshed – I have never wronged, but always defended that unfortunate" (*Paul Clifford*).

His work is much better than some of these examples might suggest, and it influenced writers like Tom Taylor and Dion Boucicault as well as film-makers like Griffith and De Mille. Equally interesting are his technical innovations on stage, of which the four rooms in the inn seen simultaneously (in *Jonathan Bradford*) is the best-known example.

—Leonard R. N. Ashley

FRERE, John Hookham.   English.   Born in London, 21 May 1769. Educated at Eton College, where he met his life-long friend, George Canning, 1785–89 (Founder/Editor, with Canning and others, *The Microcosm*, 1786–87); Caius College, Cambridge, 1789–92 (Members Prize for Latin Essay, 1792), B.A. 1792, M.A. 1795. Married Elizabeth Jemima Blake, widow of the Earl of Errol, 1816 (died, 1831). Fellow, Caius College, Cambridge, 1793–1816; entered the British Foreign Office as a Clerk, 1795; Member of Parliament for West Looe, Cornwall, 1796–1802, and Under-Secretary of State in the Foreign Office, 1799; contributor, with Canning and others, to *The Anti-Jacobin; or, The Weekly Observer*, 1797–98; British Envoy to Portugal, 1800–02; Ambassador to Spain, 1802–04; Privy

Councillor, 1805; Minister to the Junta in Spain, during the invasion of Napoleon, 1808–09. Succeeded to the family estates, 1807. Retired to Malta, 1818. *Died 7 January 1846.*

PUBLICATIONS

Collections

Works in Verse and Prose. 2 vols., 1872; edited by W. E. Frere, 3 vols., 1874.

Verse

The Anti-Jacobin (verse selections), with others, edited by W. Gifford. 2 vols., 1799; *The Poetry of the Anti-Jacobin,* edited by L. Rice-Oxley, 1924.
Prospectus and Specimen of an Intended National Work Relating to King Arthur. 2 vols., 1817–18; as *The Monks and the Giants,* 1818; edited by R. D. Waller, 1926.
Fables for Five-Year-Olds. 1830.
Psalms. 1839(?).
Parodies and Other Burlesque Pieces, with George Canning and George Ellis, edited by H. Morley. 1890.

Other

The Microcosm, with others. 1788.
Theognis Restitutus: The Personal History of the Poet, with a Translated Section. 1842; as *The Works of Theognis,* 1856.

Translator, *The Frogs,* by Aristophanes. 1839.
Translator, *The Acharnians, The Knights, and the Birds,* by Aristophanes. 1840.

Reading List: *Frere and His Friends* by Gabrielle Festing, 1899; *Frere: Sein Leben und Seine Werke, Sein Einfluss auf Byron* by A. von Eichler, 1905.

*   *   *

John Hookham Frere came of a Norfolk landowning family which contributed a number of able men to public life. His own career in politics and diplomacy was distinguished, though it came to a rather sudden end in 1809. Writing was a pastime, but one in which he showed outstanding talent. It was at Eton, in close friendship with George Canning, that he began to display his gifts as a humorous writer, in *The Microcosm,* a remarkably sophisticated weekly periodical. Canning's contributions at this stage were more brilliant than Frere's, just as he was later to outshine him in the world of affairs.

The two joined forces again in 1797 when Canning, by that time Under-Secretary of State at the Foreign Office, initiated *The Anti-Jacobin; or, The Weekly Examiner.* This directed its attack against what the Tory wits saw as dangerous absurdities in both political thinking and contemporary literary practice. It is now remembered chiefly for its verse, which has been collected and republished more than once. "The Friend of Humanity and the Needy Knife-grinder" ridicules simultaneously the politico-moral indignation and the halting Sapphics of Southey. Godwin was repeatedly pilloried as Mr. Higgins of St. Mary Axe, a philanthropist

62 FRERE

who hoped by didactic poems to spread his belief in universal benevolence and the sovereignty of Reason. "The Progress of Man" and "The Loves of the Triangles," with their pedestrian critical apparatus, are hilarious parodies of Godwin's ideas and Erasmus Darwin's verse. Contemporary German drama is also caricatured in "The Rovers," a fragment in which Frere's vein of high-spirited nonsense is reminiscent of Sheridan's in *The Critic*.

Twenty years later, when Frere's early retirement left him plenty of leisure for literary pursuits, he published *The Monks and the Giants*. He was an excellent linguist, and made some lively translations of Aristophanes; but this *ottava rima* poem sprang from his enjoyment of Pulci's racy *Morgante Maggiore*. Reading the Renaissance Florentine poet, Frere conceived the idea of treating an Arthurian theme in a deliberately homespun and comic way. The narrative purports to be the work of the brothers Whistlecraft, harness-makers of Stowmarket. It is a splendid piece of learned foolery, mildly satirical, in which off-hand colloquial diction is effortlessly combined with an elaborate stanza form. Byron was so delighted by the first two cantos, that he at once set about writing *Beppo*, "in or after the excellent manner of Mr. Whistlecraft (whom I take to be Frere)" as he wrote to John Murray, Frere's publisher as well as his own. Frere could hardly believe that the anonymous *Beppo* (1818) could be by the Romantic author of *Childe Harold*. When convinced by Murray, he commented "Lord Byron has paid me a compliment indeed." It is not too much to say that *Don Juan* also is considerably indebted to the Whistlecraft model. The resourcefulness of Frere's rhyming, his easy handling of dialogue, above all his confidential, button-holing manner, helped to set Byron on the road to his most brilliant achievements in comic narrative and satire.

—Margaret Bottrall

HAZLITT, William. English. Born in Maidstone, Kent, 10 April 1778; lived with his family in the United States, 1783–87, and in Wem, Shropshire, from 1787. Educated privately at home; studied for the Unitarian ministry at Hackney Theological College, London, 1793–94, then returned to his father's house at Wem, and continued his studies, mainly in philosophy, on his own; met Coleridge, 1798, subsequently visited him at Stowey, and, with Coleridge, visited Wordsworth at Lynton; gave up theological studies; studied painting with his brother and in Paris, 1802–03; gave up art in 1805. Married 1) Sarah Stoddart in 1808 (separated, 1819; divorced, 1822), one son; 2) Mrs. Bridgewater in 1824 (separated, 1825). Writer from 1792; divided his time between Wem and London, 1805–08; through Coleridge and Wordsworth, met Lamb and Godwin; supported Godwin in the controversy with Malthus, 1807; settled in Winterslow, near Salisbury, 1808; returned to London, 1812: lectured on philosophy at the Russell Institution; Parliamentary Reporter, 1812–13, and Dramatic Critic, 1814, for the *Morning Chronicle*; contributed to the *Edinburgh Review*, 1814 until his death; also wrote for the *Champion*, *The Times*, Leigh Hunt's *Examiner*, *London Magazine*, *Liberal*, and the *New Monthly*; lectured at the Surrey Institution, 1818–20; toured France and Italy, 1824–25. *Died 18 September 1830*.

PUBLICATIONS

Collections

Complete Works, edited by P. P. Howe. 21 vols., 1930–34.
Selected Writings, edited by Ronald Blythe. 1970.

Prose

An Essay on the Principles of Human Action, Being an Argument in Favour of the Natural Disinterestedness of the Human Mind. 1805.

Free Thoughts on Public Affairs; or, Advice to a Patriot. 1806.

A Reply to the Essay on Population by Malthus, in a Series of Letters. 1807.

A New and Improved Grammar of the English Tongue for the Use of Schools. 1810.

Memoirs of the Late Thomas Holcroft, completed by Hazlitt. 3 vols., 1816; edited by Elbridge Colby, as *The Life of Holcroft,* 2 vols., 1925.

The Round Table: A Collection of Essays on Literature, Men, and Manners, with Leigh Hunt. 2 vols., 1817.

Characters of Shakespeare's Plays. 1817; edited by C. Morgan, in *Liber Amoris and Dramatic Criticisms,* 1948.

A View of the English Stage; or, A Series of Dramatic Criticisms. 1818.

Lectures on the English Poets. 1818.

A Letter to William Gifford. 1819.

Lectures on the English Comic Writers. 1819; edited by A. Johnson, 1965.

Political Essays. 1819.

Lectures, Chiefly on the Dramatic Literature of the Age of Elizabeth. 1820.

Table-Talk; or, Original Essays. 2 vols., 1821–22.

Liber Amoris; or, The New Pygmalion. 1823; edited by C. Morgan, 1948.

Characteristics, in the Manner of Rochefoucault's Maxims. 1823.

Sketches of the Principal Picture Galleries in England with a Criticism on Marriage A-la-mode. 1824.

The Spirit of the Age; or, Contemporary Portraits. 1825; edited by E. D. Mackerness, 1969.

The Plain Speaker: Opinions on Books, Men, and Things. 2 vols., 1826.

Notes of a Journey Through France and Italy. 1826.

The Life of Napoleon Buonaparte. 4 vols., 1828–30.

Conversations of James Northcote, R.A. 1830; edited by Frank Swinnerton, 1949.

Literary Remains. 2 vols., 1836.

Sketches and Essays, Now First Collected by His Son. 1839; as *Men and Manners,* 1852.

Criticisms on Art and Sketches of the Picture Galleries of England, edited by William Hazlitt, Jr. 2 vols., 1843–44; as *Essays on the Fine Arts,* 1873.

Winterslow: Essays and Characters Written There, edited by William Hazlitt, Jr. 1850.

A Reply to Z, edited by Charles Whibley. 1923.

New Writings, edited by P. P. Howe. 2 vols., 1925–27.

Hazlitt in the Workshop: The Manuscript of "The Fight," edited by Stewart C. Wilcox. 1943.

Editor, *An Abridgement of the Light of Nature Pursued,* by Abraham Tucker. 1807.

Editor, *The Eloquence of the British Senate.* 2 vols., 1807.

Editor, *Select British Poets.* 1824.

Bibliography: *Bibliography of Hazlitt* by Geoffrey Keynes, 1931.

Reading List: *Hazlitt* by J. B. Priestley, 1960; *Hazlitt* by Herschel Baker, 1962; *Hazlitt and the Creative Imagination* by W. P. Albrecht, 1965; *Hazlitt and the Spirit of the Age* by Roy Park, 1971; *Hazlitt* by Ralph M. Wardle, 1971; *Hazlitt, Critic of Power* by John Kinnaird, 1978.

*   *   *

64   HAZLITT

William Hazlitt was an essayist pure and simple. He never published poems or fiction or drama, and his only excursion into the so-called creative arts was an abortive attempt as a young man to become a painter, which left him with a deep understanding of a craft he found he could not practice and thus made him one of the best early art critics in England and a true precursor of Ruskin. Yet, though he mainly restricted himself to criticism and reminiscence, with an occasional foray into political radicalism (to which he remained faithful when many of his friends, like Wordsworth and Coleridge, were alarmed by events in France into turning to the Right), Hazlitt raised the personal essay to the level of an art, and it is difficult to think of anyone except his friend and contemporary Charles Lamb who has excelled him in this genre.

Hazlitt was condemned by his poverty to be a perpetual journalist. He found the time to write few long, sustained books, and those which he did complete, like his amateurish *Essay on the Principles of Human Action*, his ponderous *Life of Napoleon* and the Rousseauish confessions of *Liber Amoris*, the tale of his unhappy love affair with Sarah Walker, are all relative failures. It was the lengthy essay – often a long review article – of the type which literary magazines of the time favoured, that showed Hazlitt at his best. There he could develop his flashes of insight without becoming involved in scholarly elaborations that would have revealed the lack of education and broad reading of which his enemies – with some justice – often accused him. Certainly he made up for these deficiencies by a strong intuitive understanding of both painters and writers. He stressed the importance of the emotion aroused by an open-hearted response to a work of literature or art, and declared that his critic's role was "to feel what is good and give reasons for the faith that is in me." He tended to ignore what other critics might have said, and made a virtue out of this by claiming that he was trying to show an original response to original work – to "that which was never imagined or expressed before."

Hazlitt's best books are all collections of essays and lectures, often with a unity of approach that links them, and within the limitations of such a form he acted not merely as a pioneer critic but also as a pioneer literary historian, reaching back into almost the whole past and present of English literature. Much of his best writing is about men he knew and their work. In essays like "My First Acquaintance with Poets" and "The Conversation of Poets" he not only portrays his own development as a young writer fascinated with the personality of Coleridge, but he also gives insights into the personalities of the Lake poets that go beyond the biographical into an understanding of the sources of their poetry.

At the same time, in volumes like *Characters of Shakespeare's Plays*, *Lectures on the English Poets*, *Lectures on the English Comic Writers*, and *Lectures on the Dramatic Literature of the Age of Elizabeth*, Hazlitt contributed greatly to the nineteenth-century rehabilitation of English writers of the sixteenth, seventeenth and early eighteenth centuries. He wrote very well on men he understood empathically, such as Milton, Fielding and Cervantes (whom Hazlitt cavalierly included among the English comic writers), and the Restoration comedians of manners like Wycherley and Congreve, but where his sympathies did not reach he was inclined to be silent, and perhaps his greatest omission as a critic-historian of English writing up to his time lay in his neglect of the Metaphysical poets.

Yet, for all his perceptiveness in understanding writers of the past, Hazlitt was undoubtedly at his best in writing of the world he knew from direct experience. *The Spirit of the Age*, with its sharp critical portraits of his contemporaries, despite occasional flashes of prejudice, is one of the best books to give the flavour of the English literary world at the end of the Napoleonic Wars, making verdicts on men and their works which posterity has on the whole sustained, and *The Plain Speaker*, ranging somewhat more widely, is equally fresh in its approach.

"Well, I've had a happy life," are Hazlitt's recorded last words. To those who knew the difficulties and disappointments he had endured, it seemed an astonishing statement. Yet an indefatigable zest for life was part of Hazlitt's nature, emerging in some of his best essays, like the splendid piece "On Going a Journey" (which begins characteristically: "One of the pleasantest things in the world is going a journey; but I like to go by myself"), the robust accounts of popular pleasures in "The Fight" and "The Indian Jugglers," and the two essays that balance each other, "On the Feeling of Immortality in Youth" and "On the Fear of Death," which concludes that "The most rational cure after all for the inordinate fear of death is to set a just value on life." The value Hazlitt set on life is shown in his love of English words and the rhythms of speech, in his love of the common life of Englishmen, and in his power to enter the mind of a creator, whether writer or artist, whether Wordsworth or Poussin.

In the way meant by Wilde, Hazlitt was pre-eminently the critic as artist; he never merely dissected or described, but in the best sense recreated what he discussed.

—George Woodcock

HEMANS, Felicia (Dorothea, née Browne). English. Born in Liverpool, 25 September 1793; moved with her family to Abergele, North Wales, 1800. Privately educated at home. Married Captain Alfred Hemans in 1812 (separated, 1818); five sons. Lived in Wales, and devoted herself to her family and to writing; moved to Wavertree, near Liverpool, 1828; visited Scotland, and met Sir Walter Scott, and the English lakes, and met Wordsworth, 1829; moved to Dublin, 1831. Recipient: Royal Society of Literature prize, 1821. *Died 16 May 1835.*

PUBLICATIONS

Collections

    Works, edited by Harriet Hughes. 7 vols., 1839.
    Poetical Works, edited by W. M. Rossetti. 1873.

Verse

    Poems. 1808.
    England and Spain; or, Valour and Patriotism. 1808.
    The Domestic Affections and Other Poems. 1812.
    The Restoration of the Works of Art to Italy. 1816.
    Modern Greece. 1817.
    Translations from Camoens and Other Poets. 1818.
    Wallace's Invocation to Bruce. 1819.
    The Sceptic. 1820.
    Stanzas to the Memory of the Late King. 1820.
    Dartmoor. 1821.
    Welsh Melodies. 1822.
    The Siege of Valencia: A Dramatic Poem, The Last Constantine, with Other Poems. 1823.

66   HEMANS

The Forest Sanctuary and Other Poems.   1825; revised edition, 1829.
Lays of Many Lands.   1825.
The League of the Alps, The Siege of Valencia, The Vespers of Palermo, and Other Poems,
   edited by A. Norton.   2 vols., 1826–27.
Poems.   1827.
Hymns on the Works of Nature for the Use of Children.   1827.
Poetical Works.   2 vols., 1828.
Records of Woman with Other Poems.   1828.
Songs of the Affections with Other Poems.   1830.
Hymns for Childhood.   1834.
National Lyrics and Songs for Music.   1834.
Scenes and Hymns of Life with Other Religious Poems.   1834.
Poetical Remains.   1836.
Early Blossoms.   1840.

Play

The Vespers of Palermo (produced 1823).   1823.

Reading List: *Memorials of Mrs. Hemans* by Henry F. Chorley, 2 vols., 1836; *Hemans Lyrik*
by W. Ledderbogen, 1913; *Une Femme Poète au Déclin du Romantisme Anglais: Hemans* by
Edith Duméril, 1929 (includes bibliography).

*   *   *

Though of considerable renown as a poet in her day, both at home and abroad, Felicia
Hemans is now remembered less for her writings than for her friendships – first as the
recipient of the persistent attentions of the youthful Shelley, later as the visitor of Scott and
guest of Wordsworth. Other prominent admirers included such diverse figures as Lord
Byron, Lord Jeffrey, John Wilson, Reginald Heber, and Joanna Baillie. Such high regard
cannot have been entirely misplaced, and it is an injustice to her talents to associate her only
with the stately homes of England and the boy on the burning deck.

The chief attraction of Mrs. Hemans' verse is its variety: there are historical and legendary
tales, Greek and Welsh melodies, patriotic effusions, devotional sonnets, nature lyrics,
children's verses, hymns, songs and translations. Her collected poems, the product of over 30
years of writing, fill some 700 pages of fine print, and while there is much in them that is
frankly imitative (now of Wordsworth and Coleridge, now of Bryon and Tom Moore), and
much that is sweetly sentimental (chivalry, childhood, and the Church), there is nevertheless
a good deal to surprise and delight, especially among her shorter pieces. Poems like "The
Rock of Cader Idris," "Woman on the Field of Battle," "The Voice of Spring," "The Landing
of the Pilgrim Fathers," "The Shadow of a Flower," "The Willow Song," and "I would we
had not met again ..." are representative of her genuinely lyrical voice. Among the more
interesting of her longer poems are "The Abencerrage" (a Spanish tale), "The Maremma" (an
Italian tale, after Dante), "The Forest Sanctuary" (her own favourite), and the collection
entitled *Records of Woman* (celebrating such feminine worthies as Joan of Arc, Arabella
Stuart, and Properzia Rossi). The opening lines of "The Abencerrage" (1819) are a good
example of the poet's exotic scene-setting:

> Lonely and still are now thy marble halls,
>   Thou fair Alhambra! there the feast is o'er;
> And with the murmur of thy fountain-falls
>   Blend the wild tones of minstrelsy no more.

Hushed are the voices that in years gone by
 Have mourned, exulted, menaced, through thy towers;
Within thy pillared courts the grass waves high,
 And all uncultured bloom thy fairy bowers.

Unheeded there the flowering myrtle blows,
 Through tall arcades unmarked the sunbeam smiles,
And many a tint of softened brilliance throws
 O'er fretted walls and shining peristyles.

C. H. Herford wrote in *The Age of Wordsworth* (1897) that: "Of all the English Romantic poets, Mrs. Hemans expresses with the richest intensity the more superficial and transient elements of Romanticism." Pathos, primitivism, and the picturesque abound in her verses, and indeed they quickly pall on the taste, but Mrs. Hemans has a rightful place in any anthology of the period.

—Greg Crossan

HOOD, Thomas. English. Born in London, 23 May 1799. Educated at private schools in London; apprenticed to a merchant's counting house in the City of London, 1812–15; lived with relatives in Dundee, 1815–18; returned to London and was articled to his uncle, an engraver, 1818–20; left the profession for a literary career. Married Jane Reynolds in 1825; one son, one daughter. Sub-Editor, *London Magazine*, 1821–23; became acquainted with Lamb, Hazlitt, and De Quincey; Editor and Contributor, *The Gem*, London, 1829, and the *Comic Annual*, London, 1830–40; lived in Coblentz, 1835–37, and Ostend, 1837–40; Editor, *New Monthly Magazine*, London, 1841–43; Co-Owner, *Hood's Monthly Magazine*, 1844–45. *Died 3 May 1845.*

PUBLICATIONS

Collections

Works, edited by Thomas Hood, Jr., and Frances Broderip.   10 vols., 1869–73.
Poems, edited by Walter Jerrold.   1906.
Selected Poems, edited by John Clubbe.   1970.
Letters, edited by Peter F. Morgan.   1971.

Verse

Odes and Addresses to Great People, with J. H. Reynolds.   1825.
Whims and Oddities in Prose and Verse.   2 vols., 1826–27.
The Plea of the Midsummer Fairies, Hero and Leander, Lycus the Centaur, and Other Poems.   1827.
The Epping Hunt.   1829.

68   HOOD

The Dream of Eugene Aram. 1831.
Whimsicalities: A Periodical Gathering (verse and prose). 2 vols., 1844; revised edition, 1870.
The Headlong Career and Woeful Ending of Precocious Piggy, edited by Frances Broderip. 1858.

Plays

Mr. Sims (produced 1829).
York and Lancaster (produced 1829).

Fiction

National Tales. 1827.
Tylney Hall. 1834.

Other

Hood's Own; or, Laughter from Year to Year. 1839; second series, edited by Thomas Hood, Jr., 1861.
Up the Rhine. 1840.
Fairy Land; or, Recreation for the Rising Generation (juvenile), with Jane Hood, edited by Frances Broderip. 1860.
Hood and Charles Lamb: The Story of a Friendship, Being the Literary Reminiscences of Hood, edited by Walter Jerrold. 1930.
Letters from the Dilke Papers in the British Museum, edited by Leslie Marchand. 1945.

Reading List: *Hood* by J. M. MacIlrath, 1935; *Hood* by Laurence Brander, 1963; *Hood* by John C. Reid, 1963; *Victorian Forerunner: The Later Career of Hood* by John Clubbe, 1968.

*   *   *

Thomas Hood began his career as a Regency man, and handled words with Romantic gusto. He shared the Romantic preference for dealing with extremes of human experience, and for stories of a supernatural world beyond those limits, taken from folk-lore and legend. The Gothic ambience of haunted houses and hag-ridden murderers had a strong appeal for him; and he couched these tales in varieties of narrative verse derived, directly or via Wordsworth and Coleridge, from ballad and romance. The fertility of his metrical and verbal invention is clear in his serious poems of this kind; but it fully emerges in his comic verse. This derives from the same sources: it is an unexpected, illuminating twist upon serious subjects, and treats of death, despair, revenant ghosts, and suicides. These tales too are often in the ballad form, drawing upon supernatural associations and the comic potential of jingling broadside metres for resonant comic contrasts.

Contrast, or incongruity, is the basic comic device in Hood's ballads. He juxtaposes the trivial and the extraordinary with such an appearance of naturalness that we are startled into a new, and comic, vision of each. His ghosts are very corporeal, concerned with the fate of their bodies as if with important luggage they are obliged to leave lying around; conversely, his pining lovers are hampered in their soaring aspirations by unromantic flesh, too fat or too tall or too old for their passionate spirits. A paternal ode on an angelic three-year-old is punctuated by the infant's hair-raising physical activities; a stag-hunt is conducted by tradesmen who cannot ride. For incongruous effects Hood utilises all the resources of the poet: verbal music, elaborate patterns of stanza and of rhyme, choruses, adaptations of "the real language of men" are all turned on their heads. But the device which Hood made especially his own and bequeathed to all his Victorian progeny of comic versifiers was the pun. Puns are the epitome of his comic style: they are an incongrous juxtaposition captured in a single word.

Hood's comic ballads achieved the accolade of authenticity coveted by Wordsworth for the *Lyrical Ballads*, becoming current in popular circulation on broadsides. He continued to use ballad styles when his rumbustious comic vein gave way abruptly, under the influence of the consciousness of the 1840's, to a mood of social protest. His "Song of the Shirt," published in *Punch* in 1843, was written as a popular song, and so passed into the consciousness of the nation. The London seamstress became the representative of the oppressed poor, and Hood's poem about her the model for an outburst of a new kind of writing, with a social purpose and message. We now find the fervour with which this and subsequent protest songs were received as strange as is the cruelty of some of his comic writing; but in both Hood reflected his times, and has much to tell us about its sensibility.

—J. S. Bratton

HUNT, (James Henry) Leigh.   English.   Born in Southgate, Middlesex, 19 October 1784. Educated at Christ's Hospital, London. Married Marianne Kent; seven children. Journalist for all of his life: contributor to the *Traveller*, before 1805; Editor, *The News*, 1805–07; contributor to the *Statesman*, 1806, and the *Times*, 1807; Editor, *The Examiner: A Sunday Paper*, 1808–21, and contributor until 1825; Editor, *The Reflector*, 1810–11; imprisoned for libelling the Prince Regent, 1813–15; Editor, *The Indicator*, 1819–21, and *The Literary Pocket-Book; or, Companion for the Lover of Nature and Art*, 1819–23; joined Shelley in Italy to establish *The Liberal: Verse and Prose from the South*, 1822; after Shelley's death lived with Byron at Pisa; returned to London, 1825; contributor to the *New Monthly Magazine*, 1825–26, and occasionally until 1850; Editor, *The Companion*, 1828; contributor to *Atlas*, 1828–30; Editor, *The Chat of the Week*, 1830, and *The Tatler: A Daily Journal of Literature and the Stage*, 1830–32; contributor to *True Sun* and *Weekly True Sun*, 1833–34; Editor, *Leigh Hunt's London Journal*, 1834–35, *The Monthly Repository*, 1837–38, and *Leigh Hunt's Journal*, 1850–51; Contributor to *Spectator*, 1858–59, and to the *Morning Chronicle* throughout his career. Granted Civil List pension, 1847. *Died 28 August 1859.*

PUBLICATIONS

Collections

Poetical Works, edited by H. S. Milford.   1923.

Fiction

Sir Ralph Esher; or, Adventures of a Gentleman of the Court of Charles II. 1832.
Tales, edited by William Knight. 1891.

Play

A Legend of Florence (produced 1840). 1840.

Verse

Juvenilia. 1801.
The Feast of the Poets and Other Pieces. 1814; revised edition, 1815.
The Descent of Liberty: A Mask. 1815.
The Story of Rimini. 1816.
Foliage; or, Poems Original and Translated. 1818.
Hero and Leander, and Bacchus and Ariadne. 1819.
Poetical Works. 3 vols., 1819; revised edition, 1832, 1844.
Amyntas: A Tale of the Woods, from the Italian of Tasso. 1820.
Ultra-Crepidarius: A Satire on William Gifford. 1823.
Bacchus in Tuscany: A Dithyrambic Poem, from the Italian of Redi. 1825.
Captain Sword and Captain Pen. 1835.
The Palfrey: A Love-Story of Old Times. 1842.
Stories in Verse Now First Collected. 1855.
Ballads of Robin Hood, edited by L. A. Brewer. 1922.

Other

Critical Essays on the Performers of the London Theatres. 1807.
An Attempt to Show the Folly and Danger of Methodism. 1809.
*The Prince of Wales v. The Examiner: A Full Report of the Trial of John and Leigh
   Hunt.* 1812.
The Reflector (periodical, 1810–11). 2 vols., 1812.
Musical Copyright: Whitaker Versus Hume. 1816.
The Round Table: A Collection of Essays on Literature, Men, and Manners, with William
   Hazlitt. 2 vols., 1817.
The Months, Descriptive of the Successive Beauties of the Year. 1821; edited by R. H.
   Bath, 1929.
The Indicator. 1822.
Lord Byron and Some of His Contemporaries. 1828; revised edition, 1828.
Christianism; or, Belief and Unbelief Reconciled, edited by John Forster. 1832; revised
   edition, as *The Religion of the Heart,* 1853.
The Indicator and The Companion: A Miscellany for the Fields and Fireside. 2 vols.,
   1834.
Hunt's London Journal 1834–35. 2 vols., 1834–35.
The Seer; or, Commonplaces Refreshed. 2 vols., 1840–41.
Imagination and Fancy, with an Essay in Answer to the Question What Is Poetry? 1844;
   edited by Edmund Gosse, 1907.
Stories from the Italian Poets. 2 vols., 1846.
Men, Women, and Books. 2 vols., 1847.
A Jar of Honey from Mount Hybla. 1848.

HUNT 71

The Town: Its Memorable Characters and Events. 2 vols., 1848.

Autobiography. 3 vols., 1850; revised edition, 1860; edited by J. E. Morpurgo, 1949; *The Earliest Sketches* edited by Stephen F. Fogle, 1959.

Table Talk. 1851.

The Old Court Suburb; or, Memorials of Kensington. 2 vols., 1855; revised edition, 1855.

A Saunter Through the West End. 1861.

Correspondence, edited by Thornton Hunt. 2 vols., 1862.

A Tale for a Chimney Corner and Other Essays, edited by E. Ollier. 1869.

A Day by the Fire and Other Papers Hitherto Uncollected, edited by J. E. Babson. 1870.

The Wishing-Cap Papers, Now First Collected, edited by J. E. Babson. 1873.

Essays and Poems, edited by R. B. Johnson. 2 vols., 1891.

Dramatic Essays, edited by William Archer and R. W. Lowe. 1894.

The Love of Books, edited by L. A. and E. T. Brewer. 1923.

Marginalia, edited by L. A. Brewer. 1926.

Prefaces, Mainly to His Periodicals, edited by R. B. Johnson. 1927.

My Hunt Library: The Holograph Letters, edited by L. A. Brewer. 1938.

The Dissidence of Dissent (Monthly Repository 1837–38), edited by F. E. Mineka. 1944.

Dramatic Criticism, Literary Criticism, and *Political and Occasional Essays,* edited by L. H. and C. W. Houtchens. 3 vols., 1949–62.

Musical Evenings; or, Selections, Vocal and Instrumental, edited by David R. Cheney. 1964.

Hunt on Eight Sonnets of Dante, edited by D. Rhodes. 1965.

Editor, *Classic Tales, Serious and Lively, with Critical Essays.* 5 vols., 1806–07.

Editor, *The Masque of Anarchy,* by Shelley. 1832.

Editor, *The Dramatic Works of Sheridan.* 1840.

Editor, *The Dramatic Works of Wycherley, Congreve, Vanbrugh, and Farquhar.* 1840.

Editor, with R. H. Horne, *The Poems of Chaucer Modernized.* 1841.

Editor, *One Hundred Romances of Real Life.* 1843.

Editor, *The Foster Brothers: A Tale of the Wars of Chiozza,* by Thornton Hunt. 3 vols., 1845.

Editor, *Wit and Humour, Selected from the English Poets.* 1846.

Editor, with J. B. Syme, *Readings for Railways.* 2 vols., 1849–53.

Editor, *A Book for a Corner.* 1849.

Editor, *Beaumont and Fletcher* (selections). 1855.

Editor, with S. Adams Lee, *The Book of the Sonnet.* 2 vols., 1867.

Reading List: *Hunt and His Circle* by Edmund Blunden, 1930; *Hunt* by Louis Landré, 1936 (includes bibliography); *Byron, Shelley, Hunt, and The Examiner* by W. H. Marshall, 1960.

*   *   *

It is impossible to ignore Leigh Hunt, yet it is uncommonly difficult to "place" his contribution to Literature. He was a splendidly competent editor whose journals failed to realise their potential. He was an essayist overshadowed by Lamb, a critic overshadowed by Hazlitt and a poet overshadowed by Shelley, Byron, Keats, Wordsworth, and Tennyson among others. As a reformer he had the moral courage to accept imprisonment for his views and to remain true to his beliefs. His only reward for this was a Civil List pension when the party of "Reform" became the government.

Dickens pilloried him as Skimpole in *Bleak House*, drawing him as "a sentimentalist, brilliant, vivacious and engaging, but thoroughly selfish and unprincipled." Byron thought him boring and prosaic, yet Shelley considered him "gentle, honourable, innocent and brave" and Carlyle made no bones about referring to him as "a Man of Genius." The Victorians over-praised his verse; today it appears the work of a competent man-of-letters. There is no doubting the generosity of his critical judgement even though the sceptic might claim that he picked winners by backing every horse in the race. It was his lack of judgement in supporting his claims which was damaging, the indiscriminate nature of his enthusiasm.

Nevertheless he has left at least one book of considerable interest. Carlyle rated *The Autobiography of Leigh Hunt* as "by far the best book of the autobiographic kind ... in the English language," and it is likely to remain his most lasting achievement. It is a surprisingly cool look at literature, politics, and society by a man who knew most of the literary figures of the first half of the nineteenth century. It is written with charm and perception and it is, as J. E. Morpurgo has rightly said, "a magnificently arranged selection of journalistic writing."

He has been called a hack. If his response to the need to provide for himself and his family lays him open to this charge, he was surely the most splendid hack in literary journalism.

—John Stuart Williams

KEATS, John. English. Born in London, 31 October 1795. Educated at Reverend John Clarke's private school, Enfield, Middlesex; after death of his parents apprenticed to Thomas Hammond, surgeon and apothecary, Edmonton, London, 1810; also studied medicine at Guy's Hospital, London, 1815–16, and qualified as an apothecary 1816. Encouraged by Leigh Hunt, abandoned medicine for poetry, 1816; made walking tour of the Lake District, and Scotland and Ireland, 1818. Consumptive: went to Italy for his health, 1820, and died in Rome. *Died 23 February 1821.*

PUBLICATIONS

Collections

> *Poetical Works and Other Writings,* edited by H. Buxton Forman.   8 vols., 1938–39.
> *Poetical Works,* edited by H. W. Garrod.   1939; revised edition, with J. Jones, 1959.
> *The Letters,* edited by H. E. Rollins.   2 vols., 1958.
> *Complete Poems,* edited by John Barnard.   1973.

Verse

> *Poems.*   1817.
> *Endymion: A Poetic Romance.*   1818.
> *Lamia, Isabella, The Eve of St. Agnes, and Other Poems.*   1820.
> *Another Version of Keats's Hyperion,* edited by R. M. Milnes.   1857.

Bibliography: *Keats: A Bibliography and Reference Guide* by J. R. MacGillivray, 1949.

KEATS 73

Reading List: *Studies in Keats* by J. Middleton Murry, 1930, revised edition as *Keats,* 1955; *The Evolution of Keats's Poetry* by Claude Finney, 2 vols., 1936; *The Stylistic Development of Keats,* 1945, and *Keats,* 1963, both by Walter Jackson Bate; *The Mask of Keats: A Study of Problems* by Robert Gittings, 1956; *Keats: A Reassessment* edited by Kenneth Muir, 1958; *Keats and the Dramatic Principle* by Bernice Slote, 1958; *Keats: The Making of a Poet* by A. Ward, 1963; *Aesthetic and Myth in the Poetry of Keats* by W. E. Evert, 1964; *Keats* by Douglas Bush, 1966; *Keats and Embarrassment* by Christopher Ricks, 1974.

* * *

The first works of a young poet are more frequently expressions of the intent to be a poet than exercises of a poet's powers. They are also, almost necessarily, derivative; in John Keats's case the influence of Spenser is pervasive, not the homely, English, and moral Spenser but the cultivator of the enamelled and the musical. These early poems also exhibit, often with pitiless clarity, the modes of sensibility current at the time. The character of those of Keats's time may be inferred from a remark in a letter from Haydon to Keats about *Endymion*: "I have read your delicious poem with exquisite enjoyment." The influence of Spenser is one likely to play quite happily on poetry which is "delicious" and designed to provide "exquisite enjoyment." The poems published in 1817 are generally notable for their lack of organisation: of structure they have little more than the external verse pattern and a single generalisation or introductory remark followed by a long catalogue of more or less pertinent examples. The characteristic mood is one of romantic pain, "sweet desolation" – "balmy pain"; the characteristic pose is one of indulgent relaxation. The staple of the idiom is composed of such phrases as warm desires, coy muse, quaint jubilee, curious bending, luxuries bright, milky, soft and rosey, luxurious wings, pleasant smotherings. The unexpressed premise of these poems is that poetry is a drug, a more refined form of alcohol.

Undoubtedly a part of Keats's mind, the more critical and intelligent part, was in abeyance during the composition of these poems. But not wholly so. There are moments when the indolence gives way to a more energetic, a more keenly apprehensive grasp, when the fumes of indulgence are dispersed by a fresher air. At these moments the verse shows a more biting sense of reality, a firmer rhythm, a more particularised sort of imagery, and a use of language at once more strenuous and more controlled. There are other lines enlivened by an unpretentious gaiety and simplicity in the manner of Herrick. And there is that more modest, objective, and very successful poem "On the Grasshopper and the Cricket." Keats was becoming aware that a poet could not remain content to loll a prisoner of his own senses; his sensations must be filtered through a judging mind and be informed by deliberate thought.

Mawkish was the epithet Keats himself applied to *Endymion*. It is not, however, gross in any way. It is fluent, facile, sweetly insipid. There is no leading idea, unless we call Endymion's search for pleasure one, and little is remarkable in the detail. It appears to be the result of no particular pressure and engages nothing that exists at a deeper level than the decorative. Its structure is vague, its development sketchy, its length (except that Keats took length as a test of a poet's powers) pointless.

There would be no need to qualify these remarks very radically to have them apply with equal force to "Isabella; or, The Pot of Basil." This is a poetical version of an anecdote drawn from one of Keats's favourite books, *The Anatomy of Melancholy*, itself an essentially literary and academic work, the purposes of which conform closely to the ends that Keats conceived at this time as proper to poetry. "Lamia" also derives from Burton and uses a myth with a long history stretching back in English literature to the late fourteenth or early fifteenth century *Thomas of Erceldoune*. But "Lamia" differs from "Isabella" in that it is meant to present a serious idea; it is a poem written to the formula of the "vast idea." It is still plangent and melancholy but slower and fuller in movement. The poem endeavours to represent – but as in a tableau rather than a drama – the conflict between illusory beauty and the hallucination of pleasure and the life of the intellect and moral dignity. Lycius, the normal man, is caught and destroyed between the two. But there is an excessive disproportion

74   KEATS

between the important ideas formally involved and the essentially literary idiom and manner. That discrepancy is abolished in "The Eve of St. Agnes." The poem is much less pretentious than "Lamia": no vast idea rolls before the poet's eye. He remains within the limitations of a subject which gives him without pressing or manipulation natural opportunities for realising his extraordinary perception of glow, richness, and colour in the physical world. The exigencies of the narrative, slight as they are, control his delight in luxury and give it due subordination as one element in experience. Keats successfully resists the temptation merely to indulge his "sensual vision." The figure of Madeline, delicate and uncharacterised as it is, is more than an example of what Keats called the "tendency to class women in my books with roses and sweet-meats." Throughout the poem the imagery has, even in those scenes which could easily become occasions for uncritical, relaxed indulgence, a certain quality of coolness and crispness and a scope of metaphorical reference which save it from any descent into the ludicrous or into mere sensuality.

Between "The Eve of St. Agnes" and the great Odes Keats was, it is clear, astonishingly transformed, advancing from the status of a charming minor talent to that of a genius of the first order.

The fruit of Keats's maturing mind and sensibility is the set of four poems, "Ode on Melancholy," "Ode to a Nightingale," "Ode on a Grecian Urn," and "To Autumn" written in 1819, the first three during the early months of the year. (The "Ode to Psyche" was also written in 1819, but it does not belong in the same class with the others.) These poems are different in kind from their predecessors; while the earlier ones are merely decorative, these are tragic: they are enlarged, complicated by a dimension of human experience unknown in the former. Their distance from the earlier poems may be indicated by saying that while Spenser is the dominant influence there, here it is Shakespeare; and not Shakespeare as the supplier of external literary tricks like Shelley's Shakespeare in *The Cenci*, but a Shakespeare who is grasped, subordinated to Keats's purposes, and dissolved in Keats's own idiom. To say this is not to claim for these poems, or for all of them, a complete maturity. Leavis defined the sort of inadequacy which persists in them when he said: "It is as if Keats were making major poetry out of minor – as if, that is, the genius of a major poet were working in the material of a minor poetry." And there are, without doubt, positive weaknesses in these poems, remnants of decay, touches of nostalgic softness, and moments of regression to a less disciplined past.

The unfinished *Hyperion* brings up the name of Milton, its literary ancestor. It is easy to see why Milton should have appealed as a model to a poet of Keats's character, and one engaged like Keats in an effort, intense and sustained, "to refine his sensual vision." There was a strong Miltonic current running in the eighteenth century, especially among those minor writers who were later to be thought of as writers of "true poetry," the predecessors of Romanticism. Then, with the rejection of Augustanism, Milton came to stand for all that was lofty, epic, and severe in the English tradition. He was the solitary giant, looming and self-sufficient, and the distracted second-generation Romantics were profoundly impressed by his heroic individuality, his calm assumption of the poet's public robes, and the untroubled confidence with which he undertook his enormous theme. Above all he represented a poet in his role as moral teacher and spiritual healer. But although we can see *why* Milton should have attracted Keats, we can also see *how*, in the event, Keats's choice of Milton as an exemplar was a disastrous one, as Keats himself admitted when he abandoned his project: "Life to him would be death to me." No two poets could have been so radically different, so constitutionally unsympathetic to one another, no two poetic styles could have been so naturally antagonistic. Keats's use of language which accommodated itself so easily to the influence of Shakespeare was denuded of all its proper virtue when associated with Milton's. *Hyperion* was intended to be an extension of Keats's poetic experience, an effort in a new direction, and also a stage in his spiritual progress, an exercise in moral discipline; in fact, it turned out to be a contraction of the one and a retrogressive step in the case of the other. What was meant to be as strict and ascetic as Milton proved to be as ornamental as Spenser, as relaxed as Tennyson. What was designed to be a central commentary on human life disclosed itself as merely marginal and elegiac, not a vehicle for wisdom but a symptom of weakness.

The true line of Keats's development, lost in *Hyperion* in a waste of misdirected energy, misguided submission, and frustrated purpose, is recovered in the Odes. These are the poems of a sensibility both powerful and exquisite, on the point of attaining its majority, on the point of completing its self-education. And because of this Keats is liable momentarily to be guilty of certain imperfections. But our recognition of these will only make us wonder all the more at the triumph of the spirit, the triumph of the lacerated spirit, which these poems, written at an unpropitious time and in the most tragic conditions, represent.

—William Walsh

KEBLE, John. English. Born in Fairford, Gloucestershire, 25 April 1792. Educated at home; Corpus Christi College, Oxford, 1807–10, double first 1810. Married Charlotte Clarke in 1835. Fellow, Oriel College, Oxford, 1811 (English essay prize and Latin essay prize, 1812); College Tutor, 1818–23; initiated the Oxford Movement, 1833; Professor of Poetry, Oxford University, 1832–41; Keble College, Oxford, erected as memorial, 1870. Ordained deacon, 1815; Curate, Eastleach, Gloucestershire, 1815–23; Curate, Southrop, Gloucestershire, 1823–25, Hursley, Hampshire, 1825–27, for his father at Coln St. Aldwyn, Gloucestershire, 1827–35, and Rector of Hursley, from 1835. Examiner, East India House examinations, 1830, 1832. Co-Editor, a Library of the Fathers of the Holy Catholic Church series, from 1838. *Died 29 March 1866.*

PUBLICATIONS

Collections

   The Christian Year, Lyra Innocentium and Other Poems, edited by J. C. Sharp.   1914.

Verse

   The Christian Year: Thoughts in Verse for Sundays and Holydays Throughout the Year.   1827.
   Lyra Apostolica, with others.   1836.
   The Psalter or Psalms of David in English Verse.   1839.
   Lyra Innocentium: Thoughts in Verse on Christian Children.   1846.
   Miscellaneous Poems, edited by G. Moberly.   1869.

Other

   On Translation from Dead Languages.   1812.
   Tracts for the Times.   8 vols., 1834–41.
   The Case of Catholic Subscription to the Thirty-Nine Articles.   1841.

76   KEBLE

Praelectiones Poeticae. 1844; translated by E. K. Francis, as *Lectures on Poetry,* 2 vols., 1912.
Sermons, Academical and Occasional. 1847.
A Very Few Plain Thoughts on the Proposed Addition of Dissenters to the University of Oxford. 1854.
On Eucharistical Adoration. 1868.
Sermons, Occasional and Parochial. 1868.
Village Sermons on the Baptismal Service, edited by E. B. Pusey. 1868.
Letters of Spiritual Counsel and Guidance, edited by R. F. Wilson. 1870; edited by B. W. Randolph, 1904.
Sermons for the Christian Year. 11 vols., 1875–80.
Occasional Papers and Reviews, edited by E. B. Pusey. 1877.
Studia Sacra, edited by J. P. Norris. 1877.

Editor, *Works of Richard Hooker.* 3 vols., 1836.
Editor, with John Henry Newman, *Remains of R. H. Froude.* 4 vols., 1838–39.
Editor, *A Selection from the Sermons and Poetical Remains of George James Cornish.* 1850.

Reading List: *Musings over "The Christian Year" and "Lyra Innocentium"* by Charlotte Yonge, 1871; *Keble* by William E. Daniels, 1948; *Keble's Literary and Religious Contributions to the Oxford Movement* by W. J. A. M. Beek, 1959; *Keble: A Study in Limitations* by Georgina Battiscombe, 1963; *Keble, Priest, Professor, and Poet* by Brian W. Martin, 1976.

*   *   *

John Keble's reputation does not depend primarily on his achievement as a poet. The Oxford college that bears his name commemorates the scholarly divine whose influence shaped the revival of Anglicanism that began with the Tractarians. Keble was an older contemporary of Newman and Pusey. He might have had a brilliant career as an academic, but from filial devotion he withdrew to a country parish. He did, however, hold the Oxford Professorship of Poetry from 1832–41, and delivered a series of Latin lectures which Newman considered his greatest literary work. Dedicated to Wordsworth, though entirely concerned with Greek and Latin poets, these lectures reveal Keble as a Romantic critic. Sharing Wordsworth's belief that poetry originates in the overflow of powerful feelings, he emphasises the dominant role of the imagination in assimilating and ordering impressions. Keble made much of the analogies between religion and poetry, but clearly distinguished between the two.

The lectures, not translated into English till 1912, were addressed to a restricted, highly cultivated audience. The work that brought Keble literary fame was *The Christian Year,* published in 1827. This collection of poems was intended to supplement the Book of Common Prayer, by strengthening the attachment of church-goers to Christian doctrine and practice. The book had an immense success. In later life, Keble himself sometimes spoke disparagingly of it; but it was constantly reprinted throughout the nineteenth century. Today, only a very few of Keble's poems are current, thanks to their inclusion in hymn-books; and even these are selected verses from more diffuse compositions, not integral poems.

To the Victorians, Keble seemed another George Herbert. The parallels are indeed striking. Both were exceptionally gifted men who dedicated their poetic powers to the service of God. Both were exemplary country parsons, graced by rare beauty of character. But comparable as they are in the spheres of moral virtue and religious devotion, as poets they can only be compared to Keble's detriment. He admired Herbert, and occasionally echoed him; but his piety was unaccompanied by wit, and his diction is mostly limp and undistinguished. The self-awareness and subtle modulation of temper and tone which commend Herbert's poems to readers who care little for their Christian content are not to be found in *The Christian Year*.

Keble in 1846 published *Lyra Innocentium*, a volume of poems about childhood (another indication of his admiration for Wordsworth). He also translated the Psalter into English verse, and edited a selection of the writings of Richard Hooker, the great Elizabethan divine. Keble's place in the hierarchy of English churchmen is unquestionably eminent; but it seems unlikely that his lyrics will ever regain the reputation they once enjoyed.

—Margaret Bottrall

KNOWLES, James Sheridan. Irish. Born in Cork, 12 May 1784; son of the lexicographer James Knowles; moved with his family to London, 1793. Educated at his father's school in Cork, 1790–93; studied medicine at the University of Aberdeen, M.D. Married 1) Maria Charteris in 1809 (died, 1841), one son; 2) Miss Elphinstone in 1842. Abandoned medicine for the stage, and appeared as an actor in Bath, Dublin, and Belfast, 1808–11; schoolmaster in his own school in Belfast, which subsequently transferred to Glasgow, 1811–28; also conducted the literary department of the *Free Press*, Glasgow, 1824–25; returned to acting, 1832–43; evangelical preacher from 1844. Awarded Civil List pension, 1848. *Died 30 November 1862.*

PUBLICATIONS

Collections

> *Various Dramatic Works.* 2 vols., 1874.
> *Dramatic Works.* 1883.

Plays

> *Leo; or, The Gypsy* (produced 1810).
> *Brian Boroihme; or, The Maid of Erin* (produced 1812). 1872.
> *Caius Gracchus* (produced 1815). 1823.
> *Virginius; or, The Liberation of Rome* (produced 1820). 1820.
> *The Fatal Dowry*, from the play by Massinger (produced 1825). 1825.
> *William Tell* (produced 1825). 1825.
> *The Beggar's Daughter of Bethnal Green* (produced 1828). 1828; revised version, as *The Beggar of Bethnal Green* (produced 1834), 1834.
> *Alfred the Great; or, The Patriot King* (produced 1831). 1831.
> *The Hunchback* (produced 1832). 1832.
> *The Vision of the Bard* (produced 1832). 1832.
> *The Wife: A Tale of Mantua* (produced 1833). 1833.

78 KNOWLES

The Daughter (produced 1836; also produced as *The Wrecker's Daughter*). 1837.
The Bridal, from the play *The Maid's Tragedy* by Beaumont and Fletcher (produced 1837). 1837.
The Love-Chase (produced 1837). 1837.
Woman's Wit; or, Love's Disguises (produced 1838). 1838.
The Maid of Mariendorpt (produced 1838). 1838.
Dramatic Works. 1838; revised edition, 2 vols., 1856.
Love (produced 1839). 1840.
John of Procida; or, The Bridals of Messina (produced 1840; also produced as *The Bride of Messina*). 1840.
Old Maids (produced 1841). 1841.
The Rose of Arragon (produced 1842). 1842.
The Secretary (produced 1843). 1843.
The Rock of Rome; or, The Arch Heresy. 1849.
Alexina; or, True unto Death (produced 1866). 1866.

Fiction

Fortesque. 1846.
George Lovell. 1847.
Tales and Novelettes, revised and edited by F. Harvey. 1874.

Verse

The Welsh Harper: A Ballad. 1796.
Fugitive Pieces. 1810.

Other

The Elocutionist: A Collection of Pieces in Prose and Verse, Peculiarly Adapted to Display the Art of Reading. 1823(?).
The Idol Demolished by Its Own Priest: An Answer to Cardinal Newman's Lectures on Transubstantiation. 1851.
The Gospel Attributed to Matthew Is the Record of the Whole Original Apostlehood. 1855.
Lectures on Dramatic Literature, edited by S. W. Abbott and F. Harvey. 2 vols., 1873.

Reading List: *Knowles and the Theatre of His Time* by Leslie H. Meeks, 1933.

*   *   *

The plays that brought James Sheridan Knowles his reputation as a modern Shakespeare are the tragedies and mawkish melodramas properly remembered alongside his uneasy relationship with the actor William Charles Macready (1793–1873). It was Macready's decision to propose *Virginius* for performance at Covent Garden in 1820 that transformed both men's careers. *Virginius* is a five-act tragedy, written, like all Knowles's plays, in blank verse which pays consistent homage to Shakespeare and the Elizabethans. It tells the story of Appius and Virginia, but with the focus on Virginius. He is a simple, recognisable father, whose very familiarity makes more affecting the climactic murder of his own daughter to save her honour. Fatherhood is as much a nineteenth century theme as motherhood, and

Macready, in private life a passionate and suffering father, was its supreme theatrical portrayer. Knowles, too, would bluster fondly about the riches of paternity. He wrote for Macready another success about the arch-father, *William Tell*, and intended Macready for the title-role of his later paternal tragedy, *John of Procida*. *William Tell* is a melodrama, told without distinction, certainly with no sense of place. Like all Knowles's serious semi-historical plays, it celebrates in regular rhetorical verse the over-easy triumph of liberty over the forces of repression. His villains are of cardboard, and easily torn apart. The patched-up friendship with Macready reached a new height in a collaboration on *The Bridal*, an adaptation of *The Maid's Tragedy* (by Beaumont and Fletcher), but petered out again after a brief run of *The Secretary*, an historical romance in which Macready played the uncle of an orphan, since the plot, taken from a novel by G. P. R. James, allowed no nearer approach to fatherhood.

To those who have followed the lead of nineteenth-century opinion by viewing Knowles as a writer of tragedies, his reputation has seemed laughably inflated. But his real strength is elsewhere. There are suggestions of it in *The Hunchback*, in which the courting of the two young couples has a genuine sprightliness. The influence of Fletcherian romance is developed in *The Beggar of Bethnal Green* and *Woman's Wit*, but the best evidence of a largely uncelebrated skill in comedy is in *The Love-Chase* and *Old Maids*. In each of them, the various fortunes of three courtships are adroitly plotted. In the earlier play, the taming of Wildrake and the marrying of Widow Green to Sir William Fondlove, and in the later, Lady Anne's teasing love of Sir Philip Brilliant provide scenes of real comic verve. If only Knowles had been prepared to forego blank verse, he might have written a comedy quite as long-lived as Boucicault's *London Assurance*. As it is, Lord Lytton's letter of 1838 to Macready makes fair comment: "I say, when a door is to be shut, 'Shut the door.' Knowles would say, as I think he has said somewhere, 'Let the room be airless.' "

—Peter Thomson

LAMB, Charles. English. Born in the Inner Temple, London, 10 February 1775. Educated at Christ's Hospital, London, 1782–89. Worked in the office of the merchant Joseph Paice, 1790, and in the Examiner's Office of South Sea House, 1791–92; worked in the Accountant's Office of the East India Company, 1792 until he retired, with a pension, 1825; writer from 1795; a friend of Wordsworth, Coleridge, and Hazlitt; guardian of his sister Mary, who was periodically insane, from 1796; contributed to *London Magazine*, 1820–25. *Died 27 December 1834.*

PUBLICATIONS

Collections

> *Works,* edited by T. Hutchinson. 2 vols., 1908.
> *The Letters of Lamb, to Which Are Added Those of His Sister Mary Lamb,* edited by E. V. Lucas. 3 vols., 1935.
> *The Portable Lamb,* edited by John Mason Brown. 1964.

80 LAMB

A Lamb Selection: Letters and Essays, edited by F. B. Pinion. 1965.
Letters of Charles and Mary Anne Lamb, edited by Edwin W. Marrs, Jr. 1975–

Fiction

A Tale of Rosamund Gray and Old Blind Margaret. 1798.

Plays

John Woodvil: A Tragedy. 1802.
Mr. H—; or, Beware a Bad Name (produced 1806). 1813.
The Wife's Trial; or, The Intruding Widow, in *Blackwood's Magazine,* December 1828.
The Pawn-Broker's Daughter, in *Blackwood's Magazine,* January 1830.

Verse

Blank Verse, with Charles Lloyd. 1798.
Poetry for Children, Entirely Original, with Mary Lamb. 2 vols., 1809; edited by A. W. Tuer, 2 vols., 1892.
Prince Dorus; or, Flattery Put Out of Countenance: A Poetical Version of an Ancient Tale (juvenile). 1811; edited by J. P. Broscoe, 1896.
Beauty and the Beast; or, A Rough Outside with a Gentle Heart: A Poetical Version of an Ancient Tale (juvenile). 1811.
Album Verses. 1830.
Satan in Search of His Wife. 1831.

Other

Original Letters of Sir John Falstaff and His Friends, with J. White. 1796; edited by Israel Gollancz, 1907 (possibly not by Lamb).
The King and Queen of Hearts (juvenile). 1805; edited by E. V. Lucas, 1902.
Tales from Shakespeare Designed for the Use of Young Persons, with Mary Lamb. 2 vols., 1807; edited by J. C. Trewin, 1964.
The Adventures of Ulysses (juvenile). 1808; edited by Ernest A. Gardner, 1921.
Mrs. Leicester's School; or, The History of Several Young Ladies Related by Themselves (juvenile), with Mary Lamb. 1809.
Works. 2 vols., 1818.
Elia: Essays Which Have Appeared under That Signature in the London Magazine. 1823; *Second Series,* 1828; both series, 2 vols., 1835; edited by W. Macdonald, 2 vols., 1929.
The Last Essays of Elia. 1833.
Recollections of Christ's Hospital. 1835.
Eliana, Being Hitherto Uncollected Writings, edited by J. E. Babson. 1864.
Mary and Charles Lamb: Poems, Letters, and Remains, edited by W. C. Hazlitt. 1874.
Lamb on Shakespeare, edited by Joan Coldwell. 1978.

Editor, *Sentimental Tablets of the Good Pamphile,* by J. C. Gorjy, translated by P. S. Dupuy. 1795.
Editor, *Specimens of English Dramatic Poets Who Lived about the Time of Shakespeare.* 1808; edited by Israel Gollancz, 1893.

LAMB 81

Bibliography: *Bibliography of the Writings of Charles and Mary Lamb* by J. C. Thomson, 1908.

Reading List: *The Lambs: A Study of Pre-Victorian England* by K. Anthony, 1945; *Lamb* by Edmund Blunden, 1954; *The Life of Lamb* by R. Fukuhara, 1963; *A Study of Lamb's Essays of Elia* by T. Fukuda, 1964; *Lamb and the Theatre* by Wayne McKenna, 1978.

*   *   *

Charles Lamb's life has become universal property both from his autobiographical genius (often mischievously perverted) and from the circle of literary greatness that looked to him as to its focus. "His genius is talent," wrote Coleridge, "and his talent is genius, and his heart is as whole and one as his head." Both the admiration and the affection were echoed by Wordsworth, Hazlitt, Hunt, Hood, and De Quincey.

Loved by his friends and reverenced by his admirers as *sui generis*, nevertheless Lamb displayed qualities that appeal to the English zeal for convention. He was essentially middle-class, born away from the handicap of poverty and never achieving the shame of riches. In practical terms he was as unadventurous as he was daring in imagination. He worked for thirty years as a clerk in the East India House. He lived all his life in London or its suburbs, venturing only once to the Continent, and he went to the country only when he could not avoid the invitations of friends, confessing himself to be "not romance-bit about *Nature*."

Conservative in his love of familiar things, friends, books, and places, he was nevertheless ardent to reform wrongs done or intended, and his early lampoons, written mostly for Leigh Hunt's *Examiner*, were as vitriolic as anything produced in an age of sharp political satire.

Lamb made his literary debut as a poet, contributing four sonnets to Coleridge's *Poems on Various Subjects* (1796), and in 1798 Lamb with Charles Lloyd published *Blank Verse*, a collection which included his most memorable poem, "The Old Familiar Faces." Also in 1798 he tried his hand at a novel, *Rosamund Gray*, an effort that is best forgotten even by his most fervent admirers. His attempts to make his mark as a dramatist are scarcely more admirable. *John Woodvil* is a dubious imitation of Jacobean tragedy and *Mr. H—* was hissed off the stage, "the author hissing as loud as any."

The *Tales from Shakespeare* has retained a certain world-wide popularity from 1807 to the present day but (perhaps fortunately for his reputation) most of the book is by Charles's sister Mary; his part in it was contributed rather from a sense of duty – of support for a tragic woman who had brought tragedy into his life but whom he loved dearly – than from any literary enthusiasm.

He was still at hack work, editing a volume of selections from Elizabethan and Jacobean dramatists when at last he found the subject-matter which allowed him the scope of his originality. The critical essays which he added to his selection (and a subsequent series written for Hunt's *Reflector*) reinstated the English in their own domain, resurrected for them the beauties of the English Renaissance, "saving and salving Webster, Jonson, Marlowe, Middleton – even Shakespeare himself" after two centuries of neglect or ill-usage by iconoclasts. Lamb's friends Coleridge and Hazlitt were shrewder and perhaps finer critics, but Lamb was more truly a man of the theatre.

By 1818 he had made his reputation, but not his fortune. His reputation was enhanced but his fortune not at all when in that year his scattered contributions in verse and prose were gathered together under the portentous title of *The Works of Charles Lamb*. There followed an invitation to contribute occasional essays to the *London Magazine* and (though he said later that he wished to be remembered "as the first to draw the public attention to the old English dramatists") it was these "Elia" essays (collected as *Essays* and *The Last Essays of Elia*) which made his fame with his contemporaries and have held it against all changes in taste, settling him amongst the incomparable few of English literature.

Humour was his consolation for sorrow but, as with all great men, his apprehension of humanistic pathos and even tragedy were never quite submerged by his sense of comedy.

Before he became Elia, he had masked himself with a number of pseudonyms, he had written of Charles Lamb as if he were a chance acquaintance, and he even borrowed the person though not the personality of Coleridge, but at last in the cheerful pen-life of Elia he escaped the burdensome sadness of life as Lamb. There is no writer like Elia. His English "stammers like his speech" but the consequence is beauty. He chases an insignificant idea and makes it significant; he "makes of an interloping inspiration a literary occasion." He relishes archaisms, scholarly asides, private jokes, but he is never precious.

And if Elia is not enough, there are still Lamb's letters to buy for him a palace high on the slopes of the English Parnassus.

—J. E. Morpurgo

LANDOR, Walter Savage. English. Born in Warwick, 30 January 1775. Educated at Rugby School, and privately; Trinity College, Oxford, 1793–94 (rusticated). Led a private regiment against Napoleon in Spain, 1808. Married Julia Thuillier in 1811 (separated, 1835). Writer from 1793; lived in South Wales on an income from his father from 1795, then inherited considerable wealth on his father's death, 1805; purchased Llanthony Abbey, 1809; lived in France, 1814, and in Italy, 1815–35, in Florence, 1821–35; returned to England, and lived in Bath, 1835–58; involved in an action for libel, 1858, and resided in Italy again until his death. *Died 17 September 1864.*

PUBLICATIONS

Collections

> *Letters,* edited by Stephen Wheeler. 1899.
> *The Complete Works,* edited by T. Earle Welby and Stephen Wheeler. 16 vols., 1927–36.
> *Poems* (selection), edited by Geoffrey Grigson. 1964.
> *A Biographical Anthology,* edited by Herbert Van Thal. 1973.

Prose

> *To the Burgesses of Warwick.* 1797; edited by R. H. Super, 1949.
> *Three Letters Written in Spain to D. Francisco Riguelme.* 1809.
> *Commentary on Memoirs of Mr. Fox.* 1812; edited by Stephen Wheeler, as *Charles James Fox: A Commentary on His Life and Character,* 1907.
> *Letters Addressed to Lord Liverpool and the Parliament on the Preliminaries of Peace.* 1814.
> *Letter from Mr. Landor to Mr. Jervis.* 1814.
> *Imaginary Conversations of Literary Men and Statesmen.* 5 vols., 1824–29; edited by R. H. Boothroyd, 1936.
> *Citation and Examination of William Shakespeare Before the Worshipful Sir Thomas*

Lucy Knight Touching Deer Stealing, to Which Is Added a Conference of Master Edmund Spenser, a Gentleman of Note, with the Earl of Essex Touching the State of Ireland. 1834.
Pericles and Aspasia. 2 vols., 1836; edited by G. Ravenscroft Dennis, 1903.
The Letters of a Conservative, in Which Are Shown the Only Means of Saving What Is Left of the English Church. 1836.
The Pentameron and Pentalogia. 1837.
To Robert Browning. 1845.
The Works. 2 vols., 1846.
Imaginary Conversation of King Carlo-Alberto and the Duchess Belgioioso on the Affairs and Prospects of Italy. 1848.
Popery, British and Foreign. 1851.
On Kossuth's Voyage to America. 1851.
Tyrannicide, Published for the Benefit of the Hungarians in America. 1851.
Imaginary Conversations of Greeks and Romans. 1853.
The Last Fruit Off an Old Tree. 1853.
Letters of an American Mainly on Russia and Revolution. 1854.
Antony and Octavius: Scenes for the Study. 1856.
Letter to Emerson. 1856.
Selections from the Writings (prose), edited by G. S. Hilliard. 1856.
Collection of Autograph Letters and Historical Documents: The Blessington Papers, edited by A. Morrison. 1895.
Letters and Other Unpublished Writings, edited by Stephen Wheeler. 1897.
Garibaldi and the President of the Sicilian Senate. 1917.
An Address to the Fellows of Trinity College Oxford on the Alarm of Invasion. 1917.
Landor: Last Days, Letters, and Conversations, edited by H. C. Minchin. 1934.

Plays

Count Julian. 1812.
Andrea of Hungary and Giovanni of Naples. 1839.
Fra Rupert. 1840.
The Siege of Ancona, in *Works.* 1846.

Verse

Poems. 1795.
Moral Epistle Respectfully Dedicated to Earl Stanhope. 1795.
Gebir: A Poem in Seven Books. 1798; translated by Landor, as *Gebirus Poema,* 1803; edited by Arthur Symons, with *The Hellenics,* 1907.
Poems from the Arabic and Persian. 1800.
Poetry. 1800; augmented edition, 1802.
Iambi Incerto Auctore. 1802(?).
Simonidea. 1806.
Ode ad Gustavum Regem: Ode ad Gustavum Exulem. 1810.
Idyllia Nove Quinque Heroum atque Heroidum. 1815.
Sponsalia Polyxenae. 1819.
Idyllia Heroica Decem Librum Phaleuciorum Unum. 1820.
Gebir, Count Julian, and Other Poems. 1831.
Terry Hogan: An Eclogue. 1836.
A Satire on Satirists and Admonition to Detractors. 1836.
Poemata et Inscriptiones. 1847.

The Hellenics Enlarged and Completed. 1847; revised edition, 1859; edited by Arthur Symons, with *Gebir,* 1907.
The Italics. 1848.
Savagius Landor Lamartino. 1848.
Epistola ad Pium IX Pontificem. 1849.
Ad Cossuthum et Bemum. 1849.
Dry Sticks, Fagoted by Landor. 1858.
Savonarola 'e il Priore di San Marco. 1860.
Heroic Idyls with Additional Poems. 1863.
A Modern Greek Idyl. 1917.
To Elizabeth Barrett Browning and Other Verses. 1917.

Bibliography: *The Publication of Landor's Works* by R. H. Super, 1954.

Reading List: *Landor* by M. Elwin, 1941, revised edition, as *Landor: A Replevin,* 1958; *Landor: A Biography* by R. H. Super, 1954; *Landor* by G. R. Hamilton, 1960; *L'Oeuvre de Landor* by P. Vitoux, 1964; *Landor* by E. Dilworth, 1971.

*   *   *

According to Ezra Pound in *How to Read*, "the decline of England began on the day when Landor packed his trunks and departed to Tuscany." And Yeats concluded his fine poem "To a Young Beauty" with the proud claim:

> There is not a fool can call me friend,
> And I may dine at journey's end
> With Landor and with Donne.

Yet Landor remains little read. We may indeed feel that what both Pound and Yeats were primarily responding to was a certain patrician high-handedness in Landor's character which found its neatest expression in his "Dying Speech of an Old Philosopher":

> I strove with none, for none was worth my strife:
> Nature I loved, and next to Nature, Art:
> I warmed both hands before the fire of life;
> It sinks; and I am ready to depart.

This has an admirable crispness and clarity, the qualities which Landor found most congenial in the Classics that he knew so well. But it may be doubted whether it shows much depth of self-knowledge in one whose whole life was spent in striving with others usually for very good reasons. After all, Landor was rusticated from Oxford for shooting his fowling-piece at the windows of an "obnoxious Tory" who was making too much noise, and served as the original of Dickens's Boythorn in *Bleak House* who sets his estate about with notices warning "That any person or persons audaciously presuming to trespass on this property will be punished with the utmost severity of private chastisement, and prosecuted with the utmost rigour of the law."

Nevertheless, as if in proof of Yeats's belief that a writer expresses a view of life antithetical to his public behaviour, Landor sought a style in prose and verse which would embody the classical ideas of lucidity and balance. Outside the epigrams – including the well-known tribute to his loved Rose Aylmer – Landor succeeded best in prose. The early blank-verse narrative poem *Gebir* lacks the force of either narrative or characterisation to sustain it, and the same is true of his plays, which lack dramatic power and can hardly be envisaged on the stage.

It was in the *Imaginary Conversations* that Landor, perhaps encouraged by his friend Southey who was then beginning his Colloquies, found his appropriate form. In these he could bring together related or contrasting historical characters and use the juxtaposition to bring out what seems to him significant ideas about life and conduct. At first sight, the *Conversations* might seem to parallel the dramatic monologues of his later friend Browning, but in fact their aims were different. Whereas Browning was interested above all in the varieties of human character, Landor's interest lay in the presentation of ideas and attitudes. Yet there is enough variety in Landor's knowledge of history and his breadth of interests to sustain these literary dialogues, some of which have been effectively broadcast. At his best, as in "Elizabeth and Cecil," "Southey and Porson," "Washington and Franklin," "Epictetus and Seneca," and the longer *Pericles and Aspasia*, Landor shows great skill in giving expression to what is basically his own philosophy, a high-toned classical republicanism, sweetened by a sense of beauty and transience.

A neglected aspect of Landor is his excellence as a letter writer. Should the reader begin to lose interest on the formality of the *Conversations*, he will find in the letters more of the ebullient character who appealed to many close friends throughout a long life. The published *Letter to Emerson* was an expression of Landor's pleasure and interest in Emerson's recent *English Traits*. Characteristically Landor was both polite and firm in his response, going through the references to his own conversation and explaining their implications. He also clarified his own political attitude: "I was always Conservative; but I would eradicate any species of evil, political, moral or religious, as soon as it springs up, with no reference to the blockheads who cry out, '*What would you substitute in its place?*' When I pluck up a dock or a thistle, do I ask any such question?"

It is in his less formal letters that Landor's unique combination of scholarship, irascibility, and humanity finds its fullest expression.

—Peter Faulkner

MONCRIEFF, William Thomas. English. Born in London, 24 August 1794. Clerk in a solicitor's office, c. 1804, then entered the service of the solicitor Moses Hooper, London; began writing songs and subsequently plays; became manager of the Regency Theatre, subsequently known as the Queen's Theatre, then as the Prince of Wales Theatre; when the theatre close worked as a law stationer, and contributed drama criticism to the *Satirist* and the *Scourge*; Manager of Astley's, then of the Coburg Theatre; wrote for Elliston at Drury Lane, 1820–24; Manager, Vauxhall Gardens, 1827; opened a music shop with John Barnett in Regent Street, London, 1828; lessee of the City Theatre, 1833; wrote for the Strand Theatre, 1837–38; went blind by 1843; brother of the Charterhouse from 1844. *Died 3 December 1857.*

PUBLICATIONS

Plays

Moscow (produced 1820).

The Diamond Arrow; or, The Postmaster's Wife and the Mayor's Daughter, music by G. W. Reeve (produced 1815). 1816.
All at Coventry; or, Love and Laugh (produced 1816). 1816.
Joconde; or, Le Prince Troubadour (produced 1816). 1816.
John Adams; or, The Mutineers of the High Seas (produced 1816).
Giovanni in London; or, The Libertine Reclaimed (produced 1817). 1817.
Rochester; or, King Charles the Second's Merry Days (produced 1818). 1819.
The Dandy Family and the Ascot Jockies (produced 1818).
The Monk's Cowl; or, The Child of Mystery (produced 1818).
Wanted a Wife; or, A Cheque on My Bankers (produced 1819). 1819.
Pigeons and Crows (produced 1819).
The Bride of Lammermuir (produced 1819).
The Green Dragon; or, I've Quite Forgot (produced 1819).
Modern Collegians; or, Over the Bridge (produced 1820). 1820.
Ivanhoe; or, The Jewess (produced 1820). 1820.
The Lear of Private Life; or, Father and Daughter, from the novel *The Father and Daughter* by Mrs. Opie (produced 1820). N.d.
The Shipwreck of the Medusa; or, The Fatal Raft! (produced 1820). N.d.
The Ravens of Orleans; or, The Forest of Cercotte (produced 1820). N.d.
The Vampire (produced 1820). n.d.
What Are You At? What Are You After? or, There Never Was Such Times (produced 1820).
The Actor in Distress; or, How to Raise Your Salary (produced 1820).
The Smuggler's Dog; or, The Blind Boy's Murder (produced 1820).
Giovanni in Ireland, music by Tom Cooke (produced 1821). 1824.
Tereza Tomkins; or, The Fruits of Geneva (produced 1821). 1821.
The Spectre Bridegroom; or, A Ghost in Spite of Himself (produced 1821). 1821.
Monsieur Tonson (produced 1821). 1821.
The Lost Life (produced 1821).
Tom and Jerry; or, Life in London, from the work by Pierce Egan (produced 1821). 1826.
Adventures of a Ventriloquist; or, The Rogueries of Nicholas (produced 1822). 1822.
Actors al Fresco; or, The Play in the Pleasure Garden, music by Jonathan Blewitt and C. E. Horn (produced 1823). Songs published 1827.
The Party Wall (as *The Secret; or, The Hole in the Wall,* produced 1823). 1823.
Fazio (produced 1823).
The Cataract of the Ganges! or, The Rajah's Daughter (produced 1823). 1823.
Zoroaster; or, The Spirit of the Star (produced 1824). 1824.
The Bashful Man (produced 1824). 1827.
Jack Sheppard the Housebreaker; or, London in 1724 (produced 1825).
The Kiss and the Rose; or, Love in the Nursery Grounds (produced 1827). 1827.
Home for the Holidays (produced 1828).
The Somnambulist; or, The Phantom of the Village, from a play by Scribe (produced 1828). 1828.
The Irresistibles (produced 1828). N.d.
The Hollow Way; or, The Hidden Treasure (produced 1828).
Monsieur Mallet; or, My Daughter's Letter, music by John Barnett (produced 1829). 1851.
Father and Daughter; or, The Victim of Seduction (produced 1829).
The Pestilence of Marseilles; or, The Four Thieves, from a play by Pixérécourt (produced 1829). 1829.
Van Diemen's Land; or, Settlers and Natives (produced 1830). 1888.
The Heart of London; or, A Sharper's Progress (produced 1830). 1839.
The Beggar of Cripplegate; or, The Humours of Bluff King Hal (produced 1830). 1830.

MONCRIEFF 87

Shakespeare's Festival; or, The New Comedy of Errors (produced 1830). 1830.
Old Heads on Young Shoulders; or, The House in the Forest (produced 1830).
Electioneering; or, Village Politicians (produced 1830).
The Devil's Walk; or, Pluto in London (produced 1830).
The Man-Wolf; or, The Loup-Garçon of the Odenwald (produced 1831).
What a Shocking Bad Hat! (produced 1831).
The Monkey That Has Seen the World (produced 1831).
Courting by Mistake; or, A Trip to the Coronation (produced 1831).
Favourites in Town; or, Stage Arrivals (produced 1831).
Bringing Home the Bride; or, The Husband's First Journey, from a French play (produced 1838).
Reform; or, John Bull Triumphant (produced 1831). 1831.
Gipsy Jack; or, The Napoleon of Humble Life (produced 1831). N.d.
Eugene Aram; or, St. Robert's Cave, from the novel by Bulwer-Lytton (produced 1832). N.d.
The Peer and Peasant (produced 1832). 1832.
Lochinvar; or, The Bridal of Netherby (produced 1832). N.d.
Victor Dene; or, I'll Sleep on It (produced 1832).
The World as It Runs; or, Fancy's Freaks (produced 1832).
One Fault (produced 1833). N.d.
How to Take Up a Bill; or, The Village Vauxhall, from a play by Melesville (produced 1833). 1833.
The Birth Day; or, The Parson's Nose, music by G. B. Chapman, from a play by Désaugiers (produced 1835). 1833; as *The Parson's Nose,* 1837.
The Waggoner of Westmorland (produced 1834).
Mount St. Bernard; or, The Headsman (produced 1834). N.d.
The Revolt of the Seraglio on the Other Side of the Pole (produced 1834).
The Court of Queen Anne; or, The Prince and the Breeches Maker (produced 1834). N.d.
The Smuggler's Haunt; or, The Fireside Story (produced 1835).
What's in a Name; or, Black's White (produced 1835).
Lestocq, music by Tom Cooke, from a play by Scribe, music by Auber (produced 1835). N.d.
The Jewess; or, The Council of Constance, music by Tom Cooke, from an opera by Scribe, music by Halévy (produced 1835). N.d.
The Winterbottoms! or, My Aunt the Dowager (produced 1837). 1837.
Sam Wellers; or, The Pickwickians (produced 1837). 1837.
A Down East Bargain; or, Love in New York (produced 1837).
The Blind Father; or, The Peasant Marchioness (produced 1837).
The Fitzpatricks; or, Lovers from Tipperary (produced 1838).
The Tobit's Dog! (produced 1838). 1838.
Tarnation Strange; or, More Jonathans (produced 1838). 1842.
Sam Weller's Tour; or, The Pickwickians in France (produced 1838).
Shakespeare and Burbage (produced 1838).
Up and Down; or, The Road of Life (produced 1838).
Nicholas Nickleby and Poor Smike; or, The Victim of the Yorkshire School (produced 1839).
Popularity (produced 1839).
Foreign Airs and Native Graces (produced 1839).
The Ballad Singer (produced 1839).
The Devil's in the Room (produced 1840).
Harlequin and Jack of Newberry; or, Baa, Baa, Black Sheep and the Old Woman of Berkeley (produced 1840).
The Queen of a Day, from a play by Scribe and J. N. Verney de St. Georges, music by

88 MONCRIEFF

Alphonse Adam (produced 1840).
Harlequin and My Lady Lee; or, Goosey, Goosey Gander and the Spell-Bound Goslings (produced 1840).
The Tribute of a Hundred Virgins (produced 1840).
Giselle; or, The Phantom Night Dancers, from the ballet with music by Alphonse Adam (produced 1842). 1842.
Love and Laugh; or, The M.P. (produced 1842).
Perourou, The Bellows Mender and the Beauty of Lyons (produced 1842). N.d.
Far Off; or, The Royal Visit to Edinburgh (produced 1842).
The Red Farm; or, The Well of St. Marie (produced 1842). 1885.
The Wood Wolf of the Black Mountains; or, The Milo of Brittany (produced 1842).
The Scamps of London; or, The Cross Roads of Life, from a novel by Eugène Sue (produced 1843). 1851.
Borrowing a Husband; or, Sleeping Out (produced 1843). With *My Wife's Out* by George Rodwell, 1885.
An Armful of Bliss (produced 1843).
The Favourite of the Derby; or, The Life of Man and Horse (produced 1844; as *The Royal Foxhunt; or, The Life and Death of Tom Moody*, produced 1847).
Caesar the Watch Dog of the Castle; or, The Sword of My Father (produced 1844). 1886.
The Mistress of the Mill, from a play by Melesville (produced 1849). 1850.
The Mayor of Rochester, with *The Omnibus* by Isaac Pocock. 1886.
Bonnie Prince Charlie; or, The Gathering of the Clans. 1887.
William's Visits. N.d.

Verse

Prison Thoughts: Elegy Written in King's Bench, in Imitation of Gray. 1821.
Songs, Duets, and Glees Sung at the Royal Gardens, Vauxhall. 1827.
Poems. 1829.
The March of Intellect. 1830.
Old Booty: A Serio-Comic Sailor's Tale. 1830.
The Triumph of Reform. 1832.
An Original Collection of Songs. 1850.

Other

The New Guide to the Spa or Leamington Priors. 1822.
Excursion to Stratford upon Avon, with a Compendious Life of Shakespeare. 1824.

Editor, *Richardson's New Minor Drama.* 4 vols., 1828–31.

* * *

William Thomas Moncrieff wrote according to the requirements of the theatre of his time. His experience as a dramatic critic and theatre manager was inextricably linked with his dramatic work. If the craze was for fairy plays he would write *Giselle*. Since the dramatizing of Scott suited the box-office, he would write a version of *Ivanhoe*. When the vaudeville reached England, Moncrieff wrote an early example, *The Kiss and the Rose*. He was also concerned enough to distinguish vaudeville from burletta as "a dramatic story in verse, rather than prose, illustrated and carried on by means of the songs and melodies of the day rather than original compositions." His most famous play was an adaptation of Pierce Egan's documentary novel, *Life in London*. Moncrieff called his version *Tom and Jerry*, and openly exploited a naive taste for realism by presenting a sequence of scenes set in familiar London places. The characters as written by Egan are already dramatic cameos. It was comparatively easy for a theatrical expert like Moncrieff to exploit such material. He had already shown an ability to anticipate as well as to follow trends. His *Shipwreck of the Medusa* in 1820 was possibly the first nautical melodrama. In the same year his tear-jerking adaptation of a novel by Mrs. Opie, *The Lear of Private Life*, advertised the possible uses of Shakespearean plots in modern settings. Moncrieff was modest enough to accept a place as part of a theatrical team. In *The Cataract of the Ganges* that place was secondary to the scene-designer's. Clarkson Stanfield's real waterfall was the sensation that made this play such a triumph at Drury Lane. The life of a moderately talented working dramatist in the early decades of the nineteenth century is vividly presented in the evidence Moncrieff gave to the Select Committee which met in 1832 under Lord Lytton's chairmanship to enquire into the state of the theatre. His introductions to the plays in Richardson's *New Minor Drama* are also quite useful indicators of contemporary evaluation.

—Peter Thomson

MOORE, Thomas.   Irish.   Born in Dublin, 28 May 1779. Educated at Whyte's School, Dublin 1786–93; Dr. Carr's Latin School, Dublin, 1794; Trinity College, Dublin, 1795–98, B.A. 1799; Middle Temple, London, 1799. Married Bessie Dyke in 1811; three daughters and two sons. Appointed Admiralty Registrar in Bermuda, 1803: after visiting the islands, and America, committed his official duties to a deputy and returned to England, 1806; became a popular and fashionable songwriter in England, and national lyricist of Ireland with publication of *Irish Melodies*, 1808–34; met Lord Byron, 1811; made liable for funds his deputy in Bermuda had embezzled, and travelled to Italy and France to avoid arrest, 1819; given memoirs by Byron in Venice; returned to England, when the Bermuda debt had been settled, 1822, and retired to Bowood, Wiltshire; destroyed Byron's memoirs, 1824, but published a life of Byron, 1830; worked on his *History of Ireland* until 1846. Granted Civil List pension, 1835. *Died 25 February 1852.*

PUBLICATIONS

Collections

> *Memoirs, Journal, and Correspondence,* edited by Lord John Russell.   8 vols., 1853–56; *Journal* edited by Peter Quennell, 1964.
> *The Poetical Works,* edited by A. D. Godley.   1910
> *Letters,* edited by Wilfred S. Dowden.   2 vols., 1964.

Verse

Odes of Anacreon. 1800.
The Poetical Works of the Late Thomas Little, Esq. 1801.
A Candid Appeal to Public Confidence. 1803.
Songs and Glees. 1804(?).
Epistles, Odes, and Other Poems. 1806.
Corruption and Intolerance: Two Poems with Notes, Addressed to an Englishman by an Irishman. 1808.
A Selection of Irish Melodies, with Symphonies and Accompaniments, music by John Stevenson and Henry Bishop. 10 vols. and supplement, 1808–34; words alone published as *Irish Melodies,* 1822.
The Sceptic: A Philosophical Satire. 1809.
A Melologue upon National Music. 1811.
Parody of a Celebrated Letter. 1812.
Intercepted Letters; or, The Two-Penny Post-Bag. 1813.
Sacred Songs. 2 vols., 1816–24.
Lalla Rookh: An Oriental Romance. 1817.
The Fudge Family in Paris. 1818.
National Airs. 6 vols., 1818–27.
Melodies, Songs, Sacred Songs, and National Airs. 1818.
The Loves of the Angels. 1823; revised edition, as *The Loves of the Angels: An Eastern Romance,* 1823.
Fables for the Holy Alliance; Rhymes for the Road. 1823.
Evenings in Greece. 2 vols., 1826–32.
Odes upon Cash, Corn, Catholics, and Other Matters, Selected from Columns of the Times Journal. 1828.
The Summer Fête: A Poem with Songs. 1831.
The Fudges in England, Being a Sequel to The Fudge Family in Paris. 1835.
Alciphron: A Poem, with The Epicurean, illustrated by J. M. W. Turner. 1839.
The Poetical Works. 10 vols., 1840–41.

Plays

The Gipsy Prince, music by Michael Kelly (produced 1801). 1801.
M.P.; or, The Blue Stocking, music by the author (produced 1811). 1811.
Montbar; or, The Buccaneers. 1804.

Fiction

The Epicurean. 1827.

Other

A Letter to the Roman Catholics of Dublin. 1810.
Tom Crib's Memorial to Congress (includes verse). 1819.
Memoirs of Captain Rock, the Celebrated Irish Chieftain. 1824.
Memoirs of the Life of Richard Brinsley Sheridan. 1825.
Letters and Journals of Lord Byron, with Notices of His Life. 2 vols., 1830.
The Life and Death of Lord Edward Fitzgerald. 2 vols., 1831.
Travels of an Irish Gentleman in Search of a Religion. 2 vols., 1833.

The History of Ireland. 4 vols., 1835–46.
Notes from the Letters of Moore to His Music Publisher, James Power, edited by T. C. Croker. 1854.
Prose and Verse, Humorous, Satirical, and Sentimental, with Suppressed Passages from the Memoirs of Lord Byron, edited by R. H. Shepherd. 1878.

Bibliography: *A Bibliographical Hand-List of the First Editions of Moore* by M. J. MacManus, 1934.

Reading List: *The Harp that Once* (biography) by Howard Mumford Jones, 1937; *Moore* by Miriam A. De Ford, 1967; *Bolt Upright: The Life of Moore* by Judith Wilt, 2 vols., 1975; *Moore, The Irish Poet* by Terence de Vere White, 1977.

* * *

No poet of his age enjoyed greater contemporary popularity than Thomas Moore. His reputation was based primarily on his long oriental poem *Lalla Rookh* and on lyrics written for traditional melodies. The former is largely (and perhaps justifiably) ignored, while his mastery of the song lyric is now generally recognized.

During his lifetime ten editions (or "numbers") of his *Irish Melodies* were published from 1808 through 1834. Arrangements and "accompaniments" for the melodies were made by Sir John Stevenson and Sir Henry Bishop, two of the most successful musicians of their day. He also produced a collection of *National Airs* (consisting mostly of lyrics written for traditional continental music) and of *Sacred Songs.* George Thomson, a pioneer in the field of collecting and arranging melodies of England, Scotland, Wales, and Ireland, asked Moore to contribute verses to his massive collection of airs; but he never produced music which satisfied the meticulous lyricist. Moore and Robert Burns (who did write for Thomson) must be placed at the top of the list of those who worked in this genre.

Moore also wrote satire, some of which would have enjoyed lasting success had it not been primarily occasional in nature. Nevertheless, his wit and satiric irony can be seen in the "squibs" and "lampoons" he wrote for the *Morning Chronicle* and other London newspapers and in his verse satire in epistolary from entitled *The Fudge Family in Paris.*

Irish nationalism is a recurring theme in his work. Most of the *Irish Melodies* have as their purpose the awakening of national consciousness, and such prose works as the *Memoirs of Captain Rock* and his *Letter to the Roman Catholics of Dublin* deal with Irish patriotism and Catholic Emancipation.

Moore's biographies of Richard Brinsley Sheridan and Lord Edward Fitzgerald, which are still mined for their contemporary insights, are examples of the best of nineteenth-century biography. His life of Byron compares favorably with Lockhart's *Life of Scott* as a highly respectable and still respected memoir of a major literary figure. Add to these works his four-volume *History of Ireland,* written for Dr. Lardner's *Cabinet Encyclopedia,* and his contributions to such literary journals as the *Edinburgh Review* and we see that he produced a body of prose work almost equal to that of his poetry. He was offered the editorship of the *Edinburgh Review* and was once asked to take on the task of writing lead articles for the *Times.*

There seems little doubt that the discovery of the MS and the publication of Moore's Journal offers a new perspective on the Irish poet. The modern edition restores passages bowdlerized by the first editor, Lord John Russell, and tends to justify Terence de Vere White's tribute to him as "after Daniel O'Connell, the greatest Irishman of his day."

—Wilfred S. Dowden

92 MORTON

MORTON, Thomas. English. Born in Durham c. 1764. Educated at Soho Square School, London; entered Lincoln's Inn, 1784, but was not subsequently admitted to the bar. Married; one daughter and two sons, including the playwright John Maddison Morton. Full-time playwright from 1792. Senior Member of Lord's, London; Honorary Member, Garrick Club, 1837. *Died 28 March 1838.*

PUBLICATIONS

Plays

Columbus; or, A World Discovered (produced 1792). 1792.

The Children in the Wood, music by Samuel Arnold (produced 1793). 1794.

Zorinski, music by Samuel Arnold (produced 1795). 1795.

The Way to Get Married (produced 1796). 1796.

A Cure for the Heart-Ache (produced 1797). 1797.

Secrets Worth Knowing (produced 1798). 1798.

Speed the Plough (produced 1800). 1800; edited by Allardyce Nicoll in *Lesser English Comedies of the Eighteenth Century,* 1931.

The Blind Girl; or, A Receipt for Beauty, music by Joseph Massinghi and William Reeve (produced 1801). Songs published 1801.

Beggar My Neighbour; or, A Rogue's a Fool, from a play by A. W. Iffland (produced 1802; as *How to Tease and How to Please,* produced 1810).

The School of Reform; or, How to Rule a Husband (produced 1805). 1805.

Town and Country (produced 1807). 1807.

The Knight of Snowdoun, music by Henry Bishop, from the poem "The Lady of the Lake" by Scott (produced 1811). 1811.

Education (produced 1813). 1813.

The Slave, music by Henry Bishop (produced 1816). 1816.

Methinks I See My Father; or, Who's My Father? (produced 1818). 1850(?).

A Roland for an Oliver, from a play by Scribe (produced 1819). 1819.

Henri Quatre; or, Paris in the Olden Time, music by Henry Bishop (produced 1820). 1820.

A School for Grown Children (produced 1827). 1827.

The Invincibles, music by A. Lee (produced 1828). 1829.

The Sublime and Beautiful (produced 1828).

Peter the Great; or, The Battle of Pultawa, with James Kenney, music by Tom Cooke and William Carnaby, from a play by Frédéric du Petit-Mère (produced 1829).

Separation and Reparation (produced 1830).

The King's Fireside (produced 1830).

The Writing on the Wall!, with J. M. Morton (produced 1852). N.d.

*   *   *

Thomas Morton's first five-act comedy, *The Way to Get Married,* gave good acting parts to Lewis, Quick, Munden, and Fawcett. It also established his method, which is to embed a pathetic tale of poverty and remorse amid comic episodes and eccentric characters. Scenes of convulsive anguish alternate with amusing encounters and adventures whose general intention is to commend generosity and expose the mercenary motives of a heartless society. Morton was, in effect, writing melodrama before the word had reached the English theatre. He had, generally, the tact to give his comedians more stage time than his "heavies," and to allow one of his comic men to make the crucial discovery that makes all well. *Secrets Worth*

Knowing is an exact example of the style. The comedy survives well, but the suffering resists contemporary staging. The same is true of Morton's best play, *Speed the Plough*, in which the real life belongs to the characters least involved in the main plot. Sir Philip Blandford's remorse over a dead wife, lost child, and murdered brother is tediously related in embarrassingly pompous prose. The child (not lost), the brother (not murdered), and the daughter also speak in grandiose archaisms. By extraordinary contrast, the uxorious Sir Abel Handy, his well-intentioned son, his wife, Farmer and Mrs. Ashfield, and their daughter are all finely observed and provided with sprightly dialogue. It is Mrs. Ashfield's obsessive concern with what Mrs. Grundy (who never appears) may say that has provided Morton's best known monument. *The School of Reform* is an attempt to repeat the success of *Speed the Plough*, but the influence of the German dramatists, particularly of Kotzebue's guilt-laden stories of sexual sin, swamps most of Morton's own talent. The character of Robert Tyke, and the final sensation scene in a Gothic chapel, underline the close relations between contemporary comedy and melodrama. *A Cure for the Heart-Ache* is the only one of Morton's comedies to suit the description, though even that play is not without pathetic attitudinising.

—Peter Thomson

O'KEEFFE, John. Irish. Born in Dublin, 24 June 1747. Educated at a Jesuit school in Saul's Court, Dublin; afterwards studied art in the Dublin School of Design. Married; one daughter and two sons. Originally an actor: member of Henry Mossop's stock company, Dublin, 1762–74; wrote for the stage from 1767; settled in London, c. 1780, and thereafter wrote comic pieces for the Haymarket and Covent Garden theatres; blind from the mid-1780's; received an annuity from Covent Garden, 1803, and a royal pension, 1820. *Died 4 February 1833.*

PUBLICATIONS

Plays

> *The She Gallant; or, Square-Toes Outwitted* (produced 1767). 1767; revised version, as *The Positive Man*, music by Samuel Arnold and Michael Arne (produced 1782), in *Dramatic Works*, 1798.
> *Colin's Welcome* (produced 1770).
> *Tony Lumpkin in Town* (produced 1774). 1780.
> *The Poor Soldier* (as *The Shamrock, or, St. Patrick's Day*, produced 1777; revised version, as *The Poor Soldier*, music by William Shield, produced 1783). 1785.
> *The Son-in-Law*, music by Samuel Arnold (produced 1779). 1783.
> *The Dead Alive*, music by Samuel Arnold (produced 1781). 1783.
> *The Agreeable Surprise*, music by Samuel Arnold (produced 1781). 1784.

The Banditti; or, Love's Labyrinth, music by Samuel Arnold (produced 1781). Songs published 1781; revised version, as *The Castle of Andalusia* (produced 1782), 1783; revised version (produced 1788).

Harlequin Teague; or, The Giant's Causeway, music by Samuel Arnold (produced 1782). Songs published 1782.

Lord Mayor's Day; or, A Flight from Lapland, music by William Shield (produced 1782). Songs published 1782.

The Maid the Mistress, from a play by G. A. Federico (produced 1783). Songs published 1783.

The Young Quaker (produced 1783). 1784.

The Birthday; or, The Prince of Arragon, music by Samuel Arnold, from a play by Saint-Foix (produced 1783). 1783.

Gretna Green (lyrics only), play by Charles Stuart, music by Samuel Arnold (produced 1783). 1791.

Friar Bacon; or, Harlequin's Adventures in Lilliput, Brobdignag etc. (lyrics only), play by Charles Bonner, music by William Shield (produced 1783; as *Harlequin Rambler*, produced 1784). Songs published 1784.

Peeping Tom of Coventry, music by Samuel Arnold (produced 1784). 1786.

Fontainbleau; or, Our Way in France, music by William Shield (produced 1784). 1785.

The Blacksmith of Antwerp (produced 1785). In *Dramatic Works*, 1798.

A Beggar on Horseback, music by Samuel Arnold (produced 1785). In *Dramatic Works*, 1798.

Omai; or, A Trip round the World, music by William Shield (produced 1785). Songs published 1785.

Love in a Camp; or, Patrick in Prussia, music by William Shield (produced 1786). 1786.

The Siege of Curzola, music by Samuel Arnold (produced 1786). Songs published 1786.

The Man Milliner (produced 1787). In *Dramatic Works*, 1798.

Love and War, from the play *The Campaign* by Robert Jephson (produced 1787).

The Farmer, music by William Shield (produced 1787). 1788.

Tantara-Rara, Rogues All, from a play by Dumaniant (produced 1788). In *Dramatic Works*, 1798.

The Prisoner at Large (produced 1788). 1788.

The Highland Reel, music by William Shield (produced 1788). 1789.

Aladdin; or, The Wonderful Lamp, music by William Shield (produced 1788). Songs published 1788.

The Lie of the Day (as *The Toy*, produced 1789; revised version, as *The Lie of the Day*, produced 1796). In *Dramatic Works*, 1798.

The Faro Table, from the play *The Gamester* by Mrs. Centlivre (produced 1789).

The Little Hunch-Back; or, A Frolic in Bagdad (produced 1789). 1789.

The Czar Peter, music by William Shield (as *The Czar*, produced 1790; as *The Fugitive*, produced 1790). In *Dramatic Works*, 1798.

The Basket-Maker, music by Samuel Arnold (produced 1790). In *Dramatic Works*, 1798.

Modern Antiques; or, The Merry Mourners (produced 1791). 1792.

Wild Oats; or, The Strolling Gentleman (produced 1791). 1791; edited by Clifford Williams, 1977.

Tony Lumpkin's Ramble to Town (produced 1792).

Sprigs of Laurel, music by William Shield (produced 1793). 1793; revised version, as *The Rival Soldiers* (produced 1797).

The London Hermit; or, Rambles in Dorsetshire (produced 1793). 1793.

The World in a Village (produced 1793). 1793.

Life's Vagaries (produced 1795). 1795.

The Irish Mimic; or, Blunders at Brighton, music by William Shield (produced 1795). 1795.

Merry Sherwood; or, Harlequin Forester (lyrics only), play by Mark Lonsdale and William Pearce, music by William Reeve (produced 1795). Songs published 1795.

The Wicklow Gold Mines; or, The Lad of the Hills, music by William Shield (produced 1796). 1814; revised version, as *The Wicklow Mountains* (produced 1796), 1797.

The Doldrum; or, 1803 (produced 1796). In *Dramatic Works,* 1798.

Alfred; or, The Magic Banner (produced 1796). 1796.

Olympus in an Uproar; or, The Descent of the Deities, from the play *The Golden Pippin* by Kane O'Hara (produced 1796).

Britain's Brave Tars; or, All for St. Paul's, music by Thomas Attwood (produced 1797).

She's Eloped (produced 1798).

The Eleventh of June; or, The Daggerwoods at Dunstable (produced 1798).

A Nosegay of Weeds; or, Old Servants in New Places (produced 1798).

Dramatic Works. 4 vols., 1798.

Verse

Oatlands; or, The Transfer of the Laurel. 1795.

A Father's Legacy to His Daughter, Being the Poetical Works, edited by Adelaide O'Keeffe. 1834.

Other

Recollections of the Life of O'Keeffe, Written by Himself. 2 vols., 1826.

*   *   *

John O'Keeffe wrote for a living, and was the slave of a public about which he must sometimes have grumbled but which he hated to upset. Between 1778, when the elder Colman bought for the Haymarket his opportunistic afterpiece *Tony Lumpkin in Town,* and 1800, when Thomas Harris awarded him a benefit at Covent Garden, O'Keeffe was a provider of theatrical pieces for those two theatres. Most of these pieces depend as much on song as on dialogue. Of the some 60 he admits to in his *Recollections,* over 20 are called "operas," a way of assuring contemporary audiences that the dialogue would be frequently interrupted by songs. In the three acts of *The Castle of Andalusia* there are over 20 such interruptions. The music for this popular piece was arranged by Dr. Arnold, but borrowed from Italy, Ireland, and the London streets. The plot calls for a noble bandit, a resourceful rogue, two pairs of lovers, an ageing and covetous widow, and the audience's ready acceptance of the convention of gullibility without which plays of mistaken identity will crumble about their ears. In *Fontainbleau* there are fewer songs and a greater dependence on bright dialogue and quirky characters like Colonel Epaulette, the anglophile Frenchman who makes his first entrance singing "Rule Britannia, Britannia rule de vay." The Jonsonian "humour" is close to journey's end in mere risible eccentricity, although there is comic resource and energy in O'Keeffe's handling of a slender story. He was bound by convention to attempt the more exacting five-act comedy form. *The Young Quaker* was moderately successful at the small Haymarket, and *The Toy,* later reduced to three acts as *The Lie of the Day,* was an effective vehicle for William Lewis, Quick, and Aickin.

But it was *Wild Oats* that made and has preserved O'Keeffe's reputation as a writer of comedy. The play depends on an alias, a carefully contrived mistaken identity, a sequence of coincidences, and a lost baby miraculously rediscovered in the person of the leading character, a strolling player conditionally named Rover. Plot and characters are not original, but if not of invention, there is a sufficient freshness of deployment to explain the success of the 1976 revival by the Royal Shakespeare Company. Rover, who has a dramatic quotation for every emergency, was created by Lewis and has proved the play's main attraction in the theatre. In a reading, the hostility towards Quaker puritanism and a veiled egalitarianism are quite as striking. O'Keeffe was proud to boast of Sheridan's calling him "the first that turned the public taste from the dullness of sentiment ... towards the sprightly channel of comic humour." He was *not* the first, but *Wild Oats* is a substantial alternative to the sentimental plays that surrounded it. Of the three other five-act comedies performed in his lifetime, *She's Eloped* survived only one night while *The World in a Village* and *Life's Vagaries* were moderately successful.

—Peter Thomson

PLANCHÉ, James Robinson. English. Born in Piccadilly, London, 27 February 1796. Studied at the Reverend Farrer's school, then at Monsieur de Court's school, London; articled to a bookseller, 1810. Married Elizabeth St. George in 1821 (died, 1846); two daughters. Began acting, as an amateur, at various private theatres in London, and began writing for the theatre in 1818; wrote for the Adelphi Theatre, 1820–21; wrote first opera, 1822, and designed costumes and supervised the production of the revival of Shakespeare's *King John* at Drury Lane, 1823; manager of the musical arrangements at the Vauxhall Gardens, 1826–27; wrote regularly for Covent Garden from 1828; managed the Adelphi Theatre, 1830; in partnership with the actress/manager Madame Vestris, first at the Olympic Theatre, then at Covent Garden, and then at the Lyceum, as resident writer and director of costumes, 1831–56; continued to write for other managements until 1872; also gained a reputation as an antiquary and scholar of heraldry and costume: Rouge Croix Pursuivant of Arms at the College of Heralds, 1854–66; Somerset Herald, 1866 until his death. Fellow, Society of Antiquaries, 1829; helped to found the British Archaeological Association, 1843. Granted Civil List pension, 1871. *Died 30 May 1880.*

PUBLICATIONS

Collections

    Extravaganzas 1825–71, edited by T. F. Dillon Croker and Stephen Tucker. 5 vols., 1879.

Plays

    Amoroso, King of Little Britain, music by Tom Cooke (produced 1818). 1818.
    Rodolph the Wolf; or, Columbine Red Riding Hood (produced 1818). 1819.
    The Troubadours; or, Jealousy Out-Witted (produced 1819).
    Abudah; or, The Talisman of Oromanes, music by Michael Kelly (produced 1819).

PLANCHÉ 97

The Czar; or, A Day in the Dockyards, from a French play (produced 1819).
The Caliph and the Cadi; or, Rambles in Bagdad (produced 1819).
Fancy's Sketch; or, Look Before You Leap (produced 1819).
Odds and Ends; or, Which Is the Manager? (produced 1819).
The Vampyre; or, The Bride of the Isles, from a French play (produced 1820). 1820.
A Burletta of Errors; or, Jupiter and Alcmena (produced 1820). Songs published 1820.
Who's to Marry Her? or, What's Bred in the Bone Won't Come Out of the Flesh (produced 1820).
The Deuce Is in Her! or, Two Nights in Madrid (produced 1820).
Zamoski; or, The Fortress and the Mine (produced 1820).
Dr. Syntax; or, Harlequin in London (produced 1820).
Giovanni the Vampire; or, How Shall We Get Rid of Him? (produced 1821).
Kenilworth Castle; or, The Days of Queen Bess, from the novel by Scott (produced 1821).
Lodgings to Let (produced 1821).
Half an Hour's Courtship; or, Le Chambre à Coucher (produced 1821).
Sherwood Forest; or, The Merry Archers (produced 1821).
The Mountain Hut; or, The Tinker's Son (produced 1821).
Peter and Paul; or, Love in the Vineyards (produced 1821). 1887.
The Witch of Derncleuch, music by William Reeve, from the novel *Guy Mannering* by Scott (produced 1821).
Capers at Canterbury (produced 1821).
The Corsair's Bride; or, The Valley of Mount Etna (produced 1821).
Love's Alarum (produced 1821).
Le Solitaire; or, The Unknown of the Mountains (produced 1821).
Marplot in Spain, music by William Reeve, from the play by Mrs. Centlivre (produced 1821; as *Too Curious by Half,* produced 1823).
The Pirate (produced 1822). 1822.
All in the Dark; or, The Banks of the Elbe, music by B. Livius, from a play by H. J. B. D. Victor (produced 1822). 1822.
The Fair Gabrielle, music by B. Livius (produced 1822). 1822.
Ali Pacha; or, The Signet-Ring, from a play by John Howard Payne (produced 1822). 1822.
Maid Marian; or, The Huntress of Arlingford, music by Henry Bishop, from the novel by Peacock (produced 1822). 1822.
Clari; or, The Maid of Milan (songs only), play by John Howard Payne, music by Henry Bishop (produced 1823). 1823.
I Will Have a Wife!, music by William Reeve (produced 1823).
Cortez; or, The Conquest of Mexico, music by William Reeve (produced 1823). 1823.
St. Ronan's Well, from the novel by Scott (produced 1824).
Military Tactics, music by William Reeve, from a French play (produced 1824).
The Frozen Lake, music by William Reeve, from a play by Scribe (produced 1824). Songs published 1824.
Der Freischutz; or, The Black Huntsman of Bohemia, music by B. Livius, from the opera by J. F. Kind, music by Weber (produced 1824). 1825.
A Woman Never Vext; or, The Widow of Cornhill, from the play by William Rowley (produced 1824). 1824.
The Coronation of Charles X of France (produced 1825).
Lilla (produced 1825).
Jocko; or, The Brazilian Monkey (produced 1825).
Success; or, A Hit If You Like It (produced 1825). In *Extravaganzas 1,* 1879.
Oberon; or, The Elf-King's Oath, from a poem by Wieland, music by Weber (produced 1826). 1826.
Returned Killed, from a French play (produced 1826). 1826.
All's Right; or, The Old School-Fellow (produced 1827).

98 PLANCHÉ

Pay to My Order; or, A Chaste Salute (produced 1827).
The Recontre; or, Love Will Fine Out the Way (produced 1827).
You Must Be Buried, from a French play (produced 1827).
Paris and London; or, A Trip Across the Herring Pond (produced 1828). 1829.
The Merchant's Wedding; or, London Frolics in 1638, from the plays *The City Match* by Jasper Mayne and *Match Me at Midnight* by William Rowley (produced 1828). 1828.
Carron Side; or, Fête Champêtre (produced 1828).
My Daughter, Sir; or, A Daughter to Marry, from a French play (as *A Daughter to Marry,* produced 1828; as *My Daughter, Sir,* produced 1832). 1830(?).
The Green-Eyed Monster, from a French play (produced 1828). 1830(?).
The Mason of Buda, music by George Rodwell (produced 1828). 1828.
Charles XII; or, The Siege of Stralsund (produced 1828). 1830(?).
Thierna-na-Oge; or, The Prince of the Lakes, music by Tom Cooke (produced 1829).
The Partisans; or, The War of Paris in 1649, from a French play (produced 1829).
Manoeuvring, with Charles Dance, from a French play (produced 1829). 1829.
Der Vampyr, music by William Hawes, from an opera by W. A. Wohlbrück, music by Heinrich Marschner (produced 1829).
The Brigand (produced 1829). 1830(?).
Hofer; or, The Tell of the Tyrol, from an opera by Jouy, Bis, and Marrast, music by Rossini (produced 1830). 1830.
The National Guard; or, Bride and No Bride, from an opera by Scribe, music by Auber (produced 1830). Songs published 1830.
The Dragon's Gift; or, The Scarf of Flight and the Mirror of Light, music by Tom Cooke (produced 1830).
The Jenkinses; or, Boarded and Done For (produced 1830). 1853.
Olympic Revels; or, Prometheus and Pandora, with Charles Dance (produced 1831). 1834; in *Extravaganzas 1,* 1879.
The Romance of a Day, music by Henry Bishop (produced 1831). 1831.
My Great Aunt; or, Relations and Friends (produced 1831). 1846.
The Legion of Honour, from a French play (produced 1831).
A Friend at Court (produced 1831).
The Army of the North; or, The Spaniard's Secret (produced 1831).
The Love Charm; or, The Village Coquette, from an opera by Scribe, music by Auber (produced 1831).
Olympic Devils; or, Orpheus and Eurydice, with Charles Dance (produced 1831). 1831; in *Extravaganzas 1,* 1879.
The Compact (produced 1832).
His First Campaign (produced 1832).
The Paphian Bower; or, Venus and Adonis, with Charles Dance (produced 1832). In *Extravaganzas 1,* 1879.
Little Red Riding Hood; or, The Fairy of the Silver Lake (produced 1832).
Promotion; or, A Morning at Versailles (produced 1833). 1852.
Reputation; or, The Court Secret (produced 1833). 1833.
The Students of Jena; or, The Family Concert, from a German opera, music by Hippolyte Chelard (produced 1833).
The Court Masque; or, Richmond in the Olden Time, music by William Hawes, from an opera by F. A. F. de Planard, music by Hérold (produced 1833).
High, Low, Jack, and the Game; or, The Card Party, with Charles Dance (produced 1833). 1833; in *Extravaganzas 1,* 1879.
Gustave III; or, The Masked Ball, music by Tom Cooke, from an opera by Scribe, music by Auber (produced 1833). 1833.
The Deep Deep Sea; or, Perseus and Andromeda, with Charles Dance (produced 1833). 1834; in *Extravaganzas I,* 1879.

The Challenge (songs only), libretto by H. M. Milner, music by Tom Cooke, from a French play (produced 1834).

Secret Service, from a play by Mélesville and Duveyrier (produced 1834). 1834.

The Loan of a Lover (produced 1834). 1834; revised version, as *Peter Spyk* (produced 1870).

My Friend the Governor (produced 1834). 1834.

The Regent, from a play by Scribe and Mélesville (produced 1834). 1834.

The Red Mask; or, The Council of Three, music by John Templeton, from an opera by A. Berrettoni, music by Marliani (produced 1834). Songs published 1834.

Telemachus; or, The Island of Calypso, with Charles Dance (produced 1834). In *Extravaganzas 1*, 1879.

The Court Beauties (produced 1835). 1835.

The Travelling Carriage (produced 1835).

The Jewess, music by Tom Cooke, from an opera by Scribe, music by Halévy (produced 1835). 1835.

Chevy Chase, music by George Macfarren (produced 1836). Songs published 1836.

Court Favour; or, Private and Confidential (produced 1836). 1838.

The Siege of Corinth, music by Tom Cooke, from an opera by C. della Valle, music by Rossini (produced 1836). Songs published 1836.

The Two Figaros (produced 1836). 1837.

Riquet with the Tuft, with Charles Dance, from a French play (produced 1836). 1837; in *Extravaganzas 1*, 1879.

A Peculiar Position (produced 1837). 1837(?).

Norma (produced 1837). 1848.

The New Servant (produced 1837).

The Child of the Wreck, music by Tom Cooke (produced 1837). 1859.

Caractacus, music by Michael Balfe, from the play *Bonduca* by Fletcher (produced 1837).

Puss in Boots, with Charles Dance (produced 1837). 1837; in *Extravaganzas 1*, 1879.

The Magic Flute, from an opera by Emanuel Schikaneder, music by Mozart (produced 1838). Songs published 1838.

The Drama's Levée; or, A Peep at the Past (produced 1838). In *Extravaganzas 2*, 1879.

The Printer's Devil (produced 1838). 1838(?).

The Queen's Horse; or, The Brewer of Preston, with M. B. Honan (produced 1838). 1839.

Blue Beard, with Charles Dance (produced 1839). 1839; in *Extravaganzas 2*, 1879.

Faint Heart Ne'er Won Fair Lady, from a French play (produced 1839). N.d.

The Garrick Fever (produced 1839). 1855.

The Fortunate Isles; or, The Triumphs of Britannia, music by Henry Bishop (produced 1840). 1840.

The Sleeping Beauty in the Wood (produced 1840). 1840; in *Extravaganzas 2*, 1879.

The Spanish Curate, from the play by Fletcher and Massinger (produced 1840). 1887.

Harlequin and the Giant Helmet; or, The Castle of Otranto (produced 1840).

The Captain of the Watch, from a play by Lockroy (produced 1841). 1841.

The Embassy (produced 1841).

Beauty and the Beast (produced 1841). 1841; in *Extravaganzas 2*, 1879.

The Marriage of Figaro, from an opera by Lorenzo da Ponte, music by Mozart (produced 1842). Songs published 1842.

The White Cat, music by J. H. Tully (produced 1842). 1842; in *Extravaganzas 2*, 1879.

The Follies of a Night (produced 1842). 1842.

The Way of the World, from the play by Congreve (produced 1842).

Fortunio; or, The Seven Gifted Servants (produced 1843). 1843; edited by Michael Booth, in *English Plays of the Nineteenth Century 5*, 1976.

100 PLANCHÉ

Who's Your Friend? or, The Queensberry Fête (produced 1843). 1843.

The Fair One with the Golden Locks (produced 1843). 1844; in *Extravaganzas 2*, 1879.

Grist to the Mill (produced 1844). 1844.

The Drama at Home; or, An Evening with Puff (produced 1844). 1844; in *Extravaganzas 2*, 1879.

Somebody Else (produced 1844). 1845.

Graciosa and Percinet (produced 1844). 1845; in *Extravaganzas 2*, 1879.

The Golden Fleece; or, Jason in Colchis and Medea in Corinth (produced 1845). 1845; in *Extravaganzas 3*, 1879.

A Cabinet Question (produced 1845). 1845.

The Bee and the Orange Tree; or, The Four Wishes (produced 1845). 1846; in *Extravaganzas 3*, 1879.

The Irish Post (produced 1846). 1846.

The Birds of Aristophanes (produced 1846). 1846; in *Extravaganzas 3*, 1879.

Queen Mary's Bower (produced 1846). 1847.

Spring Gardens (produced 1846). 1846.

Story-Telling; or, "Novel" Effects (produced 1846).

The Invisible Prince; or, The Island of Tranquil Delights (produced 1846). 1846; in *Extravaganzas 3*, 1879.

The New Planet; or, Harlequin Out of Place (produced 1847). 1847; in *Extravaganzas 3*, 1879.

The Jacobite (produced 1847). 1847.

The Pride of the Market (produced 1847). 1847.

The Golden Branch (produced 1847). 1848; in *Extravaganzas 3*, 1879.

Not a Bad Judge (produced 1848). 1848.

Theseus and Ariadne; or, The Marriage of Bacchus (produced 1848). 1848; in *Extravaganzas 3*, 1879.

The King of the Peacocks (produced 1848). 1849; in *Extravaganzas 3*, 1879.

A Romantic Idea (produced 1849). 1849.

Hold Your Tongue (produced 1849). 1849.

The Seven Champions of Christendom (produced 1849). 1849; in *Extravaganzas 3*, 1879.

A Lady in Difficulties (produced 1849). 1849.

The Island of Jewels (produced 1849). 1850; edited by Michael Booth, in *English Plays of the Nineteenth Century 5*, 1976.

Fiesco; or, The Revolt of Genoa (produced 1850).

Cymon and Iphigenia, from the play *Cymon* by Garrick (produced 1850). 1850; in *Extravaganzas 4*, 1879.

My Heart's Idol; or, A Desperate Remedy (produced 1850).

The White Hood (produced 1850).

The Day of Reckoning (produced 1850). 1852.

King Charming; or, The Blue Bird of Paradise (produced 1850). In *Extravaganzas 4*, 1879.

The Queen of the Frogs (produced 1851). In *Extravaganzas 4*, 1879.

The Prince of Happy Land; or, The Fawn in the Forest (produced 1851). 1851; in *Extravaganzas 4*, 1879.

The Mysterious Lady (produced 1852). 1853.

The Good Woman in the Wood (produced 1852). In *Extravaganzas 4*, 1879.

Mr. Buckstone's Ascent of Mount Parnassus (produced 1853). 1853(?); in *Extravaganzas 4*, 1879.

The Camp at the Olympic (produced 1853). 1854.

Harlequin King Nutcracker, with J. Halford (produced 1853). 1853.

Once upon a Time There Were Two Kings (produced 1853). 1853; in *Extravaganzas 4*, 1879.

PLANCHÉ 101

Mr. Buckstone's Voyage round the Globe (in Leicester Square) (produced 1854). In *Extravaganzas 5,* 1879.
The Knights of the Round Table (produced 1854). N.d.
The Yellow Dwarf and the King of the Gold Mines (produced 1854). In *Extravaganzas 5,* 1879.
The New Haymarket Spring Meeting (produced 1855). In *Extravaganzas 5,* 1879.
The Discreet Princess; or, The Three Glass Distaffs (produced 1855). In *Extravaganzas 5,* 1879.
Young and Handsome (produced 1856). In *Extravaganzas 5,* 1879.
An Old Offender (produced 1859).
Love and Fortune (produced 1859). In *Extravaganzas 5,* 1879.
My Lord and My Lady; or, It Might Have Been Worse (produced 1861). 1862.
Love's Triumph, music by W. V. Wallace (produced 1862). 1862.
Orpheus in the Haymarket, from an opera by H. Cremieux and L. Halévy, music by Offenbach (produced 1865). In *Extravaganzas 5,* 1879.
Queen Lucidora, The Fair One with the Golden Locks, and Harlequin Prince Graceful; or, The Carp, The Crow, and the Owl (produced 1868).
Pieces of Pleasantry for Private Performance During the Christmas Holidays. 1868.
King Christmas (produced 1871). In *Extravaganzas 5,* 1879.
Babil and Bijou; or, The Lost Regalia (songs only), play by Dion Boucicault (produced 1872).

Verse

Shere Afkun, The First Husband of Nourmahal: A Legend of Hindoostan. 2 vols., 1823.
William with the Ring: A Romance in Rhyme. 1873.
Songs and Poems from 1819 to 1879. 1881.

Other

Costumes of Shakespeare's King John (and other plays). 5 vols., 1823–25.
Lays and Legends of the Rhine. 2 vols., 1827; as *The Rhenisch Keepsake,* 1837.
Descent of the Danube from Ratisbon to Vienna During the Autumn of 1827. 1828; as *The Danube from Ulm to Vienna,* 1836.
History of British Costume. 1834.
Regal Records; or, A Chronicle of the Coronation of the Queens Regnant of England. 1838.
The Pursuivant of Arms; or, Heraldry Founded upon Facts. 1852; revised edition, 1858.
A Corner of Kent; or, Some Account of the Parish of Ash-Next-Sandwich. 1864.
Recollections and Reflections: A Professional Autobiography. 2 vols., 1872; revised edition, 1901.
The Conqueror and His Companions. 2 vols., 1874.
A Cyclopaedia of Costume; or, Dictionary of Dress. 2 vols., 1876–79.
Suggestions for Establishing an English Art Theatre. 1879.

Editor, *A Complete View of the Dress and Habits of the People of England,* by J. Strutt. 1842.
Editor, *The Regal and Ecclesiastical Antiquities of England,* by J. Strutt. 1842.

Translator, *King Nut-Cracker: A Fairy Tale.* 1853.
Translator, *Fairy Tales,* by Mme. de Aulnoy. 1855.

Translator, *Four and Twenty Fairy Tales.* 1858.

Reading List: "Planché's Classical Burlesques" by D. MacMillan, in *Studies in Philology 25,* 1928; "Exit Planché — Enter Gilbert" by Harley Granville-Barker, in *The Eighteen-Sixties,* edited by John Drinkwater, 1932; *The Rise of English Opera* by Eric Walter White, 1951; *The Burlesque Tradition* by V. C. Clinton Baddeley, 1952; "Shakespeare in Planché's Extravaganzas" by Stanley Wells, in *Shakespeare Survey 16,* 1963; "Planché and the English Burletta Tradition" by P. T. Dircks, in *Theatre Survey 17,* 1976.

*   *   *

James Robinson Planché is best known today for his crucial role in the development of Christmas pantomime. He wrote a "speaking opening" for the harlequinade *Rodolph the Wolf; or Columbine Red Riding Hood* in 1818 and, in the 1830's and following decades, produced an abundance of fairy burlettas and extravaganzas, in effect extended openings without the harlequinade. His sources were eighteenth-century French *contes féeries.* Writing mainly for Madame Vestris, who excelled in "breeches parts," he helped establish the convention of the Principal Boy in combination with the Fairy Godmother and the peculiarly human, even courtly, pantomime animal. He exercised a happy sense of balance between the familiar and fantastic, dialogue, music and spectacle, French wit and English humour; and he was never prolix. In his *Recollections and Reflections* he complained that he was increasingly "painted out" from *The Island of Jewels* (1849) onwards, and attention drawn from his skill to elaborate artistic "transformations."

Although he wrote melodramas and comedies in prose, mostly of the school of Scribe and often with settings that must have appealed to the serious historian of costume and manners in him, it is in light verse and as a librettist that Planché sparkles. *Olympic Devils* gives a fair idea of his quality. "Mythology had always possessed a peculiar fascination for me," he declared, and he brings even the darker elements of the Orpheus legend within the range of this brief piece: a choric lament from the depths ("Singing, oh! that a pool of punch had we, Instead of a flaming sulphur sea"); the Fates ("A never-ceasing game of 'snip-snap-snorum.' For help, alas, man pleads to her in vain — *Her* motto's 'Cut and *never* come again.' "); Pluto's imperiousness ("Forward, my Furies! do your work, ye Fates! And thrust the Thracian thrummer through the gates!"); and the dismemberment of Orpheus ("He seems to have a singing in his head"). The *jeux d'esprit* are organised into episodes and arias unified by some dominant trick sustained just as long as Planché can ring changes on it: so 25 lines of punning dialogue with Cerberus culminate in a musical quartet ("You mean you've howled some doggerel to the moon./No sir; I say I sing — and sing in tune!/A *bark*-a-role of course./ No sir, a glee./You take the *treble* then?/I take all three. My voice is tenor — counter-tenor — bass").

He insisted that his nonsense should be played with gravity and restraint in pleasing settings and costumes. With an abundance of graceful gestures (e.g., Paragon's *envoi* in *The White Cat,* "Here ends the tale, — *Finis coronat, O-puss!*") he offered light entertainment to cultivated audiences. His fairy world is an urbane one, his fairy princes recognisably descended from the disguised Rosalind and Viola; and it hardly requires the naming of Pope, in *High, Low, Jack, and the Game,* to identify *The Rape of the Lock* as a model from which he learnt much. His revues and his version of Aristophanes's *The Birds* reveal a limited satiric impulse, and the success of his work led to a temporary decline in the critical function of burlesque. Later writers of more critical bent who drew on the Planché tradition were W. S. Gilbert, Bernard Shaw, and Oscar Wilde.

—Margery Morgan

POOLE, John. English. Born in England in 1786. Very little is known about his family, background, or education; the dedications to his printed works suggest that he held a position in society; successful as a dramatist early in life, writing comedies and farces for the London theatres, 1811–29; an active contributor to the *New Monthly Magazine* for many years; lived in Windsor, 1831; and subsequently lived in Paris for many years; appointed a brother of the Charterhouse, London, but later gave up the position; obtained a pension through the influence of Dickens; lived in obscurity during the last 20 years of his life. *Died* (buried) *10 February 1872.*

PUBLICATIONS

Plays

Hamlet Travestie (produced 1811). 1810.
The Earls of Hammersmith; or, Infant Maturity, with Dennis Lawler (produced 1811). N.d.
Rumfuskin, King of the North Pole; or, Treason Rewarded (produced 1813). In *Bentley's Miscellany*, 1841.
The Hole in the Wall (produced 1813). 1813.
Intrigue (produced 1814). 1814.
Who's Who; or, The Double Imposture (produced 1815). 1815.
A Short Reign and a Merry One (produced 1819). 1819.
Past and Present; or, The Hidden Treasure, from a French play (as *The Hidden Treasure*, produced 1820; as *Past and Present*, produced 1830). N.d.
Match Making, from a French play (produced 1821). 1844.
The Two Pages of Frederick the Great, from a play by Nicolas Dezède (produced 1821). 1821.
Old and Young (produced 1822). 1822.
Simpson and Co. (produced 1823). 1823.
Augusta; or, The Blind Girl (produced 1823).
Deaf as a Post (produced 1823). 1823.
A Year in an Hour; or, The Cock of the Walk (produced 1824). 1824.
Married and Single; or, Belles and Bailiffs, from a French play (produced 1824). 1824.
'Twould Puzzle a Conjuror (produced 1824). N.d.
Tribulation; or, Unwelcome Visitors, from a play by A. J. M. Wafflard and J. D. F. de Bury (produced 1825). 1825.
Paul Pry (produced 1825). 1825.
The Scape-Goat (produced 1825). 1826.
'Twixt the Cup and the Lip (produced 1826).
The Wife's Strategem; or, More Frightened Than Hurt, from the play *The Gamester* by James Shirley (produced 1827). 1827.
Gudgeons and Sharks; or, Piecrust Promises (produced 1827).
The Wealthy Widow; or, They're Both to Blame, from a French play (produced 1827). 1827.
Ups and Downs; or, The Ladder of Life (produced 1828).
My Wife! What Wife? (produced 1829). N.d.
Lodgings for Single Gentlemen (produced 1829). N.d.
Turning the Tables (produced 1830). 1834(?); as *Quite the Reverse* (produced 1839).
The Bath Road (produced 1830).
Madame du Barry; or, A Glance at a Court (produced 1831).
A Nabob for an Hour, from a play by Scribe (produced 1833). 1832; as *Uncle Sam*, n.d.

104 POOLE

A Soldier's Courtship (produced 1833). 1833.
Patrician and Parvenu; or, Confusion Worse Confounded (produced 1835). 1835.
Atonement; or, The God-Daughter, from a French play (produced 1836). 1836.
Delicate Attentions (produced 1836). 1837.
Scan Mag; or, The Village Gossip. 1840(?).
The Swedish Ferryman (produced 1843).

Fiction

Sketches and Recollections. 1835; as *The Comic Sketch-Book,* 1836.
Paul Pry's Journal of a Residence at Little Pedlington. 1836.
Paul Pry's Delicate Attentions and Other Tales. 1837.
Little Pedlington and the Pedlingtonians. 1839.
Phineas Quiddy; or, Sheer Industry. 1842.
Christmas Festivities: Tales, Sketches, and Characters. 4 vols., 1845–48.

Verse

Byzantium: A Dramatic Poem. N.d.

Other

Crotchets in the Air; or, An (Un)Scientific Account of a Balloon-Trip. 1838.

Editor, *The Comic Miscellany for 1845.* 1845.

*　　*　　*

Two works distinguish John Poole from the mass of minor dramatists active in the English theatre during the early decades of the nineteeth century. The first is his *Hamlet Travestie,* and the second *Paul Pry.* This is not to deny merit to certain other pieces – *Tribulation,* for example, a comedy derived from a French original, or the two farces *Deaf as a Post* and *'Twixt the Cup and the Lip.* But these pieces neither initiated a literary fashion, as did the *Hamlet Travestie,* nor added a household name to the English language, as did *Paul Pry.* The credit for the phenomenal success of *Paul Pry* has to be shared between the author and John Liston, who played the title role. The play has a fairly conventional double-plot, but its comic centre is the interfering nosy parker Paul Pry, whose catchphrase "I hope I don't intrude?" convulsed audiences at the Haymarket for an unprecedented 114 nights in its first season. The credit for the success of *Hamlet Travestie* is Poole's alone. It was his first dramatic piece, and it was published and already into three editions before it received any performance. Much of the fun of a reading is to be gained from the "burlesque annotations, after the manner of Dr. Johnson and Geo. Steevens, Esq. and the various commentators," but the text has charms for anyone prepared to enjoy a prolonged exercise in bathos. The flavour can be judged by almost any extract, this of the King's at the opening of the first act, for example:

> Cheer up, my hearty: tho' you've lost your dad,
> Consider that your case is not so bad:
> Your father lost a father; and 'tis certain
> Death o'er your great-grandfather drew the curtain.
> You've mourned enough: 'tis time your grief to smother;
> Don't cry; you shall be king some time or other.

Most of the play's best known lines turn up, only to be pulled down to the level of colloquial, rhyming doggerel. The soliloquies are rewritten as songs, as is some of the dialogue. The extraordinary thing is that Poole sticks very close to Shakespeare's plot; and he writes with more wit than many of those who followed his lead.

—Peter Thomson

PRAED, Winthrop Mackworth. English. Born in London, 26 July 1802. Educated at Langley Broom School, near Colnbrook, 1810–14; Eton College, 1814–21 (Founder-Editor, *The Etonian*, 1820); Trinity College, Cambridge, 1821–25 (Sir William Browne Medal, 1822, 1823, 1824; Chancellor's Medal for English verse, 1823), B.A. 1825; called to the Bar, Middle Temple, London, 1829. Married Helen Bogle in 1835; two daughters. Tutor to Lord Ernest Bruce, at Eton College, 1825–27; elected Fellow, Trinity College, Cambridge, 1827; practised law on the Norfolk circuit, 1829; Conservative Member of Parliament for St. Germans, 1830–31, for Great Yarmouth, 1834–37, and for Aylesbury, 1837–39; Secretary to the Board of Control (Peel's administration), 1835. Deputy High Steward of Cambridge University. *Died 15 July 1839.*

PUBLICATIONS

Collections

> *Poems.* 2 vols., 1864; revised edition, 1885.
> *Selected Poems,* edited by Kenneth Allott. 1953.

Verse

> *Pyramides Aegyptiacae.* 1822.
> *Nugae Seria Ducunt in Mala.* 1822.
> *In Obitum T. F. Middleton.* 1823.
> *Lillian: A Fairy Tale.* 1823.
> *Australasia.* 1823.
> *Athens.* 1824.
> *Scribimus Indocti Doctique.* 1824.
> *The Ascent of Elijah.* 1831.
> *Intercepted Letters about the Infirmary Bazaar.* 4 vols., n.d.
> *Trash Dedicated Without Respect to J. Halse, Esq., M.P.* 1833.
> *Political Poems.* 1835.
> *Political and Occasional Poems,* edited by G. Young. 1888.

106 PRAED

Other

Speech in Committee on the Reform Bill, on Moving an Amendment. 1832.
Essays, edited by G. Young. 1887.
Every-Day Characters. 1896.

Reading List: *A Poet in Parliament: The Life of Praed* by Derek Hudson, 1939.

*   *   *

Winthrop Mackworth Praed was, in his own words, a "rhymer" rather than a poet. He was a gifted versifier whose talent found its best expression in light verse, poems celebrating the life of the leisured society in which he lived.

His work falls mainly into three categories, *vers de société,* verse tales, and political poems. Of these, the latter, topical in Praed's own day, are somewhat obscure to the modern reader. Written as ephemeral pieces, they were resurrected in book form almost fifty years after their author's death. Few of them are of interest today, though Kenneth Allott included the best of them in his edition of *Selected Poems.* The verse tales indicate considerable narrative skill and are most successful when Praed is not attempting to write seriously. The most serious of these tales, "The Legend of the Drachenfels," with its high morality ("Why turns the serpent from his prey?—/The Cross hath barred his terrible way") succeeds only in being ponderous and tedious. On the other hand, such a tale as "The Legend of the Teufel-haus," with its romantic subject matter, facetious treatment and somewhat macabre ending illustrates Praed's work in this vein at its best.

His most successful work, however, is to be found in his society verses, practically all of which were written in his most productive period, the late 1820's and early 1830's when Praed was studying law and establishing his political interests. The poems treat of the life and manners of the upper-middle-class society of Praed's day and vary from the series of poems on Every-day Characters to those which deal with the conversation and interests which occupy that society. He presents his characters with warmth and wit, but without sentimentality, writing often in an anti-romantic tone in order to guard himself against a seriousness which he is unable to sustain. Chronologically belonging to the Romantic era, his best work is, in fact, Augustan in flavour, though his intentions are more frivolous and his wit less acerbic. It is in his skill as a craftsman that he most resembles the Augustans, adopting their fashion of figures of speech, alliteration and assonance, puns and paradoxes. He is particularly fond of syllepsis, the extension of a pun by which one word serves two purposes, as for instance in "The Devil's Decoy" when "The startled Priest struck both his thighs,/And the abbey clock struck one." Another of his favourite devices is the bathetic ending which he employs in poems such as "The Belle of the Ball-Room," "My Partner," or "A Letter [The Talented Man]." A brilliant classical scholar, Praed's principal debt to his classical learning is his considerable metrical proficiency and a correctness in versification which is itself Augustan.

A poet who was aware of his own limitations, Praed is to be read as a purveyor of light verse, but light verse which, at its best, attains a degree of perfection which set a standard few later versifiers have equalled.

—Hilda D. Spear

ROGERS, Samuel. English. Born in Stoke Newington, London, 30 July 1763. Educated at private schools in Hackney and Stoke Newington. Entered his father's bank, Cornhill, London, 1779; Partner, 1784, and, on his father's death, Principal Partner, 1793 until his retirement, 1803; thereafter, with income from the bank, lived in society as an art collector and man of letters; acted as patron to various writers, and came to be regarded as arbiter of taste. Offered poet laureateship on death of Wordsworth, 1850, but declined. *Died 18 December 1855.*

PUBLICATIONS

Collections

   Poetical Works. 1856; edited by E. Bell, 1859.

Verse

   The Ode to Superstition with Some Other Poems. 1786.
   The Pleasures of Memory. 1792.
   An Epistle to a Friend with Some Other Poems. 1798.
   Verses Written in Westminster Abbey after the Funeral of Charles James Fox. 1806.
   The Voyage of Columbus. 1810.
   Miscellaneous Poems, with E. C. Knight and others. 1812.
   Poems. 1812; edited by S. Sharpe, 1860.
   Jacqueline. 1814.
   Human Life. 1819.
   Italy. 2 vols., 1822–28.
   Poetical Works. 1852.

Other

   Recollections of the Table-Talk of Samuel Rogers. 1856; edited by O. Stonor, 1952.
   Recollections, edited by W. Sharpe. 1859.
   Reminiscences and Table-Talk, edited by G. H. Powell. 1903.
   Italian Journal, edited by J. R. Hale. 1956.
   Rogers and William Gilpin: Their Friendship and Correspondence, edited by C. P. Barbier. 1959.

Reading List: *The Early Life of Rogers,* 1887, and *Rogers and His Contemporaries,* 2 vols., 1889, both by P. W. Clayden; *Rogers and His Circle* by R. E. Roberts, 1910; *Rogers et Son Poème "Italie"* by Ernest Gidden, 1959; *Rogers, The Poet from Newington Green* by Adam J. Shirren, 1963.

*   *   *

Hazlitt's stricture that Samuel Rogers was "elegant but feeble" is unkind though undeniable. The luxurious repose, the almost maidenly dignity with which his life was surrounded, renders his verse nerveless and withdrawn, though the poet described himself more flatteringly, in *Italy*:

> Nature denied him much,
> But gave him at his birth what he most values;
> A passionate love for music, sculpture, painting,
> For poetry, the language of the gods,
> For all things here, or grand or beautiful,
> A setting sun, a lake among the mountains,
> The light of an ingenuous countenance,
> And what transcends them all, a noble action.

Rogers was the last true disciple of the cult sensibility: his notable collection of *objects d'art* demonstrated the infallibility of his taste; invitations to his literary breakfasts were eagerly sought; and in his unusually long life he was true friend to many poets – Crabbe, Byron, Wordsworth, and Tennyson among them. His controversial sallies passed round with those of Sydney Smith and Lutrell; his enlightened social attitudes earned the respect of men as diverse as Fox and Wellington. And his contemporaries bought over 21,000 copies of *The Pleasures of Memory*, which Byron hailed as "one of the most beautiful didactic poems in our language." Yet the raw edge of suffering, the extremes of joy and grief, are missing. He is the poet of the elegant Regency salon; a cultivated but bloodless amateur, a dilettante. A contemporary *bon mot* declared that Rogers had laboured nine months over a couplet, was now brought to bed of it, and that parent and child were as well as could be expected. Such scrupulous care, not always evident in the finished work, leached from his verse the last drops of immediacy.

It may, today, be his misfortune that his longest poems are the most readable: both *Italy* and *The Pleasures of Memory* reveal a dignified grace, reflecting the dispassionate sensibility of Gray and Goldsmith, and the conscious style of Johnson. The Horatian "Epistle to a Friend" lacks the *merum sal* of its Latin models, but makes an articulate case for the leisured and gentlemanly life.

Where deep feelings such as heroism or love are involved Rogers fails. *Columbus* and *Jacqueline* demand these emotions, but demand them in vain. The engravings which he commissioned Turner and Stothard to make for his collected works capture perfectly his passive sense of beauty, his withdrawn and static observations. Lines like the following, (from *Italy*) need the accompaniment of Turner's graphic skill to render them moving:

> It was an hour of universal joy.
> The lark was up and at the gate of heaven,
> Singing as sure to enter where he came;
> The butterfly was basking in my path,
> His radiant wings unfolded. From below
> The bell of prayer rose slowly, plaintively;
> An odours such as welcome in the day,
> Such as salute the early traveller,
> And come and go, each sweeter than the last,
> Were rising. Hill and valley breathed delight;
> And not a living thing but blessed the hour!

—T. Bareham

SCOTT, Sir Walter. Scottish. Born in Edinburgh, 15 August 1771; spent his childhood in the Border country. Educated at Edinburgh High School, and the University of Edinburgh; studied law as a clerk in his father's law office; admitted to the Faculty of Advocates, 1792. Married Charlotte Charpentier in 1797 (died, 1826); four children. Writer from 1796; Sheriff-Depute of Selkirkshire, 1799–1832; Clerk of the Court of Session, 1806–30; joined his brother and James Ballantyne as a partner in a printing company, Edinburgh, 1804, which went bankrupt in 1826, involving him in the discharge of its debts for the rest of his life; founded the *Quarterly Review*, 1809; built and lived at Abbotsford from 1812. Created a baronet, 1820. *Died 21 September 1832.*

PUBLICATIONS

Collections

> *Poetical Works*, edited by J. G. Lockhart. 12 vols., 1833–34; edited by J. Logie Robertson, 1904.
> *Miscellaneous Prose Works*, edited by J. G. Lockhart. 28 vols., 1834–36; 2 additional vols., 1871.
> *The Letters*, edited by Herbert Grierson. 12 vols., 1932–37.
> *Short Stories.* 1934.
> *Selected Poems*, edited by Thomas Crawford. 1972.

Verse

> *The Chase, and William and Helen: Two Ballads from the German of Gottfried Augustus Bürger.* 1796.
> *The Eve of Saint John: A Border Ballad.* 1800.
> *The Lay of the Last Minstrel.* 1805.
> *Ballads and Lyrical Pieces.* 1806.
> *Marmion: A Tale of Flodden Field.* 1808.
> *The Lady of the Lake.* 1810.
> *The Vision of Don Roderick.* 1811.
> *Rokeby.* 1813.
> *The Bridal of Triermain: or, The Vale of St. John, in Three Cantos.* 1813.
> *The Lord of the Isles.* 1815.
> *The Field of Waterloo.* 1815.
> *The Ettrick Garland, Being Two Excellent New Songs*, with James Hogg. 1815.
> *Harold the Dauntless.* 1817.
> *New Love-Poems*, edited by Davidson Cook. 1932.

Plays

> *Goetz of Berlichingen, with The Iron Hand*, by Goethe. 1799.
> *Guy Mannering; or, The Gipsy's Prophecy*, with Daniel Terry, music by Henry Bishop and others, from the novel by Scott (produced 1816). 1816.
> *Halidon Hill: A Dramatic Sketch from Scottish History.* 1822.
> *MacDuff's Cross*, in *A Collection of Poems*, edited by Joanna Baillie. 1823.
> *The House of Aspen* (produced 1829). In *Poetical Works*, 1830.
> *Auchindrane; or, The Ayrshire Tragedy* (produced 1830). In *The Doom of Devorgoil; Auchindrane*, 1830.

110 SCOTT

The Doom of Devorgoil: A Melo-Drama; Auchindrane; or, The Ayrshire Tragedy. 1830.

Fiction

Waverley; or, 'Tis Sixty Years Since. 1814.
Guy Mannering; or, The Astrologer. 1815.
The Antiquary. 1816.
The Black Dwarf, Old Mortality. 1817; *Old Mortality* edited by Angus Calder, 1975.
Rob Roy. 1817.
The Heart of Mid-Lothian. 1818.
The Bride of Lammermoor: A Legend of Montrose. 1819.
Ivanhoe: A Romance. 1819.
The Monastery. 1820.
The Abbot; or, The Heir of Avenel. 1820.
Kenilworth: A Romance. 1821; edited by David Daiches, 1966.
The Pirate. 1821.
The Fortunes of Nigel. 1822.
Peveril of the Peak. 1823.
Quentin Durward. 1823; edited by M. W. and G. Thomas, 1966.
St. Ronan's Well. 1823.
Redgauntlet: A Tale of the Eighteenth Century. 1824.
Tales of the Crusaders (The Betrothed, The Talisman). 1825.
Woodstock; or, The Cavalier. 1826.
Chronicles of the Canongate: First Series: The Highland Widow, The Two Drovers, The Surgeon's Daughter. 1827; *Second Series: The Fair Maid of Perth,* 1828.
My Aunt Margaret's Mirror, The Tapestried Chamber, Death of the Laird's Jock, A Scene at Abbotsford. 1829.
Anne of Geierstein; or, The Maiden of the Mist. 1829.
Waverley Novels (Scott's final revision). 48 vols., 1829–33.
Count Robert of Paris, Castle Dangerous. 1832.

Other

Paul's Letters to His Kinsfolk. 1816.
The Visionary. 1819.
Provincial Antiquities of Scotland. 2 vols., 1826.
The Life of Napoleon Buonaparte: Emperor of the French, with a Preliminary View of the French Revolution. 9 vols., 1827.
Tales of a Grandfather, Being Stories Taken from Scottish History. 9 vols., 1827–29.
Miscellaneous Prose Works. 6 vols., 1827.
Religious Discourses by a Layman. 1828.
The History of Scotland. 2 vols., 1829–30.
Letters on Demonology and Witchcraft. 1830.
Tales of a Grandfather, Being Stories Taken from the History of France. 3 vols., 1830.
Letters Addressed to Rev. R. Polwhele, D. Gilbert, F. Douce. 1832.
Letters Between James Ellis and Scott. 1850.
Journal 1825–32, edited by D. Douglas. 2 vols., 1890; edited by W. E. K. Anderson, 1972.
Familiar Letters, edited by D. Douglas. 2 vols., 1894.
The Letters of Scott and Charles Kirkpatrick Sharpe to Robert Chambers, 1821–45. 1903.

SCOTT 111

The Private Letter-Books edited by W. Partington. 1930.
Sir Walter's Postbag: More Stories and Sidelights from the Collection in the Brotherton Library, edited by W. Partington. 1932.
Some Unpublished Letters from the Collection in the Brotherton Library, edited by J. A. Symington. 1932.
The Correspondence of Scott and Charles Robert Maturin, edited by F. E. Ratchford and W. H. McCarthy. 1937.
Private Letters of the Seventeenth Century, edited by D. Grant. 1948.

Editor, *An Apology for Tales of Terror.* 1799.
Editor, *Minstrelsy of the Scottish Border.* 2 vols., 1802; edited by Alfred Noyes, 1908.
Editor, *Sir Tristrem: A Metrical Romance,* by Thomas of Ercildoune. 1804.
Editor, *Original Memoirs Written During the Great Civil War,* by Sir H. Slingsby and Captain Hodgson. 1804.
Editor, *The Works of John Dryden.* 18 vols., 1808 (*Life of Dryden* published separately, 1808, edited by Bernard Kreissman, 1963).
Editor, *Memoirs of Captain George Carleton.* 1808.
Editor, *Queenhoo-Hall: A Romance, and Ancient Times: A Drama,* by Joseph Strutt. 4 vols., 1808.
Editor, *Memoirs of Robert Cary, Earl of Monmouth, and Fragmenta Regalia,* by Sir Robert Naunton. 1808.
Editor, *A Collection of Scarce and Valuable Tracts.* 13 vols., 1809–15.
Editor, *English Minstrelsy, Being a Collection of Fugitive Poetry.* 2 vols., 1810.
Editor, *The Poetical Works of Anna Seward.* 3 vols., 1810.
Editor, *Memoirs of Count Grammont,* by Anthony Hamilton. 2 vols., 1811.
Editor, *The Castle of Otranto,* by Horace Walpole. 1811.
Editor, *Secret History of the Court of King James the First.* 2 vols., 1811.
Editor, *The Works of Jonathan Swift.* 19 vols., 1814 (*Memoirs of Swift* published separately, 1826).
Editor, *The Letting of Humours Blood in the Head Vaine,* by S. Rowlands. 1814.
Editor, *Memorie of the Somervilles.* 2 vols., 1815.
Editor, *Trivial Poems and Triolets,* by Patrick Carey. 1820.
Editor, *Memorials of the Haliburtons.* 1820.
Editor, *Northern Memoirs Writ in the Year 1658,* by Richard Franck. 1821.
Editor, *Ballantyne's Novelist's Library.* 10 vols., 1821–24 (*Lives of the Novelists* published separately, 2 vols., 1825).
Editor, *Chronological Notes of Scottish Affairs from the Diary of Lord Fountainhall.* 1822.
Editor, *Military Memoirs of the Great Civil War,* by John Gwynne. 1822.
Editor, *Lays of the Lindsays.* 1824.
Editor, *Auld Robin Gray: A Ballad,* by Lady Anne Barnard. 1825.
Editor, with D. Laing, *The Bannatyne Miscellany.* 1827.
Editor, *Memoirs of the Marchioness de la Rochejaquelein.* 1827.
Editor, *Proceedings in the Court-Martial Held upon John, Master of Sinclair, 1708.* 1829.
Editor, *Memorials of George Bannatyne, 1545–1608.* 1829.
Editor, *Trial of Duncan Terig and Alexander Bane Macdonald, 1754.* 1831.
Editor, *Memoirs of the Insurrection in Scotland in 1715,* by John, Master of Sinclair. 1858.

Bibliography: *Bibliography of the Waverley Novels* by G. Worthington, 1930; "A Bibliography of the Poetical Works of Scott 1796–1832" by W. Ruff, in *Transactions of the Edinburgh Bibliographical Society 1,* 1938; *A Bibliography of Scott: A Classified and*

112 SCOTT

Annotated List of Books and Articles Relating to His Life and Works 1797–1940 by J. C. Corson, 1943.

Reading List: *Scott as a Critic of Literature* by M. Ball, 1907; *Scott: A New Life* by Herbert Grierson, 1938; *Scott* by Una Pope-Hennessy, 1948; *Scott: His Life and Personality* by H. Pearson, 1954; *Scott* by Ian Jack, 1958; *The Heyday of Scott* by Donald Davie, 1961; *Witchcraft and Demonology in Scott's Fiction* by C. O. Parsons, 1964; *Scott* by T. Crawford, 1965; *Scott's Novels* by F. R. Hart, 1966; *The Wizard of the North: The Life of Scott* by Carola Oman, 1973; *Scott* by Robin Mayhead, 1973.

*   *   *

Walter Scott was born in Edinburgh in 1771. His father, who is affectionately satirized as Saunders Fairford, the "good old-fashioned man of method" in *Redgauntlet*, was a respected solicitor. His mother, the daughter of a well-known medical professor at the University, had brains and character, and it is tempting to believe that from her Scott inherited the ability which put him for a time at the very top of the tree. He had his education at the High School of Edinburgh and at Edinburgh University. Of formative importance, however, were the months he spent at his paternal grandfather's Border farm as a small boy recuperating from the illness (probably poliomyelitis) which left him permanently lame. The tales he heard there of old, unhappy, far-off things, and the skirmishes in which his own ancestors had fought, lit in him the love of the Scottish past which was the enduring passion of his life.

As Sheriff of Selkirkshire and a Clerk of the Court of Session, Scott was obliged to divide his time between Edinburgh and his Sherifdom; and it was near Selkirk that he built Abbotsford, the "Conundrum Castle" of a house which he embellished with all manner of historical trophies and curiosities. His two official salaries combined to give him a modest competence. They were not, however, enough to let him live in the style of the wealthier Edinburgh lawyers, the *noblesse de la robe* so important to Scottish society, nor of the landowners of the Border country round Abbotsford. That, literature alone could provide.

The literary task to which he devoted his youth was the collection of the Border ballads. His taste had run that way since early youth; he loved the country through whose remoter parts he rode in the quest for those who could recite or sing to him the old songs he wanted; he had a fantastically retentive memory and above all the endearing faculty of talking to people of all kinds. *The Ministrelsy of the Scottish Border*, inspired by the example of Percy's *Reliques*, is not, by modern standards, scholarly. There are valuable discursive notes, but modern imitations are accorded a place alongside genuine ballads, and Scott was not interested in variant readings, nor above improving or adding a verse or two. Nonetheless *The Minstrelsy* confirmed Scott's bent towards the historic past, and it established his reputation as a rising man.

One poem, originally intended for the *Ministrelsy*, grew under Scott's hand into his first major independent work. *The Lay of the Last Minstrel* is a narrative poem of magic and border chivalry which, although imperfect in construction and seldom rising to real poetry, exactly struck the growing taste for the mediaeval and the supernatural. The poem's successors *Marmion* and *The Lady of the Lake* were also instantly successful; *Rokeby, The Lord of the Isles*, and *Harold the Dauntless* were less so.

Although the range of Scott's poetry is narrow, it has considerable merits. It is muscular, manly verse; its galloping rhythms suit his subjects, and it passes the first test of narrative verse that it should tell the story well. The narrative poetry reaches its heights in moments of action:

> The stubborn spearmen still made good,
> Their dark, impenetrable wood,
> Each stepping where his comrade stood,
> The instant that he fell

or in the elegiac sadness:

> Of the stern strife, and carnage drear,
> Of Flodden's fatal field,
> Where shiver'd was fair Scotland's spear,
> And broken was her shield.

Scott's best-known poems, however, are the songs interspersed with the narrative in both poems and novels. Thousands who have never read Scott are familiar with Schubert's settings of "Ave Maria" and the other lyrics from *The Lady of the Lake*.

In July 1814 a three-volume novel entitled *Waverley* was published anonymously in Edinburgh. Within five weeks it had sold out, and by the following January it was into its fifth edition. If Scott's real motive had been to protect his reputation as a poet should the novel fail, he had no need to keep up the mystery; but speculation about the unknown author amused him, and he did not acknowledge his authorship of the Waverley novels, which were published at the rate of two a year, until twelve years later.

Scott's reputation has suffered from judgements based on the mass of his work rather than the best of it. At his best – in *The Antiquary, Rob Roy, Old Mortality, The Heart of Mid-Lothian, The Bride of Lammermoor*, and *Redgauntlet* (some would add *Waverley, Guy Mannering* and *The Fair Maid of Perth*) – he was writing of a country whose history and people he knew intimately. *Redgauntlet* begins in the Edinburgh of his youth; the trial of Effie Deans is set in a court-room he knew well; Scott's grandmother remembered being carried as a child to a covenanters' field-preaching, and Scott himself had talked with a man who had been "out" with the Jacobites in 1715 and 1745. The Scottish novels are Scott's real achievement. They inspired writers as diverse as Hugo, George Eliot, Tolstoy, and James Fenimore Cooper. In a sense, they created Scotland as it is known today. They introduced to the world a new form of fiction, the historical novel.

The great historical characters – James VI, Cromwell, Mary and Elizabeth, Prince Charlie, Rob Roy – are seldom central to the novels in which they appear, for Scott's technique is to follow the fortunes of an ordinary man caught up in great events, but they are striking portraits of breathing, fallible human beings. "Sir Walter not only invented the historical novel," says Trevelyan, "but he enlarged the scope and revolutionized the study of history itself." After reading the Waverley novels men could no longer content themselves with broad generalizations about the past; Scott had taught them that it was peopled by real men and women.

As a creator of character his range is enormous. He is the first novelist in English to bring the lower orders of society to life on the page, not as figures of fun but as part of humanity. Fairservice, Ochiltree, Mucklebackit, Balderstone and Davie Deans – as well as Bailie Jarvie the merchant, lawyers like Pleydell and Fairford, and small lairds like Dumbiedykes – are both of their age and for all time.

Scott's marvellous command of the Scottish dialect, his eye for the telling detail, and the humorous yet affectionate way in which he allows his characters to reveal themselves in speech, led his contemporaries to compare him with Shakespeare. "Not fit to tie his brogues," was Scott's characteristic disclaimer. In one respect, however, he is Shakespeare's superior. His common people – his servants and gardeners and beggars – are better. To Shakespeare they are seen *de haut en bas*. There is no similar condescension in Scott.

The subtleties of Jane Austen, whom he greatly admired, were not within Scott's range. As he said in his *Journal*, his was "the Big Bow-wow strain" of writing, and he prided himself on his "hurried frankness of composition." As a story-teller, he is at his best over the shorter distance of "Wandering Willie's Tale" in *Redgauntlet* or of great scenes like the trials of McIvor and Cuddie Headrigg, the appeal of Jeanie Deans to Queen Caroline, or the fight in the Clachan of Aberfoyle.

Again and again he returns to the conflict between old ways and new. By temperament and by upbringing Scott was both a romantic and a realist. In the novels he thrills to the

114 SCOTT

Jacobite past; but he settles ultimately for the age of reason, for Hume and Adam Smith rather than Rob Roy and Charles Edward Stuart. The tension of opposites characteristic of eighteenth-century Scotland remains his theme in the novels set further back in time or further off in place: Cavaliers and Roundheads in *Woodstock*, Saxons and Normans in *Ivanhoe*, Royalists and Covenanters in *Old Mortality*. The truth, for Scott, habitually lies somewhere between the extremes. He is one of the sanest of great writers.

"The greatest figure he ever drew is in the *Journal*," wrote John Buchan, "and it is the man Walter Scott." In 1825, when Scott began to keep a journal, his reputation was at its height. A few months later the slump of 1826 ruined his printer and publisher and, in those days before limited liability, Scott himself. Legally he could have declared himself bankrupt, but he would not. "My own right hand shall do it," he said, and he set himself to work, mornings and evenings, week days and Sundays, term time and holidays, to pay off the joint debt of £126,000. Thanks mainly to the collected editions of his work to which he contributed notes, the debt was finally paid off, but Scott himself, hastened to an early grave by worry and overwork, did not live to see it. Carlyle's famous sentence was fully earned: "No sounder piece of British manhood was put together in that eighteenth century of Time."

—W. E. K. Anderson

SEWARD, Anna. Known as the "Swan of Lichfield." English. Born in Eyam, Derbyshire, 12 December 1742; moved with her family to Lichfield, Staffordshire, 1754, and remained there for the rest of her life. Educated privately; encouraged to write by Dr. Erasmus Darwin. Lived at home, caring for her father; acquainted with Dr. Johnson and his circle at Lichfield; met Boswell c. 1776 and supplied him with anecdotes about Johnson; inherited the family estate, 1790; met Scott, 1807, who became her literary executor and editor. *Died 25 March 1809.*

PUBLICATIONS

Collections

> *Poetical Works,* edited by Walter Scott. 3 vols., 1810.
> *Letters 1784–1807,* edited by A. Constable. 6 vols., 1811.

Verse

> *Elegy on Captain Cook, to Which Is Added an Ode to the Sun.* 1780; revised edition, 1784.
> *Monody on Major André.* 1781.
> *Poem to the Memory of Lady Miller.* 1782.
> *Louisa: A Poetical Novel in Four Epistles.* 1784.
> *Ode on General Elliott's Return from Gibraltar.* 1787.
> *Llangollen Vale with Other Poems.* 1796.
> *Original Sonnets on Various Subjects, and Odes Paraphrased from Horace.* 1799.
> *Blindness.* 1806.

SHELLEY 115

Other

Variety: A Collection of Essays. 1788.
Memoirs of the Life of Dr. Darwin. 1804.
Memoirs of Abelard and Eloisa. 1805.
Monumental Inscriptions in Ashbourn Church, Derbyshire, with B. Boothby. 1806.
Miss Seward's Enigma. 1855.

Reading List: *The Singing Swan: An Account of Seward* by Margaret Ashmun, 1931; *Seward: An Eighteenth-Century Handelian* by R. M. Myers, 1947.

* * *

Anna Seward was known as the Swan of Lichfield, and, as the term suggests, she did produce a considerable body of forgettable poems. Her *Poetical Works,* published after her death, came to three volumes, and her *Letters* came to six. A contemporary critic refers to all this literary work as "written almost throughout with a disgusting affectation of verbal ornament, and everywhere tinctured with personal, political, and poetical prejudices." Nevertheless, she was a brilliant woman who never achieved a major literary accomplishment; and a reason may have been that she was part of a provincial literary circle that despised the London literary world of Samuel Johnson. Further, she received too much flattery within that limited circle of her friends in the Midlands, William Hayley, Cowper, Erasmus Darwin, without ever having to confront the major literary world of London. She was a minor writer by choice, and as such she presaged the tendency in our society for minor writers deliberately to break off into regional groupings.

One major contribution that she did make to English literature, however, came through her friendship and sometime infatuation with Erasmus Darwin, who had helped teach her to make poems when she was a girl growing up in Lichfield and who also chose deliberately to be a regional and minor writer with all the self-consciousness and sense of limits that go with that choice. Her *Memoirs of the Life of Dr. Darwin* is written in a less affected and more direct manner. She makes incisive and critical statements in that book about him and about the whole literary world of the Midlands. The book, in fact, may be her most valuable contribution to our literary heritage. During her lifetime she received the most fame for her two elegiac poems *Elegy on Captain Cook* and *Monody on Major André.* She probably received help on the Captain Cook elegy from Dr. Darwin just as she helped him with the opening lines of his poem *The Botanic Garden.* The avowedly minor writers at this time often worked together establishing the sense of small community that provided some compensation for the realization that epic works were not being produced. In this sense, Anna Seward, the assertive woman and minor writer, seems very modern.

—Donald M. Hassler

SHELLEY, Percy Bysshe. English. Born at Field Place, near Horsham, Sussex, 4 August 1792. Educated at Syon House School, Isleworth, Middlesex, 1802–04; Eton College, 1804–10; University College, Oxford, 1810–11 (expelled for pamphlet *The Necessity of Atheism*). Eloped with and married Harriet Westbrook, 1811 (died, 1816), two children, left her in 1814 for Mary Wollstonecraft Godwin (i.e., Mary Shelley) daughter of William Godwin, married in 1816, one daughter and two sons. Visited Ireland, 1812; returned to

116   SHELLEY

London, became a friend of William Godwin, 1813; left England for Italy, 1818, and settled in Pisa, 1820; died by drowning. *Died 8 July 1822.*

PUBLICATIONS

Collections

Complete Poetical Works, edited by Thomas Hutchinson.   1904; revised edition, edited by G. M. Matthews, 1970.
Complete Works, edited by Roger Ingpen and W. E. Peck.   10 vols., 1926–30.
Shelley's Prose; or, The Trumpet of Prophecy, edited by D. L. Clark.   1954.
Alastor, Prometheus Unbound, Adonais, and Other Poems, edited by P. H. Butter.   1970.
Complete Poetical Works, edited by Neville Rogers.   2 vols. (of 4), 1972–75.
Poetry and Prose, edited by Donald H. Reiman and Sharon Powers.   1977.

Verse

Original Poetry by Victor and Cazire, with Elizabeth Shelley.   1810.
Posthumous Fragments of Margaret Nicholson.   1810.
Queen Mab: A Philosophical Poem, with Notes.   1813.
Alastor; or, The Spirit of Solitude, and Other Poems.   1816.
Laon and Cythna; or, The Revolution of the Golden City: A Vision of the Nineteenth Century in the Stanza of Spenser.   1817; revised edition, as *The Revolt of Islam: A Poem in Twelve Cantos,* 1818.
Rosalind and Helen: A Modern Eclogue, with Other Poems.   1819.
Epipsychidion.   1821.
Adonais: An Elegy on the Death of John Keats.   1821.
Posthumous Poems, edited by Mary Shelley.   1824.
The Masque of Anarchy: A Poem Now First Published.   1832.
The Daemon of the World: The First Part as Published in 1816 with Alastor, the Second Part Deciphered and Now Printed from His Manuscript Revision and Interpolations, edited by H. Buxton Forman.   1876.
The Wandering Jew, edited by B. Dobell.   1887.
The Notebook in the Harvard Library, edited by G. E. Woodberry.   1929.
The Esdaile Notebook: A Volume of Early Poems, edited by Kenneth N. Cameron.   1964; edited by Neville Rogers, as *The Esdaile Poems,* 1966.

Plays

The Cenci (produced 1886).   1819.
Prometheus Unbound: A Lyrical Drama, with Other Poems.   1820; the play edited by L. J. Zillman, 1959, 1968.
Oedipus Tyrannus; or, Swellfoot the Tyrant, from the play by Sophocles.   1820.
Hellas: A Lyrical Drama.   1822.

Fiction

Zastrozzi: A Romance.   1810; edited by Eustace Chesser, 1965.

St. Irvyne; or, The Rosicrucian: A Romance. 1811.

Other

The Necessity of Atheism, with T.J. Hogg. 1811; edited by Eustace Chesser, 1965.
An Address to the Irish People. 1812.
*Proposals for an Association of Those Philanthropists Who Convinced of the Inadequacy
of the Moral and Political State of Ireland to Produce Benefits Which Are Nevertheless
Attainable Are Willing to Unite to Accomplish Its Regeneration.* 1812.
A Letter to Lord Ellenborough. 1812.
*A Vindication of Natural Diet, Being One in a Series of Notes to Queen Mab: A
Philosophical Poem.* 1813.
A Refutation of Deism, in a Dialogue. 1814.
*A Proposal for Putting Reform to the Vote Throughout the Kingdom, by the Hermit of
Marlow.* 1817.
*History of Six Weeks' Tour Through a Part of France, Switzerland, Germany and
Holland,* with Mary Shelley. 1817; abridgement edited by C. I. Elton, 1894.
The Shelley Papers. 1833.
Essays, Letters from Abroad, Translations, and Fragments, edited by Mary Shelley. 2
vols., 1840.
Shelley Memorials, from Authentic Sources, to Which Is Added An Essay on Christianity,
edited by Lady Shelley and R. Garnett. 1859.
Relics of Shelley, edited by R. Garnett. 1862.
*Notes on Sculptures in Rome and Florence Together with a Lucianic Fragment and a
Criticism of Peacock's Poem Rhododaphne,* edited by H. Buxton Forman. 1879.
A Philosophical View of Reform, edited by T. W. Rolleston. 1920.
On the Vegetable System of Diet, edited by Roger Ingpen. 1929.
Verse and Prose from the Manuscripts, edited by Sir J. C. E. Shelley-Rolls and Roger
Ingpen. 1934.

Translator, *Plato's Banquet,* edited by Roger Ingpen. 1931.
Translator, *Shelley's Translations from Plato: A Critical Edition,* edited by J. A.
Notopoulos, in his *Platonism of Shelley.* 1949.

Bibliography: *A Bibliography of Studies of Shelley 1823–1950* by Clement A. E. Dunbar,
1976.

Reading List: *Shelley* (biography) by Newman Ivey White, 2 vols., 1940; *Shelley's Major
Poetry* by Carlos Baker, 1948; *The Young Shelley: Genesis of a Radical,* 1950, and *Shelley:
The Golden Years,* 1974 both by Kenneth N. Cameron; *Shelley's Mythmaking* by Harold
Bloom, 1959; *Shelley and His Circle 1773–1822* (texts) edited by Kenneth N. Cameron and
D. H. Reiman, 6 vols. (of 8 or more), 1961–73; *Shelley: A Critical Reading* by Earl R.
Wasserman, 1971; *Shelley: The Pursuit* by Richard Holmes, 1974; *The Dark Angel: Gothic
Elements in Shelley's Works* by John V. Murphy, 1974; *Shelley: The Critical Heritage* edited
by James E. Barcus, 1975; *Shelley: A Voice Not Understood* by Timothy Webb, 1978.

*   *   *

"An enthusiasm for Shelley seems to me to be an affair of adolescence," said T. S. Eliot. No
harm in that in itself, of course. If his rush of images, his lyrical intensity, his "passion for
reforming the world," his idealism excite the young, that will at least start their reading of
poetry in the right way, from enjoyment. But can he not remain also "the companion of
age"? Did he not mature as an artist? Apart from juvenilia each volume of poetry which he

118   SHELLEY

published consisted of a long poem, to which sometimes a few short ones were tacked on. As he presented himself he was not primarily a lyric poet pouring out personal feelings, but one trying to deal with large themes in long poems, mostly of a dramatic or narrative kind.

Take *Alastor*, for instance, the first longish poem in which he approaches maturity. Read as autobiography it would seem sentimental, self-indulgent; but clearly it should not be so read. The unnamed protagonist should not be identified with the author (who might be accused more justly of rash involvement in relationships than of "self-centred seclusion"). *Alastor* not only movingly celebrates the romantic idealist quester, it criticises him too; it combines boundless aspiration with scepticism; it displays a remarkable ability to create symbolic landscapes suggestive of the protagonist's emotional states; and it shows a more assured handling of the verse than in earlier poems. The artist in Shelley is gaining control, but has not yet fully attained it. At the end balance is lost, and the dying hero is too extravagantly praised for qualities which have not been sufficiently created in the poem.

A more mature poem, in which again idealism and scepticism are confronted, is "Julian and Maddalo," written three years later. Here one of the characters, Julian, is openly based on Shelley himself, or on part of himself. Julian is an idealist, believing that "we might be all / We dream of, happy, high, majestical," and is confronted with Maddalo, based on Byron, showing the reality of evil and suffering. Again, more skilfully and naturally than in *Alastor*, the argument is sustained by description of scenery. The bare strip of sand on which Julian and Maddalo ride suggests the potentiality which Julian wishes to believe in; the sunset over the hills and Venice suggests the realisation of that potentiality and the possible at-oneness of heaven and earth; and the black tower in which the madman is imprisoned thrusts itself questioningly into that sunset. The language is conversational, fitted skilfully and with apparent ease into couplets. The tone, except in the madman's monologue, is light, controlled, urbane. The artist Shelley is now more fully in control, giving a fair say to Maddalo as well as to Julian and tactfully distancing the weaker side of himself in the madman.

One could try to demonstrate Shelley's maturing by continuing the survey of his poems of medium length through the delightful fantasy "The Witch of Atlas" and "Adonais" up to "The Triumph of Life," which shows a greater strength and precision in language and imagery than ever before. One could show his mastery of a wide variety of styles and metrical forms appropriate to different kinds of poem. But his claim to major status must rest mainly on his greatest complete poem, *Prometheus Unbound*. This, on the whole successfully, combines at least three levels of meaning. Psychologically, the reunion of Prometheus and Asia is the reintegration of the split human personality, like the reunion of Blake's Albion and his emanation Jerusalem. Politically, the overthrow of Jupiter is a revolution leading to the establishment of a free, expansive society. Mystically, the journey of Asia and Panthea to the cave of Demogorgon is a casting aside of the veils of illusion and an approach towards a vision of ultimate reality. By using and adapting an existing myth Shelley devised a more satisfactory surface to carry the deeper meanings than Blake usually did. His myth sustains itself better; he does not need to explain himself. Much is conveyed by sound, and by recurring images which come to have complex symbolic, seldom crudely allegorical, meanings. One can still point to weaknesses, however. Having added the fourth act he could with advantage have shortened the third, which in any case continues too long after the downfall of Jupiter and loses dramatic impact. Sometimes he loses control of his long sentences, and sometimes he is content to waft us along on a stream of sound, conveying only a vague and generalised meaning. Nevertheless this is the greatest of English romantic mythological poems.

By transferring the argument to the realm of myth Shelley was able to let Julian win, but he still knew, as his next long work, *The Cenci*, shows, what Maddalo might have to say in answer. Beatrice is a failed Prometheus, who becomes what she beholds, answering her Jupiter with murder rather than pity. It was a sign of maturity to wish to write this harshly realistic work immediately after, indeed, concurrently with, *Prometheus*. But it shows also Shelley's limitations. Like most others who have tried poetic drama, he could not escape the influence of the Elizabethans, especially Shakespeare, and create a language and a style for modern drama; and he was only to a limited extent successful in creating living, believable characters.

This last is perhaps his main limitation. It is unfair to say that all his characters are himself, but they are representative of aspects of himself or of ideas, attitudes, feelings rather than flesh-and-blood people – appropriately so in some poems, less so in others. He had a passion for ideas, and an unusual capacity to embody them concretely in images. He had a genuine passion for reforming the world, expressed in sacrificial action as well as in words, but in some degree spoiled by impatience and self-absorption, which limited him both as man and poet.

The same process of maturing as in the longer poems can be seen in the shorter – from the declamatory juvenilia through the uneven "Hymn to Intellectual Beauty" (the weak "I shrieked, and clasped my hands in ecstasy" after the strong opening stanzas) to the well-controlled use of personal experience in relation to larger themes in "Ode to the West Wind." The lyrics show a considerable range – of subject, tone, and metrical form. Some are "metaphysical" poems, using science (as in "The Cloud") and philosophical ideas (as in "Ode to Heaven") with grace and urbanity. Some (as "An old mad, blind, despised and dying king") use plain language to comment on contemporary politics. Some are dramatic, intended for private theatricals in his circle in Italy – obviously the superb "Hymn of Apollo" and "Hymn of Pan," less obviously "When the lamp is shattered." As G. M. Matthews has shown (in *Review of English Literature 2*, 1961), much of the criticism of this last poem, and of others, has been misdirected because of failure to recognise the kind of poem that it is. Many of his lyrics, quite properly, are more or less direct expressions of personal feeling. Here, when he approaches certain sensitive areas, he still tends to become strident and self-pitying; but less so towards the end. The late poems to Jane Williams, written in a quiet, conversational tone, convey a stronger sense than his earlier love poems of actual place, persons, situation. Along with the still boundless aspiration is a resigned acceptance of necessary limitation.

Shelley's prose displays a powerful, if impatient, intelligence wrestling with a wide range of problems – in religion, philosophy, morals, politics, literature, diet. Yeats called "A Defence of Poetry" "the profoundest essay on the foundation of poetry in English"; but others have found it, though eloquent, lacking in complete consistency. Mainly Shelley says that the poet, inspired, puts aside "life's dark veil" to reveal the real and ideal world behind; but his scepticism does not allow him to say this quite confidently and consistently. Sometimes he seems to say that poetry itself is a "figured curtain," which reveals, it may be, nothing external, but only "the wonder of our being." It is a common uncertainty among the romantics and their successors. Other prose works worth reading are the short philosophical essays "On Love," "On Life," "On a Future State"; *A Philosophical View of Reform*, showing him dealing quite realistically with what was immediately possible in politics as well as with more distant goals; and the translations from Plato.

"Shelley," the elderly Wordsworth said, "is one of the best artists of us all: I mean in workmanship of style." This artistry and his combination of sceptical intelligence with idealism and visionary power make him a companion for age as well as for adolescence.

—P. H. Butter

SOUTHEY, Robert. English. Born in Bristol, 12 August 1774. Educated at Westminster School, London; Balliol College, Oxford; also studied law. Married 1) Edith Fricker in 1795 (died, 1837); 2) Caroline Ann Bowles in 1839. Involved with Coleridge in an abortive scheme for a "pantisocracy" in America, 1794; visited Spain and Portugal, 1800; settled near

120 SOUTHEY

Wordsworth at Greta Hall, Keswick, 1803, and worked as a translator and journalist; contributor to the *Quarterly Review* from 1808. Poet Laureate, 1813 until his death. *Died 21 March 1843.*

PUBLICATIONS

Collections

Poetical Works. 10 vols., 1860.
Poems, edited by Edward Dowden. 1895.
Select Prose, edited by Jacob Zeitlin. 1916.

Verse

Poems, with Robert Lovell. 1795.
Joan of Arc: An Epic Poem. 1796; revised edition, 2 vols., 1798, 2 vols., 1806, 1812.
Poems. 2 vols., 1797–99; revised edition of vol. 1, 1797.
Thalaba the Destroyer. 2 vols., 1801.
Madoc. 1805.
Metrical Tales and Other Poems. 1805.
The Curse of Kehama. 1810.
Roderick, The Last of the Goths. 1814.
Odes to the Prince Regent, the Emperor of Russia, and the King of Prussia. 1814.
The Minor Poems. 3 vols., 1815.
The Poet's Pilgrimage to Waterloo. 1816.
The Lay of the Laureate: Carmen Nuptiale. 1816.
A Vision of Judgement. 1821; edited by R. E. Roberts, 1932.
A Tale of Paraguay. 1825.
All for Love, and The Pilgrim to Compostella. 1829.
Poetical Works. 1829.
The Devil's Walk, with Coleridge, edited by H. W. Montagu. 1830.
Selections from the Poems, edited by I. Moxon. 1831; as *The Beauties of the Poems,* 1833.
Poetical Works. 10 vols., 1837–38.
Oliver Newman: A New England Tale, with Other Poetical Remains, edited by H. Hill. 1845.
Robin Hood: A Fragment, with Other Fragments and Poems, with Caroline Southey. 1847.

Play

The Fall of Robespierre, with Coleridge. 1794.
Wat Tyler: A Dramatic Poem. 1817.

Fiction

The Doctor. 7 vols., 1834–47 (vols. 6 and 7 edited by J. W. Warter); edited by J. W. Warter, 1848.

SOUTHEY 121

Other

Letters Written During a Short Residence in Spain and Portugal, with Some Account of Spanish and Portuguese Poetry. 1797; revised edition, 2 vols., 1808.
Letters from England. 3 vols., 1807; edited by Jack Simmons, 1951.
History of Brazil. 3 vols., 1810–19.
The History of Europe. 4 vols., 1810–13.
Omniana; or, Horae Otiosiores, with Coleridge. 2 vols., 1812; edited by Robert Gittings, 1969.
The Origin, Nature, and Object of the New System of Education. 1812.
An Exposure of the Misrepresentations and Calumnies in Mr. Marsh's Review of Sir George Barlow's Administration at Madras. 1813.
The Life of Nelson. 2 vols., 1813; revised edition, 1814, 1830.
A Summary of the Life of Arthur Duke of Wellington. 1816.
The Life of Wesley and the Rise and Progress of Methodism. 2 vols., 1820; edited by M. H. Fitzgerald, 1925.
The Expedition of Orsua and the Crimes of Aguirre. 1821.
Life of John Duke of Marlborough. 1822.
History of the Peninsular War. 3 vols., 1823–32.
The Book of the Church. 2 vols., 1824.
Vindiciae Ecclesiae Anglicanae: Letters to Charles Butler, Comprising Essays on the Romish Religion and Vindicating the Book of the Church. 1826.
Sir Thomas More; or, Colloquies on the Progress and Prospects of Society. 2 vols., 1829.
Essays Moral and Political. 2 vols., 1832.
Selections from the Prose Works, edited by I. Moxon. 1832; as *The Beauties of the Prose Works,* 1833.
Lives of the British Admirals. 5 vols., 1833–40; vol. 1 as *The Early Naval History of England,* 1835; edited by D. Hannay, as *The English Seamen,* 1904.
The Life of the Rev. Andrew Bell, vol. 1. 1844.
Select Biographies: Cromwell and Bunyan. 1844.
Common Place Book, edited by J. W. Warter. 4 vols., 1849–51.
Selection from the Letters, edited by J. W. Warter. 1849.
Correspondence with Caroline Bowles, edited by Edward Dowden. 1881.
Southey: The Story of His Life Written in His Letters, edited by J. Dennis. 1887.
Journal of a Tour in the Netherlands in the Autumn of 1815. 1902.
Letters: A Selection, edited by M. H. Fitzgerald. 1912.
The Lives and Works of the Uneducated Poets, edited by J. S. Childers. 1925.
Journal of a Tour in Scotland in 1819, edited by C. H. Herford. 1929.
Journals of a Residence in Portugal 1800–01, and a Visit to France 1838, edited by Adolfo Cabral. 1960.
New Letters, edited by Kenneth Curry. 2 vols., 1965.

Editor, and Contributor, *The Annual Anthology.* 2 vols., 1799–1800.
Editor, with Joseph Cottle, *The Works of Chatterton.* 3 vols., 1803.
Editor, *Palmerin of England,* by Francisco de Moraes, translated by Anthony Munday. 1807.
Editor, *Horae Lyricae,* by Isaac Watts. 1834.
Editor, *The Works of William Cowper: Poems, Correspondence, and Translations, with a Life of the Author.* 15 vols., 1835–37.

Translator, *On the French Revolution,* vol. 2, by Mr. Necker. 1797.
Translator, *Amadis of Gaul,* by Vasco Lobeira. 4 vols., 1803.
Translator, *Chronicle of the Cid.* 1808.

122 SOUTHEY

Translator, *The Geographical, Natural, and Civil History of Chili,* by Abbé Don J. Ignatius Molina. 1808.
Translator, *Memoria Sobre a Litteratura Portugueza.* 1809.

Reading List: *Life and Correspondence* by C. C. Southey, 6 vols., 1849–51; *The Early Life of Southey 1774–1803* by William Haller, 1917 (includes bibliography); *Southey* by Jack Simmons, 1945; *Southey and His Age,* 1960, and *Southey,* 1964, both by Geoffrey Carnall; "The Published Letters of Southey: A Checklist," in *Bulletin of the New York Public Library,* March 1967, and *Southey,* 1975, both by Kenneth Curry; *Southey: The Critical Heritage* edited by Lionel Madden, 1972.

*   *   *

Robert Southey is now remembered mainly as a mediocre associate of Coleridge and Wordsworth, or as the fatuously self-applauding poet laureate of Byron's *Vision of Judgment,* apostate revolutionary and diligent manufacturer of books in verse and prose. Not that his work is forgotten altogether: indeed, a modified form of his version of "The Story of the Three Bears" has become one of the most familiar texts in the language, and publishers still find it worth reprinting his *Life of Nelson.* But the few acknowledged successes seldom kindle interest beyond themselves.

As a poet he is exceptionally versatile. There are irregular odes, a heroic epistle from the Fair Rosamond in the manner of Pope's "Eloisa to Abelard," sublime compositions on Biblical topics, sportive trifles on a pig and on gooseberry pie, sentimental sonnets, burlesque sonnets and elegies by the fictitious Abel Shufflebottom, lugubrious sapphics, sententiously reflective poems in blank verse, and ballads and metrical tales. In various "monodramas" he enters vehemently into the defiance of isolated and imperilled characters. In "English Eclogues" (1798–9) Southey makes his own particular experiment to discover, as Wordsworth put it, how far the language of conversation in the middle and lower classes of society is adapted to the purposes of poetic pleasure: at their best they achieve a pleasantly sardonic crispness.

The turmoil of his emotional life, of which one has tantalising glimpses in the brief record he left of some of his dreams, is nearly always firmly repressed. He wrote to escape from his emotions, not to explore them. Something slips out in his fascination with traditional stories of the Devil and his interventions in human affairs, and while most of his ballads on this theme are more humorous than terrifying, there is no mistaking the element in them of sheer nightmare. As the Devil comes to claim the old woman of Berkeley, the frenzied endeavours of piety are paralysed: "the choristers' song that late was so strong,/Grew a quaver of consternation." More commonly, Southey tells tales in which the Devil or his representatives are thwarted, as in that notable tour-de-force "The Young Dragon"; but salvation is always a miracle.

The characteristic animation of Southey's poetry is most perfectly expressed in the "rhymes for the nursery" on the cataract of Lodore, but it is equally apparent in his exotic verse narratives *Thalaba the Destroyer* and *The Curse of Kehama,* written to illustrate the Arabian and Hindu mythologies respectively. Their irregular verse and bizarre subjects were more congenial to him than the more orthodox materials of his other long poems: *Joan of Arc, Madoc,* and *Roderick, The Last of the Goths.* In these large compositions the poetry tends to be lack-lustre and featureless, giving less scope for alluring fantasies of invulnerability. Southey's deepest need was to feel invulnerable, whether in the Arabia or India of his imagination, or in his secluded life in the Lake District. His most satisfying poetry contrives to juxtapose the pleasures of domestic seclusion with the perils of an ugly world, as in the poem on the Battle of Blenheim, when an old man and two children reflect upon the dreadful slaughter many years after the event. Longer poems in a similar vein are *The Poet's Pilgrimage to Waterloo* and *A Tale of Paraguay.*

He took his role as poet very seriously, the more so when appointed Poet Laureate in 1813. He saw himself as commissioned to keep up the spirit of the country in her battles, and carry on a crusade against sedition and a heartless political economy. In the 1790's he had been equally vehement on the radical side, and *Wat Tyler*, a verse play written in 1794 but not published until it appeared in 1817 in a pirated edition, denounces the aristocracy with a splendid zest. His later political views must be studied in his prose writings, notably in some of the articles he wrote for the *Quarterly Review*, where the intensity of his indignation can generate an eloquence resembling the water coming down at Lodore. The *Colloquies on the Progress and Prospects of Society* are a temperate summing up of his convictions, developed in conversations with the ghost of Sir Thomas More, with a reassuring background of Lakeland scenery.

One of Southey's pleasantest characteristics is the wide-ranging curiosity which informs an unusually comprehensive survey of English society in *Letters from England*, finds its most wayward expression in his eccentric novel *The Doctor*, and spices his laborious histories of Brazil (1810–19) and of the Peninsular War (1823–32), not to mention the *Life of Wesley and the Rise and Progress of Methodism*. The celebrated *Life of Nelson* is on a smaller scale than these other works, and the constraint perhaps makes the book less attractive to those who enjoy Southey in a more outrageous vein. His private correspondence suffers from no such inhibitions: it supplies vivid materials for anyone who wants to understand the emotional climate of early nineteenth-century Britain.

—Geoffrey Carnall

WORDSWORTH, William. English. Born in Cockermouth, Cumberland, 7 April 1770. Educated at Hawkshead Grammar School, Lancashire; St. John's College, Cambridge, 1787–91, A.B. 1791. Lived in France during the early period of the Revolution, 1791–92: involved with Annette Villon, who bore him a daughter; married Mary Hutchinson in 1802, five children. Lived with his sister Dorothy at Racedown, Dorset, 1795–97; settled with Dorothy at Alfoxden, Somerset, near Coleridge at Nether Stowey, 1797; toured Germany with Dorothy and Coleridge, 1798–99; settled with Dorothy at Grasmere, in the Lake District, 1799, and remained there for the rest of his life; came into a legacy from his father, 1802; quarrelled with Coleridge, 1810; appointed Stamp Distributor for Westmorland, 1813; reconciled with Coleridge and toured the Rhineland with him, 1828. D.C.L.: University of Durham, 1838; Oxford University, 1839. Poet Laureate, 1843 until his death. *Died 23 April 1850.*

PUBLICATIONS

Collections

> *Poetical Works,* edited by Ernest de Selincourt and Helen Darbishire. 5 vols., 1940–49; revised edition of vols. 1–4, 1952–58.
> *Prose Works,* edited by W. J. B. Owen and Jane W. Snyder. 3 vols., 1974.

124 WORDSWORTH

The Cornell Wordsworth, edited by Stephen Parrish. 1975–
Complete Poems, edited by John O. Hayden. 2 vols., 1976.

Verse

An Evening Walk: An Epistle in Verse. 1793.
Descriptive Sketches. 1793.
Lyrical Ballads with a Few Other Poems, with Coleridge. 1798; revised edition, as
    Lyrical Ballads with Other Poems, 2 vols., 1800; 1800 text edited by R. L. Brett and A.
    R. Jones, 1963; 1798 text edited by W. J. B. Owen, 1967.
Poems. 2 vols., 1807.
The Excursion, Being a Portion of the Recluse. 1814.
The White Doe of Rylstone; or, The Fate of the Nortons. 1815.
Poems. 2 vols., 1815.
Thanksgiving Ode, January 18, 1816, with Other Short Pieces. 1816.
Peter Bell: A Tale in Verse. 1819.
The Waggoner. 1819.
The River Duddon: A Series of Sonnets, Vaudracour and Julia, and Other Poems. 1820.
Miscellaneous Poems. 4 vols., 1820.
The Little Maid and the Gentlemen; or, We Are Seven. 1820(?).
Ecclesiastical Sketches. 1822.
Memorials of a Tour on the Continent 1820. 1822.
Poetical Works. 4 vols., 1824; revised edition, 1827, 1836–42, 1845, 1846, 1849–50.
Epitaph. 1835.
Yarrow Revisited and Other Poems. 1835.
The Sonnets. 1838.
England in 1840! 1840(?).
Poems on the Loss and Re-Building of St. Mary's Church, Cardiff. 1842.
Select Pieces from the Poems. 1843.
Grace Darling. 1843.
Verses Composed at the Request of Jane Wallas Penfold. 1843.
The Prelude; or, Growth of a Poet's Mind: An Autobiographical Poem. 1850; edited by
    Ernest de Selincourt, 1926, revised by Helen Darbishire, 1959; 1805 text edited by de
    Selincourt, 1933, revised by Stephen Gill, 1970; both texts edited by J. C. Maxwell,
    1976.
The Recluse. 1888.

Play

The Borderers, in *Poetical Works.* 1842.

Other

*Concerning the Relations of Great Britain, Spain, and Portugal to Each Other and to the
    Common Enemy at This Crisis.* 1809.
A Letter to a Friend of Robert Burns. 1816.
A Description of the Scenery of the Lakes in the North of England. 1822.
Letters of the Wordsworth Family from 1787 to 1855, edited by W. Knight. 3 vols.,
    1907.
*Wordsworth and Reed: The Poet's Correspondence with His American Publisher
    1836–50*, edited by L. N. Broughton. 1933.

The Letters of William and Dorothy Wordsworth, edited by Ernest de Selincourt. 5 vols., 1935–39; revised by Chester L. Shaver and others, 4 vols., 1967–78.
Some Letters of the Wordsworth Family, Now First Published, edited by L. N. Broughton. 1941.
Pocket Notebook, edited by G. H. Healey. 1942.

Bibliography: *Wordsworth Criticism: A Guide and Bibliography* by J. V. Logan, 1947, supplemented by *Wordsworthian Criticism 1945–59* by E. F. Henley and D. H. Stam, 1960, revised edition, 1965; *The Cornell Wordsworth Collection: A Catalogue* by G. H. Healey, 1957.

Reading List: *Wordsworth* by Herbert Read, 1930, revised edition, 1949; *The Mind of A Poet: A Study of Wordsworth's Thought* by Raymond D. Havens, 1941; *Wordsworth and the Vocabulary of Emotion* by Josephine Miles, 1942; *Wordsworth and Other Studies* by Ernest de Selincourt, 1947; *The Poet Wordsworth* by Helen Darbishire, 1950; *Wordsworth: A Reinterpretation* by F. W. Bateson, 1954, revised edition, 1956; *Wordsworth's Poetry 1787–1814* by Geoffrey H. Hartman, 1964; *Wordsworth: The Chronology of the Early Years 1770–1799,* 1967, and ... *the Middle Years 1800–1815,* 1975, both by Mark L. Reed; *Imagination and Fancy: Complementary Modes in the Poetry of Wordsworth* by J. Scoggins, 1967; *Tradition and Experiment in Wordsworth's Lyrical Ballads* by Mary Jacobus, 1976; *Wordsworth: Language as Counter-Spirit* by Francis Fergusson, 1977.

*   *   *

William Wordsworth is always thought of as the pre-eminent poet of nature, though he declared himself that his subject was "the Mind of Man –/My haunt, and the main region of my song." It is true that his chief concern is with man, but he does express a belief in the regenerative power of nature to such an extent that there is some truth in the popular belief. What is not true is that Wordsworth, because of this belief, is a facile optimist who turns his eyes away from human misery. He portrays suffering humanity in many of his poems, showing a variety of causes: poverty, separation, bereavement, neglect. As Geoffrey Hartman has written "those famous misreaders of Wordsworth who say he advocates rural nature as a panacea should be condemned to read *The Excursion* once a day."

Wordsworth's eye for human unhappiness is the sharper because he has such a powerful and authentic vision of the ideal life. It is authentic because it is based on the poet's own experience and observation, and it includes a "natural" life which is based on much more than a love for the country. It is found in the experience of a child who, like Wordsworth himself, is allowed a large measure of freedom; in the lives of shepherds and independent farmers, whose work is satisfying and meaningful; and in the lives of all those who are able to love their fellow human beings, whose benevolent instincts are not thwarted by oppression, wrong habits, or an acceptance of false or trivial values. Throughout his poetry Wordsworth is the enemy of the glittering, the fashionable, and the temporary; and one feature of his belief in "nature" is a concentration on those things which would render men's feelings "more sane, pure and permanent" (letter to John Wilson, June 1802). The result is that he concentrates on the simplest and most elemental passions of the human heart: the love of a mother for her idiot child, the compassion due to the aged and the poor, a mother's grief for her lost baby. It is this consistent, austere aim to portray universal and simple emotions which lies behind the much misunderstood Preface to the 1800 edition of *Lyrical Ballads,* in which Wordsworth states as his aim the tracing of "the primary laws of our nature." It is this which is responsible for his choice of "low and rustic life," since he believed that there "the essential passions of the heart" spoke more plainly, were more simple, and were more durable. To this must be added his belief (deduced from his own experience, and fully articulated in *The Prelude*) that a mind which has been influenced by a simple and

126 WORDSWORTH

natural benevolence can survive adverse circumstances and unwholesome influences. Moments when he feels reassured in this belief, as he encounters a particularly beautiful or striking moment, are among the most memorable passages of Wordsworth's poetry, for instance in "Lines Written a Few Miles above Tintern Abbey."

In his earliest published poems, *An Evening Walk* and *Descriptive Sketches*, Wordsworth shows both his concern with simple human states and his awareness of natural beauty. Drawing on eighteenth-century traditions of the picturesque, in *An Evening Walk*, and transcending them in *Descriptive Sketches*, he gives word-paintings of Lake District and Alpine scenes respectively; yet in both poems he is also concerned with suffering humanity. In *An Evening Walk* the peaceful description is interrupted by a harrowing portrait of a homeless widow (her soldier-husband has been killed at Bunker's Hill in the American war) whose starving and frozen children die in her arms; and in *Descriptive Sketches* the sublime scenery of the Alps is contrasted with the miseries of the impoverished and oppressed Swiss.

Descriptive Sketches was written for the most part in France in 1792, and its plea for freedom indicates Wordsworth's political enthusiasm at this time for the French Revolution. His disillusion with its later stages, and his separation from his French mistress and their child, were the two chief causes of the poet's unhappiness in the years which followed his return to England in December 1792. For a time he found help in the writings of the political philosopher William Godwin, only to find that Godwin's view of man took too little account of man's deepest affections; and although critics no longer believe that Wordsworth had some kind of "breakdown" at this time, it is clear that in the years that followed he was given new faith in himself as a poet, and in mankind generally, by the love of his sister Dorothy and the friendship with Coleridge. The poetry of these years includes *The Borderers*, a verse drama of considerable psychological insight but insufficient dramatic force, which shows a good man betrayed into a great crime and subjecting another man to the same process; and "The Ruined Cottage," which shows the destruction of an innocent family by famine, sickness and war. "The Ruined Cottage" was later incorporated into Book I of *The Excursion*, with the addition of some consoling reflections; in its original form (printed by Jonathan Wordsworth in *The Music of Humanity*, 1969) it is Wordsworth's most powerful narrative of wretchedness and neglect. The understatement of its blank verse narrative allows the gradual unfolding of the tragedy to develop with a slow, accumulating force. To it was added the fragment describing the pedlar (later the Wanderer) in which the poet expresses clearly and confidently his belief in the One Life of nature (a concept derived from Coleridge) and in the ability of man to gain power from nature and to suffer with those who suffer.

Lyrical Ballads continues these themes. On the one hand there are the compassionate poems ("The Thorn," "Simon Lee," "Goody Blake and Harry Gill") dealing with misery, neglect, and old age, but on the other hand there are poems of love and care ("The Idiot Boy") and those which celebrate the harmony between man and nature ("To my Sister," "Expostulation and Reply," "The Tables Turned"). In "Tintern Abbey," the last-written and last-placed poem of the collection, Wordsworth describes the power of memory to recreate the scene, and the power of the mind to "see into the life of things"; as an expression of the sublime feelings awakened by nature, the central passage (beginning "And I have felt") is unsurpassed.

The winter of 1798–99, spent with Dorothy in Germany, is notable on two counts: the composition of the "Lucy poems," and the first attempt at what later became *The Prelude*. The "Lucy Poems," four elegiac lyrics (a fifth was composed later), describe a beautiful young girl, a child of nature: the poems celebrate her loss and her perfection, in simple language and lyric metres which nevertheless allow a complexity of response. In the first, two-part *Prelude*, the poet describes his childhood and schooltime, and the "spots of time" which act as a renovating power in later years. Between 1799 and 1805 Wordsworth extended *The Prelude* to thirteen books, including his experiences in Cambridge, the Alps, London, and France, and celebrating the loss and restoration of his imaginative power. The poem has individual passages of great beauty and energy, in which specific interactions between man and nature are shown (boat-stealing, skating, hooting to the owls, crossing the

WORDSWORTH   127

Alps, the climbing of Snowdon): these are notable, not only for their vividness, but for their variety of tone and effect. But the strength of *The Prelude* is not only in individual passages, but also in its structure: it is an epic, closely modelled on *Paradise Lost*, showing the "heroic argument" of the developing human mind. The ecstatic childhood gives way to a sober maturity, and the close-knit rural community is left behind for Cambridge and London; but what is lost is balanced by a gain in understanding and human feeling, so that, when the poet's faith in himself is restored at the end, he has a more mature and compassionate awareness of human demands. The loss of the childhood paradise thus becomes an individual "fortunate fall."

A similar process of loss and gain is found in the "Immortality Ode," where the memory of childhood serves to emphasise that its radiance has gone; yet this is replaced by an awareness of mortality, a faith that looks through death, and a philosophic mind. The "Immortality Ode" ends with thanks to "the human heart by which we live," and Wordsworth's poetry of this period is constant in its recognition of the claims of human nature. In "Resolution and Independence" he is cured of self-pity by his meeting with the leech-gatherer, a man of patience and fortitude; and in "Peele Castle" he bids farewell to "the heart that lives alone."

Wordsworth's other great achievements in the years after *Lyrical Ballads* were his sonnets, in which again he follows his great master, Milton. Wordsworth's sonnets are not so abrupt, complex, or dense as Milton's: their most notable characteristic is an arresting line, the thought of which is then developed with economy and beauty. Figurative language, especially the simile, is used to great effect, and Wordsworth uses the tight structure of the sonnet to express single ideas with a marvellous clarity and finality.

The major philosophical poem which Wordsworth published during his lifetime was *The Excursion*. It has been described by Geoffrey Hartman as a dinosaur, dying of its own weight, and although it addresses itself to matters of great importance, such as human despondency and bereavement, it does so in a way which lacks the intensity and excitement of the earlier poetry. And, with a few exceptions, the publication of *The Excursion* marks the end of Wordsworth's effective career as a poet. In the last forty years of his life he applied himself, for the most part, to conventional subjects, and treated them in a conventional way. It is idle to speculate on the causes of this decline; it is rather a matter for rejoicing that during the great decade (ending with *Poems*, 1807) Wordsworth wrote so powerfully about man in society and man in relation to nature, the unchanging passion of the human heart.

—J. R. Watson

NOTES ON CONTRIBUTORS

ANDERSON, W. E. K. Headmaster, Shrewsbury School, Shropshire. Editor of *The Journal of Sir Walter Scott*, 1972. **Essay:** Sir Walter Scott.

ASHLEY, Leonard R. N. Professor of English, Brooklyn College, City University of New York. Author of *Colley Cibber*, 1965; *19th-Century British Drama*, 1967; *Authorship and Evidence: A Study of Attribution and the Renaissance Drama*, 1968; *History of the Short Story*, 1968; *George Peele: The Man and His Work*, 1970. Editor of the *Enriched Classics* series, several anthologies of fiction and drama, and a number of facsimile editions. **Essay:** Edward Fitzball.

BAREHAM, T. Senior Lecturer in English, New University of Ulster, Coleraine. Author of *George Crabbe: A Critical Study*, 1977, *A Bibliography of Crabbe* (with S. Gattrell), 1978, and articles on Shakespeare and Malcolm Lowry. **Essays:** Robert Bloomfield; Samuel Rogers.

BERRY, Francis. Professor of English, Royal Holloway College, University of London. Author of several books of verse, the most recent being *Ghosts of Greenland*, 1966, and of critical works including *Poets' Grammar*, 1958, *Poetry and the Physical Voice*, 1962, and studies of Herbert Read, Shakespeare, and John Masefield. **Essay:** Lord Byron.

BOTTRALL, Margaret. Biographer and Critic. University Lecturer, Department of Education, and Senior Tutor, Hughes Hall, Cambridge University, until 1972. Author of *George Herbert*, 1954, and *Every Man a Phoenix: Studies in Seventeenth-Century Autobiography*, 1958. Editor of *Personal Records*, 1961, and *Songs of Innocence and Experience*, by Blake, 1970. **Essays:** John Hookham Frere; John Keble.

BRATTON, J. S. Lecturer in English, Bedford College, University of London. Author of *The Victorian Popular Ballad*, 1975. **Essay:** Thomas Hood.

BUTTER, P. H. Regius Professor of English, University of Glasgow. Author of *Shelley's Idols of the Cave*, 1954; *Francis Thompson*, 1961; *Edwin Muir*, 1962; *Edwin Muir: Man and Poet*, 1966. Editor of *Alastor, Prometheus Unbound, and Other Poems*, by Shelley, 1971, and *Selected Letters of Edwin Muir*, 1974. **Essay:** Percy Bysshe Shelley.

CARNALL, Geoffrey. Reader in English Literature, University of Edinburgh. Author of *Robert Southey and His Age*, 1960, *Robert Southey*, 1964, and *The Mid-Eighteenth Century* (with John Butt), a volume in the Oxford History of English Literature, 1978. **Essay:** Robert Southey.

CROSSAN, Greg. Lecturer in English, Massey University, Palmerston North, New Zealand. Author of *A Relish for Eternity* (on John Clare), 1976. New Zealand Contributor to *Annual Bibliography of English Language and Literature*. **Essay:** Felicia Hemans.

130 NOTES ON CONTRIBUTORS

FAULKNER, Peter. Member of the Department of English, University of Exeter, Devon. Author of *William Morris and W. B. Yeats,* 1962; *Yeats and the Irish Eighteenth Century,* 1965; *Humanism in the English Novel,* 1976; *Modernism,* 1977. Editor of *William Morris: The Critical Heritage,* 1973, and of works by Morris. **Essay:** Walter Savage Landor.

HASSLER, Donald M. Associate Professor of English, Kent State University, Kent, Ohio. Author of *Erasmus Darwin,* 1972. **Essays:** Erasmus Darwin; Anna Seward.

HEATH-STUBBS, John. Writer and Lecturer. Author of several books of verse, the most recent being *The Watchman's Flute,* 1978, a book of plays, and of *The Darkling Plain: A Study of the Later Fortunes of Romanticism,* 1950, *Charles Williams,* 1955, and studies of the verse satire, the ode, and the pastoral. Editor of anthologies and works by Shelley, Tennyson, Swift, and Pope; translator of works by Giacomo Leopardi, Alfred de Vigny, and others. **Essay:** Samuel Taylor Coleridge.

LINDSAY, Maurice. Director of the Scottish Civic Trust, Glasgow, and Managing Editor of *The Scottish Review.* Author of several books of verse, the most recent being *Walking Without an Overcoat,* 1977; plays; travel and historical works; and critical studies, including *Robert Burns: The Man, His Work, The Legend,* 1954 (revised, 1968), *The Burns Encyclopedia,* 1959 (revised, 1970), and *A History of Scottish Literature,* 1977. Editor of the Saltire Modern Poets series, several anthologies of Scottish writing, and works by Sir Alexander Gray, Sir David Lyndsay, Marion Angus, and John Davidson. **Essays:** Joanna Baillie; Thomas Campbell; Thomas De Quincey.

MORGAN, Margery. Reader in English, University of Lancaster. Author of *A Drama of Political Man: A Study in the Plays of Harley Granville-Barker,* 1961 and *The Shavian Playground: An Exploration of the Art of G. B. Shaw,* 1972. Editor of *You Never Can Tell* by Shaw, 1967, and *The Madras House* by Granville-Barker, 1977. **Essay:** James Robinson Planché.

MORPURGO, J. E. Professor of American Literature, University of Leeds. Author and editor of many books, including the *Pelican History of the United States,* 1955 (third edition, 1970), and volumes on Cooper, Lamb, Trelawny, Barnes Wallis, and on Venice, Athens, and rugby football. **Essay:** Charles Lamb.

MUIR, Kenneth. Professor Emeritus of English Literature, University of Liverpool; Editor of *Shakespeare Survey,* and Chairman, International Shakespeare Association. Author of many books, including *The Nettle and the Flower,* 1933; *King Lear,* 1952; *Elizabethan Lyrics,* 1953; *John Milton,* 1955; *Shakespeare's Sources,* 1957; *Shakespeare and the Tragic Pattern,* 1959; *Shakespeare the Collaborator,* 1960; *Introduction to Elizabethan Literature,* 1967; *The Comedy of Manners,* 1970; *The Singularity of Shakespeare,* 1977; *Shakespeare's Comic Sequence,* 1978. Editor of several plays by Shakespeare, and of works by Wyatt and Middleton; translator of five plays by Racine. **Essay:** William Blake.

O'TOOLE, Bridget. Member of the Faculty, New University of Ulster, Coleraine. **Essay:** Ebenezer Elliott.

REEVES, James. Author of more than 50 books, including verse (*Collected Poems,* 1974), plays, and books for children; critical works include *The Critical Sense,* 1956, *Understanding Poetry,* 1965, *Commitment to Poetry,* 1969, *Inside Poetry* (with Martin Seymour-Smith), 1970, and *The Reputation and Writings of Alexander Pope,* 1976. Editor of many collections and anthologies, and of works by D. H. Lawrence, Donne, Clare, Hopkins, Robert Browning, Dickinson, Coleridge, Graves, Swift, Johnson, Marvell, Gray, Whitman, and others; translator of fairy tales. **Essays:** Thomas Lovell Beddoes; George Darley.

SAMBROOK, A. J.   Reader in English, University of Southampton, Hampshire. Author of *A Poet Hidden: The Life of Richard Watson Dixon*, 1962, and *William Cobbett: An Author Guide*, 1973. Editor of *The Scribleriad*, 1967, *The Seasons and The Castle of Indolence* by James Thomson, 1972, and *Pre-Raphaelitism: Patterns of Literary Criticism*, 1974. **Essay:** William Cobbett.

SPEAR, Hilda D.   Lecturer in English, University of Dundee, Scotland. Author of *Remembering, We Forget* (on the poetry of World War I), 1978, the biographical and bibliographical sections of *The Pelican Guide to English Literature 5*, 1957, and of articles on Charles Stuart Calverley, Wilfred Owen, Siegfried Sassoon, Isaac Rosenberg, and Ford Madox Ford. Editor of *The English Poems of Calverley*, 1974, and *The Mayor of Casterbridge* by Thomas Hardy, 1978. **Essays:** Richard Harris Barham; Winthrop Mackworth Praed.

THOMSON, Peter.   Professor of Drama, University of Exeter, Devon. Author of *Ideas in Action*, 1977. Editor of *Julius Caesar* by Shakespeare, 1970; *Essays on Nineteenth-Century British Theatre* (with Kenneth Richards), 1971; *The Eighteenth-Century English Stage*, 1973; *Lord Byron's Family*, 1975. **Essays:** George Colman, the Younger; James Sheridan Knowles; William Thomas Moncrieff; Thomas Morton; John O'Keeffe; John Poole.

TIBBLE, Anne.   Free-lance Writer. Author of *African Literature*, 1964, *The Story of English Literature*, 1970, *The God Spigo* (novel), 1976, two volumes of autobiography, and books on Helen Keller, Gertrude Bell, Gordon, and John Clare. Editor of works by Clare. **Essay:** John Clare.

WALSH, William.   Professor of Commonwealth Literature and Chairman of the School of English, University of Leeds. Author of *Use of Imagination*, 1958; *A Human Idiom*, 1964; *Coleridge*, 1967; *A Manifold Voice*, 1970; *R. K. Narayan*, 1972; *V. S. Naipaul*, 1973; *Patrick White's Fiction*, 1978. **Essay:** John Keats.

WATSON, J. R.   Member of the Department of English, University of Leicester. Author of *Picturesque Landscape and English Romantic Poetry*, 1970. Editor of *Browning: "Men and Women" and Other Poems: A Casebook*, 1974, and *Victorian Poetry* (with N. P. Messenger), 1974. **Essay:** William Wordsworth.

WILLIAMS, John Stuart.   Head of the Communications Department, South Glamorgan Institute of Higher Education, Cardiff. Author of four books of verse, the most recent being *Banna Strand*, 1975. Editor of three verse anthologies. **Essay:** Leigh Hunt.

WOODCOCK, George.   Free-lance Writer, Lecturer, and Editor. Author of verse (*Selected Poems*, 1967), plays, travel books, biographies, and works on history and politics; critical works include *William Godwin*, 1946; *The Incomparable Aphra*, 1948; *The Paradox of Oscar Wilde*, 1949; *The Crystal Spirit* (on Orwell), 1966; *Hugh MacLennan*, 1969; *Odysseus Ever Returning: Canadian Writers and Writing*, 1970; *Mordecai Richler*, 1970; *Dawn and the Darkest Hour* (on Aldous Huxley), 1972; *Herbert Read*, 1972; *Thomas Merton*, 1978, Editor of anthologies, and of works by Charles Lamb, Malcolm Lowry, Wyndham Lewis, and others. **Essay:** William Hazlitt.